INFORMATION MANAGEMENT IN DIGITAL ENVIRONMENT

INFORMATION MANAGEMENT
IN DIGITAL ENVIRONMENT

Editors
RAMAN NAIR. R
K J JOHN
SREEKUMAR. N

Ess Ess Publications
New Delhi

INFORMATION MANAGEMENT IN DIGITAL ENVIRONMENT

ISBN: 978-81-934311-9-1

First Published 2018

Published by:
Ess Ess Publications
4831/24, Ansari Road,
Darya Ganj,
New Delhi-110 002.
INDIA
Phones: 23260807, 41563444
Fax: 41563334
E-mail: info@essessreference.com
www.essessreference.com

Cover Design by *Patch Creative Unit*

Printed and bound in India at Yash Printographics.

Toc H Institute of Science and Technology

TIST, Ernakulam - 682313, India

Editors (LISDA 2016 Volume)

Dr. Raman Nair

Dr. K J John

Sreekumar N

Contents

Foreword

LISDA-2016, the 'National Conference on Innovative Library services in Digital Age', held at Toc-H Institute of Science & Technology, Arakkunnam in July 2016 is obviously the very first of its kind from an institution for higher education in engineering and allied subjects. It deliberated on a contemporary relevant theme opening new vistas in the optimization of emerging digital capabilities in library content management, innovative facilities and services.

To dispense services in a modern library, its professionals ought to have thorough awareness, expertise and in-depth knowledge of electronic resources, library management software (LMS), open access resources, discovery tools and information literacy. As the role of libraries is undergoing a sea change, we ought to catch up with its fast developments. The library professionals of today have to play a dynamic role in responsible and efficient knowledge transfer. This need is felt more in the present environment of knowledge-driven economy and interdisciplinary collaborations.

At the conference, a unique conglomeration of dignitaries, practicing professionals in library science, computer science, information technology and management studies discussed and shared ideas and experiences on a wide spectrum of innovative library amd information services, opening new vistas in the optimization of emerging digital capabilities in library content management, innovative facilities and services, emerging trends in efficient retrieval and dissemination of information, incorporating technological developments in information management conducive to teaching and learning processes. The leading presentations by well known experts covered a wide range of topics ranging from digitalizing heritage, building digital libraries using greenstone, open source environment today, consortium for e-journals to make subscriptions cost-effective, and library space. Papers on information technology and public libraries, innovations in library to make processes and practices more efficent, open source and free software for academic, defense and research processes were the added attractions of the national conference.

It gives me immense pleasure to place on record my deep appreciation of the hard work done by the editors in bringing out the conference proceedings in book format.

I am fully convinced that this book will be immensely useful to all libraries for their progress and modernization.

Preethi Thekkath
Principal
Toc H Institute of Science &Technology
Arakkunnam P.O., Ernakulam-682313

Preface

The National Conference on "Innovative Library Services in Digital Age" held at Toc H Institute of Science and Technology, Arakunnam, Ernakulam in July 2016 focused on Innovative Library Services and Applications in the Digital Age. The scope of the conference included the development of the digital and virtual libraries, automation of library systems, open access library research, resource sharing networks, language technology, digitization and providing access to public records, responsibilities of government, innovations in library processes and practices, information search and retrieval for better research. The scope was also extended to the information and communication technology (ICT), being the nuts and bolts for the development of functional capabilities of digital libraries associated with the ICT services. Hence the security of ICT was also incorporated.

This conference was intended to facilitate discussion and knowledge sharing. The core of the ideas presented and discussed at the conference is captured in this volume. Conference achieved participation of eminent personalities from Indian Institute of Management, Mahatma Gandhi University, Central University of Kerala, Central, and State Government Departments and other reputed institutions. The authors comprised of specialists in the field of library science and information technologies, professors, and research students. All shared their ideas and experiences.

Whole-hearted responses to the Call-for-Papers resulted in 25 proposals. After a peer review process, 21 full papers are selected and published in the present volume. The papers cover a wide variety of topics and perspectives, including Library Automation in Contemporary Open Source Environment, Library Space, Means to Bridge the Gap Between the Recorded Knowledge and the Living Knowledge, Innovative Library Management Using Holographic Projection Technology, Techniques of Literature Search for Relevance and Efficiency in Research, Consortium for e-journals, Knowledge Based Library and Information Services in R&D Organizations, Survey on Wireless Intrusion Detection Mechanisms, Building Digital Libraries using Greenstone, and Achieving the Objectives of the Public Library Movement Using Information and Communication Technologies (ICT). Together, they represent a wide range of issues associated with Library and Information services in the digital era and are of current relevance.

Of the 21 papers presented during the 2 days of the conference, 10 were leading presentations by experts from library and information science and the other 11 promising paper presentations covered relevant areas complementary to the theme of the conference. The motto of the conference was promoting new ideas and research to ensure that library and information service professionals continuously strive to achieve more for the academic community and other groups for whom they work with.

In fact, there had been some reluctance in the beginning amongst the library staff in organizing a conference of this magnitude, probably the first ever in this region. But the timely support and co-ordination of the departments of IT & CS had invariably boosted their confidence. The conference proved to be an attractive and proactive event that stimulated collaboration and cooperation among library educators, ICT experts, academic administrators and researchers in India. A national conference such as this needed the support of many people. We take this opportunity to thank the committee members of the event, who worked hard to make the conference a success, reviewed the papers and managed all other sundry work. We acknowledge our gratitude to those experts and authors who put in their best efforts to write and present the papers and participated in the interactions.

All through our endeavors, we have been ably guided and supported by the Principal, Faculty and Toc H Society, ever bent upon synergizing the state-of-the-art infrastructure and technology to meet the challenges of technology applications and innovations.

— Editors

Contributors

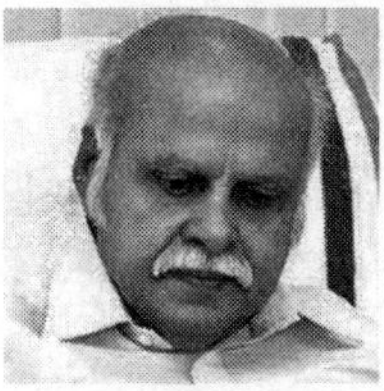

Professor (Dr.) P J Joseph, currently is President of Toc H Institute of Science & Technology and Toc H Public School, Cochin, Kerala. A teacher par excellence, he represented the country at various international fora and received numerous coveted awards. UNESCO Institute of Education, Hamburg, Germany enlisted his name in the UNESCO Exchange network for promotion of adult literacy. The Kingston University, U K, conferred on him International Visiting Fellowship. A founder member of the Commonwealth Association for adult education, he got deeply involved in slum development programmes. Author of over a dozen books, Professor Joseph has also published numerous articles in national and international journals.

Prof (Dr) Preethi Thekkath is currently officiating as Principal in- charge of Toc H Institute of Science & Technology Arakkunnam. She graduated in Electrical and Electronics Engineering from N.S.S College of Engineering in the year 1995. She obtained Ph.D in Electrical Engineering with specialisation in Power Electronics in the year 2016. In addition to her service in TIST, she has also served institutions like L.B.S College of Engineering Kasaragod and Rajalakshmi Engineering College Chennai. She is an active member of IEEE, ISTE and IEE.

Dr K J John has over three decades of experience in teaching, research, curriculum development and publication. A Ph.D. in English from Nagpur University, he has successfully guided 10 doctoral research scholars. Serving on the Board of Studies and Arts Faculty, he worked on different syllabus committees, especially of Communicative English. Currently, Dr John teaches courses on Managerial Communication & Soft Skills to MBA Students of Toc H Institute of Science& Technology. As Prof-in-charge, he oversees the overall function of TIST Libraries.

Dr. T. Mukundan obtained Ph.D. from the Indian institute of Science, Bangalore. Did Post Doctoral at the Cavendish Laboratory, University of Cambridge, UK. He has worked in HEMRL, Pune (DRDO), Virginia Tech, USA,. Presently he is in NPOL. He has edited two books published by NPOL and has about 70 research papers in national and international journals. Is a recipient of the DRDO Laboratory Scientist of the Year Award in its year of inception, the DALMIA - HEMSI Award of the High Energy Materials Society of India (HEMSI), National Science Day Oration Medal from Scientific Advisor to Defense Minister , Technology Group Award as Group Leader, and NPOL Annual Day Technology Award. He is a Fellow of the Royal Society of Chemistry (FRSC), London.

Mr. **Bino Jose** is a gold medallist for MLISc of Guru Ghasidas University in Bilaspur; obtained PhD from Berhampur University in Orissa; started career teaching at Mahatma Gandhi Chitrakoot Gramoday University in Madhya Pradesh; later moving to Allahabad Agricultural University and established the Dept of Information Science there; worked with JIIT and Shiv Nadar University in Noida; GLAITM in Mathura; Wipro Technologies in Bangalore and Asia Pacific Institute of Management in Delhi. Is presently with XLRI Jamshadpur. Areas of interest include Library Automation, User Studies, IPR and Cloud Computing etc

Dr.M.G.Sreekumar is an adjunct professor in Humanities and Liberal Arts in Management at Indian Institute of Management Kozhikode (IIMK). Is the Chief Architect of the Indian Business Museum at IIMK. He served on sabbatical as Visiting Professor in the Faculty of Computer Science & Information Technology of the University of Malaya, Kuala Lumpur, Malaysia. Has received the AIMS International Outstanding Adjunct Management Faculty Award - 2016,_Sir Ratan Tata Scholarship to Harvard University, Best Research Paper Awards of American Society for Information Science & Technology (ASIST), Salzburg, Hewlett-Packard etc. He was a Fulbright Scholar at the University of Maryland and at the NIH, Bethesda. He has been a consultant to WHO, UNESCO, and NSF Colombo. A widely traveled professional, has conducted courses, seminars and workshops in the USA, UK, Malaysia, Singapore, Hong Kong, Australia, New Zealand, Ethiopia, Austria, Sri Lanka, Nepal, Philippines and Thailand.

Dr. Sainul Abideen P did his PG and PhD from DRTC, Bangalore. Presently is heading the Library of the Indian Institute of Science Education & Research (IISER Thiruvananthapuram). Has served IIT-Kharagpur, IIITM-K, C-DoT etc. He is a VLR Scholar in S&T Information Management offered by Flemish Inter University Council, Belgium and was an invitee to the 3rd World Congress for Information Systems held in Rio De Janeiro 2008, with travel grant from the UNESCO. Dr. Sainul is a member (Representing Asia/Pacific) in the International Coordination Committee (ICCI) constituted by UNESCO. Sainul has served as the Joint Coordinator of the IISER Library Consortium and he was a member of the National Steering Committee of the INDEST Consortium and member of Senate, IISER TVM.

Mr. Akshay K is a Computer Science Student of Toc H Institute of Science & Technology, Arakkunnam, Kerala. His areas of interest include Computer Networks, Cloud computing and Data Security.

Fr. Bibi Alias has obtained B.Com, BD, and MLISc. Has 7 Years experience as Librarian in various institutions. Is now working as Librarian in Toc H Institute of Science & Technology, Arakkunnam.

Mr. Binodkumar. N has obtained Bachelors Degree in Arts and Post graduation in Library and Information Science. Has 11 Years experience as Librarian in various institutions. Is now working as Librarian in Toc H Institute of Science & Technology,Arakkunnam.

Mr. Dileep Rajan has bachelors Degree in Commerce and PG in Library and Information Science. Has 10 Years experience as Librarian in various institutions. Is now working as Librarian in Toc H Institute of Science & Technology, Arakkunnam.

Dr. P. Ganesan is presently working as Assistant Librarian at Alagappa University, Karaikudi, Tamil Nadu. Did PhD from Bharathidasan University, Tiruchirappalli and has undergone various specialized courses on IT Applications at National Centre for Science Information (NCSI), and Indian Institute of Science (IISc). He also served as Documentation Officer at University of Hyderabad where he prepared course material for IT Programmes. He has to his credit numerous papers in National/ International Journals/ Conference proceedings. He has produced 3 PhD's. Has visited Malaysia, Singapore, Thailand etc and is a member of various library science related committees in India and abroad.

Mr. Gireesh Kumar T.K. is presently Assistant Librarian, at Central University of Kerala. He MLIS from Indira Gandhi National Open University (IGNOU), New Delhi. Has cleared UGC NET and JRF. Has served International Institute of Dental Science and Research Centre at Kasaragod, Digital Library at Indian Institute of Information Technology-Kerala (IIITM-K) and International Advanced Research Centre (ARCI) (Govt. of India) at Hyderabad. Was elected as one among ten around the World for the *Doctoral Student Consortium and International Workshop* on Global Collaboration of Information Schools. Has published more than 25 research papers/ presentations /book chapters in national and international journals/ conferences/ edited volumes.

Mr. Hariharan S is a student of Information Technology at Toc H Institute of Science and Technology, Arakkunnam. His technical skills related to Operating Systems include WINDOWS, Linux, Ubuntu. He is proficient in Languages: C, C++, C#, VB, JAVA, ANDROID, PHP, HTML; Databases: SQLITE, MS SQL Server; Web Technologies: JavaScript, VB Script, SOAP, REST, word press, css, and jquery and Game Development: multi-platform- unity games Personal Qualities. Received Best Programmer Award 2012-2016.Is a AMCAT certified Data Analyst BPO/ITES Professional.

Mr. Humayoon Kabeer P. has post graduation and M.Phil in library and information science and is in the library profession for the last 23 years. Has worked as Librarian in Chalakkudy Municipality, Government Secretariat, Government Law College, Government College (Kasaragod), Thrissur, Institute of Advanced Study Government Medical College (Thrissur) and Librarian under UGC Scheme in many Government Arts and Science Colleges.

Dr. M Jayapradeep has MA in Political Science, MLISc and MPhil in Library and Information Science. Awarded PhD for his work on Fisheries Informatics from Karpagam University in 2014. He served Indian Air Force, Biotechnology Information Centre (Government of India), Kerala Agricultural University, Kerala University of Fisheries and Ocean Studies, and is presently Librarian, SVN College of Engineering, Mavelikkara, Kerala. His areas of interests are informatics and knowledge management. He is presently an Advisor of the international journal 'Informatics Studies'.

Ms. Jincy Kurian is a B Tech graduate in Information Technology from Toc H Institute of Science & Technology,Arakkunnam, Kerala. She completed her post graduation (M Tech) in Network Computing from the same institution in 2016. Her areas of interest include Computer Networks, Cloud computing and Data Security.

Fr. John Neelankavil CMI is currently Chief Librarian of DVK Central Library at Dharmaram Vidya Kshetram, Pontifical Athenaeum, Bengaluru. His academic qualifications include BA, BPh, BTh, MLISc, M.Phil. He teaches Research Informatics at DVK and in the Department of Philosophy at Christ University, Bengaluru. He also serves as Director, Centre for Environmental Studies, DVK. He has done the Conceptual and Functional Design and the Space Planning of the DVK Central Library with 45000 square feet built area, considered as a model library for space planning. He served as consultant for space design to more than 20 libraries in various institutions in India. Has also served as Production Executive of a TV Programme, namely, Mission in Africa. And is a member of the Academic Council, Syndicate, and the Senate of DVK, Bengaluru.

Mr. Josbin Simon is a Computer Science Student of Toc H Institute of Science & Technology, Arakkunnam, Kerala. His areas of interest include Computer Networks, Cloud computing and Data Security.

Kevin Rubison is a Computer Science Student of Toc H Institute of Science & Technology, Arakkunnam, Kerala. His areas of interest include Computer Networks, Cloud computing and Data Security.

Smt.Laila T Abraham : is presently University Librarian(i/c) of Mahatma Gandhi University, Kottayam, India. Is a post graduate in M.A. Linguistics. She is a rank holder in BL.Sc and MLISc from University of Kerala and has cleared UGC-NET.. Is a prolific writer in Malayalam and English.Her poems have been selected and included in the "Anthology of Women Writers in India". Has won Best paper award in the ETD International Symposium 2015 held under the auspices of UGC-INFLIBNET and NDLTD, USA.

Smt Letha M.M. is working as Scientist 'E' in Technical information Resource Center, NPOL. She has obtained her MSc (Botany) from University of Calicut and MLlSc from the Madurai Kamaraj University. She is presently with NPOL, Cochin, a Defence Research and Development Organisation establishment. She is the joint editor for two books and has numerous papers to her credit. Her areas of interest include: Knowledge management and web based information services.

Ms. Moble Jacob is a B Tech graduate in Information Technology from Toc H Institute of Science & Technology,Arakkunnam, Kerala. She completed her post graduation (M Tech) in Network Computing from the same institution in 2016. Areas of interest include Computer Networks, Cloud computing and Data Security.

Nayana Nair, a recipient of UGC- Junior Research Fellowship in Library and Information Science, took her Master's degree in Library and Information science from Tata Institute of Social Sciences with gold medal. She completed her Bachelor's Degree in English (Hons) from the English and Foreign Languages University. At Capital Centre Library, Central University of Kerala, she was involved in the development of

IRKnowledgebase, a portal and archive on International Relations. She also served as the Digital Library Coordinator for the Indian Public Library Movement Project at P.N. Panicker Foundation supported by NASSCOM and IPLM. Her areas of interest include Digitization, Conservation of Manuscript, and Metadata.

Smt.Sobhana P K has her education at Sree Kerala Verma College, Thrissur and and university of Kerala. Started her career at Kerala Agricultural University. Is presently State Librarian of Kerala and is heading Trivandrum Public Library, the oldest public library in India. She is participating in various State and Central Committees on libraries and is an active member of Indian Public Library Movement. Her areas of interest are Digitalization, Library Extension and Library Budgeting.

Mr. Sreekumar. N, has done his post graduation in Library and Information science from Annamalai University and Graduation in library and Information Science from Mahatma Gandhi University, after obtaining graduation in science. Is in the library profession for about two decades. Is now working as Chief Librarian in Toc H Institute of Science & Technology, Arakkunnam. Has organized a few conferences and workshops.

Steffy Livera has done BTech in Computer Science and Engineering in Toc H Institute of Science & Technology, Arakunnam during the year 2011-2015. Completed Internships in Robotics & Embedded System @ R&D Lab, Techjeeva and in Kerala Police Cybercell –Ernakulam. Is presently, doing M.Tech in Computer Science with specialisation in Data Security in TIST.

Ms.Teenu Jose is a B Tech graduate in Information Technology from Toc H Institute of Science & Technology,Arakkunnam, Kerala. She completed her post graduation (M Tech) in Network Computing from the same institution in 2016. Her areas of interest includes Computer Networks, Cloud computing and Data Security.

Dr. R. Raman Nair has Masters in Library and Information Science from Banaras Hindu University and PhD in Agricultural Informatics from University of Kerala. Associated with OA projects of Kerala Legislative Assembly, and Mahatma Gandhi University Online PhD Theses. Was a member of the National Committee on Submission and Access to Electronic Theses and Dissertations in Universities in India. Organized many national/ international workshops on ICT under Ministries of Science and Technology, Agriculture and Culture of Govt of India.

1

Library Automation in Contemporary Open Source Environment

T. K.Gireesh Kumar

ABSTRACT

The landscape of library automation has considerably changed over the last two decades. Computerization of libraries in the present context is no longer just an option, where the information explosion is progressing and the user's demand for innovative services are enhancing, but it becomes a necessity for the sustainability. The process of library automation has been advancing fast for the last few years and accordingly many enhancements have taken place in the functionalities of traditional automation software to cope with the contemporary issues. The present study assesses the status of library automation activities in the contemporary open source environment in India. The paper reviews the developmental activities associated with the library automation focusing its growth and justification on adopting open source integrated library system in Indian libraries. Also suggests some measures to enhance the sustainability of open source integrated library system in Indian libraries. The study was based on the perspectives of library professionals from different institutions in India performing library house-keeping operations using any open sources library packages. Online survey method was adopted to examine the perceptions of library professionals. Findings of the study revealed that managerial issues such as knowledge in open source technology, Information and Communication Technology infrastructure, in-house technical expertise, organizational policies and support, experience and training on open source software, trained manpower etc. invariably influence the rate of adoption of open source integrated library system in Indian libraries.

Keywords : Library Automation; Open Source Integrated Library System, OSILS, India

1. INTRODUCTION

Library automation in India has a long history of around five decades. It has been realized by the library professionals' decades back that move from manual practices of library housekeeping operations to integrated systems and networked operations is indisputable. Library and information centers are passing through the technological changes in automation of activities which improves its performance in all the respects especially in its innovative services to cope with the changing needs of users. In view of the transition of libraries from traditional to digital, library professionals are looking ahead to encounter more technological innovations with inexpensive tools to establish web presence to effectively serve their user communities. The changing demands of users for more efficient, effective and specialized services have now elevated the role of library professionals from custodians of resources or service providers to knowledge managers. Libraries are looking for innovative automation solutions to efficiently accommodate and manage different kinds of library materials such as print, electronic, digital and digitized and to provide access to their collection from anywhere around the globe.

Encyclopedia of Library and Information Science

defines automation "is the technology concerned with the design and development of process and system that minimize the necessity of human intervention in operation". Acquisition, Cataloguing, Circulation, Serial Control and OPAC are the major areas of library automation. Benefits of library automation software are still much debated, particularly, in the case of developing countries like India where the application moves at a slow pace. Automation of libraries also requires adequate planning as well as continuous support from technical staff to utilize computers and related technologies efficiently. However the advent of various technologies and their availability in the public domain free of cost makes library automation cheap, faster and more effective than ever. The scope of library automation has been considerably changed according to the growth of Information and Communication Technologies (ICT) and further with the adoption of Open Source Integrated Library System (OSILS). The nature of library collection keeps on changing from print to electronic to digital and so on which draws the creation of next generation automation systems with enhancements in the functionalities of the existing software.

2. LIBRARY AUTOMATION: PRESENT SCENARIO

Library automation activities underwent frequent and substantial changes during the years. If we look two decades back, there were situations where the availability of suitable software was limited and the chances of choice for standard software in terms of its cost and functions were less. Current library automation systems are metamorphosed from basic functional performers to multifunctional integrated library systems designed with rational database architecture. These applications are now capable of performing the activities of organizing and retrieving data in any desirable way to sustain in the increasingly digital world. Now libraries automate their collection and service to establish a web presence. The process and functionalities of library automation has witnessed drastic changes in the technology driven environment. In India, there are different types of softwares presently available for automation. A number of domestic and foreign integrated library systems of different categories such as commercial/proprietary, free/open, in-house/developed by others are being used in Indian libraries. Some libraries are in the verge of changing to or migrating to another ILS as they have wrongly selected the software. There are some facets which compel the libraries to adopt automation software in the present networked society: Changing nature of library collection to accommodate both electronic contents and digitized materials; Software-as-a-service (SaaS) being the objective of next generation automation system; Advancements in computer technologies such as cloud computing as the cost of hiring technical personnel to trouble shoot software issues can be saved, service-oriented architecture (SOA) and the presence of application programming interface (API); Need for innovative library services through mobile devices and smart phones; Index based smart searches and relevance ranking display as next-generation discovery services; and migration among automation platforms from propriety to OSILS or vice versa.

Further in India, libraries are increasingly recognizing the use of OSILS focusing its advantages particularly on cost and customization to automate their activities. Adoption of OSILS in libraries offers significant benefits compared to its commercial counterparts. Directorate of Technical Education of Government of Kerala has integrated Koha as its official software for computerization of libraries under Government control, Pondicherry

University has adopted Koha in the course curriculum, NewGenLib was declared open source software, ABCD integrated library system under open source category has been introduced. Training programs and courses to train LIS professionals on OSILS are happening frequently and all these activities shows the global efforts in adopting OSILS.

3. INTEGRATED LIBRARY SYSTEM

Integrated Library Systems, ILS in short, are multifunctional software which integrates multiple functions. Integrated system can either be standard or can be open source. The Astandard software is sold and supported by commercial agency where as open source can be sold and supported commercially. ILS are also named as Library Management Systems (LMS) and Automated Library System (ALS) and Library Automation Software are the synonyms used to represent ILS. Commercial/Proprietary and Free/Open Source are the two categories of ILS. There are many open sources ILS available to the public but an analysis to its suitability, utility, authority and currency in meeting the requirements of LIS shall be proper in the current scenario.

Open source ILS has changed the dimension of library and information profession and the automation process. Integrated library system in the open source stream has made inroads into the activities of libraries, its services and information management affairs. OSILS reduces the cost of installation and maintenance and enhances the efficiency of library services. In India, OSILS is actively gaining momentum among the library community. Many libraries are considering giving up their proprietary ILSs and implementing OSILS. Dissatisfaction of libraries with the performance of the software, response of their traditional vendors, hefty license and maintenance fee etc lead most of the libraries to explore OSILS for their libraries apart from the common benefits such as lower costs, more flexibility, better match and open to customization

4. LITERATURE REVIEW

The process of library automation has been developed and matured in India and are using integrated library systems over the years. The study of Kushwah et al opines that high purchase and maintenance cost, addition of new version or new feature, heavy charges for additions, lack of proper support from the vendors etc are the major problems involved in using proprietary software. Many libraries have already automated their libraries using OSILS. The literature review indicates that the tendency for embracing OSILS in the recent years has been enhancing in all kinds of libraries in India. A few studies have been published as case studies or analysis of individual software or issues on adopting OSILS by proprietary software users. Adopting OSILS provides both economical and technological benefit to the libraries in terms of its initial implementation and maintenance cost, and also freedom from vendor lock and license restrictions and is performing as an alternative to costly proprietary packages. OSILS provides technological freedom to the libraries and also helps the library professionals to provide services at low cost or free of cost. The next generation ILS is steered by the rapid advancements in the area of computer science and is adapting itself to the state-of-the-art forthcoming hardware architectures and software technologies. Jasimudeen and et.al, conducted a survey among Indian libraries and found that the primary reasons of libraries not implementing open source solutions for their automation purposes are lack of awareness, training and absence of encouraging government policies.

Indian libraries which have not automated with any of the software should consider and look forward to adopt OSILS packages. The study of Kamila concludes that it is better to use OSILS because of its many useful features such as importing of data directly from Library of Congress and other large databases which minimizes the processing work of library, main library and branch library automation facilities, MARC21, Z39.50 etc. as well as its freedom to change the source code as and when necessary which can solve the local problems of every institution. Kumar and Abraham found that the implementation of open source library management system is limited in India due to the lack of awareness and knowledge on the brighter side of open source concept among library professionals.

5. OBJECTIVE OF THE STUDY

The general objective of the study is to examine the use of OSILS in India libraries and to analyze the various factors that influence the adoption of OSILS in Indian libraries. The specific objectives of the study are as follows:

- To identify the growth of OSILS adoption in Indian libraries
- To find out the justifications for the adoption of open source software for library automation.
- To suggest some measures to enhance the growth and sustainability of OSILS in Indian libraries
- To formulate suggestions for enhancing implementation of OSILS in Indian libraries

6. METHODOLOGY

An online survey questionnaire method was adopted to gather primary data. A structured questionnaire focusing the objectives of the study was prepared using Google doc, an online survey tool of Google. The URL link of the survey was randomly disseminated to the libraries of universities, educational institutions and special or research libraries via e-mail with a request letter to participate. The target audience of the survey was library professionals within India using any kind of open source ILS. Questionnaires were composed keeping in mind the different aspects of OSILS as a library management tool. As many as 133 libraries across the country responded to the questionnaire. The responses received from various kinds of libraries were analyzed in terms of users' perception of usefulness of OSILS and the issues associated with the adoption and migration. The survey was done over a period of 8 months to have a higher response rate.

7. SCOPE AND LIMITATIONS

The study limits its horizon to those libraries in India where OSILS is being practiced. In the study it is intended to consider every library using any of the OSILS regardless of its type such as academic/research/corporate and the collection size. The questionnaire is designed to comprehend the awareness and observation of OSILS of library professions of India. The study looks upon the OSILS from its active use and services in the library point of view.

8. ANALYSIS AND FINDINGS

A. Respondents

Among 133 respondents 120 (90%) were male and 13 (10%) were female respondents. Different segments of respondents were made with regard to age of the respondents. Out of the total respondents 49% of professionals were in the age group of 31-40 years whereas the ratio of 21-30 years and 41-50 years were 20% and 26% orderly (Fig. 1.). The senior respondents beyond 51 years stood last at 5%.

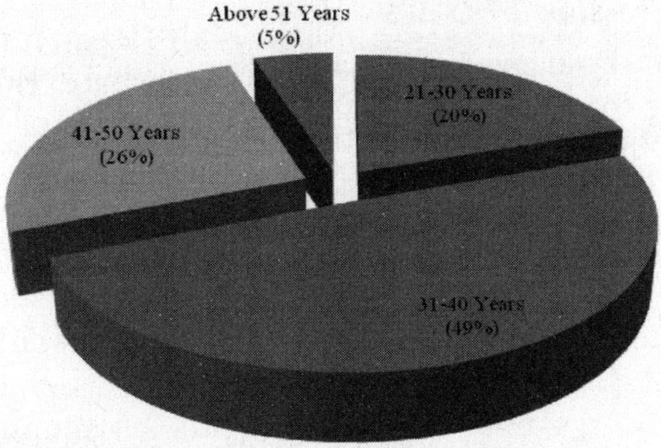

Fig. 1. Respondents' age group.

The analysis of respondents indicate that professionals in the age group of 31-40 showed better interest in responding comparing with the other three with a higher majority of male respondents, there by assumed that they are prone to technological advancement in the library.

B. Type of Libraries Responded

Different segments of libraries were made with regard to the type of libraries responded. A higher majority (77%) of respondents belonged to the academic libraries and the percentage of respondents from special and research, corporate and non-profit libraries were marked as 17%, 2% and 4% respectively (Table I).

Table 1. Type Of Libraries Responded

Library Type			
Academic	*Special/Research*	*Corporate*	*Non profit*
103 (77%)	23 (17%)	2 (2%)	5(4%)

The analysis shows that adoption rate of OSILS is more in academic libraries and corporate and non-profit libraries including public libraries yet to embrace the adoption.

C. Progression of OSILS Adoption

The extensive adoption and its constant support from the user community are influencing the other libraries to adopt OSILS. It is clear from the analysis that over a period of time an increase can be well noticed in the adoption of OSILS in Indian libraries. From the year 2012 to 2014 there has been a drastic increase in the rate of adoption. The trend of OSILS adoption has been highly progressive which is 47% in 2012-2014 (Fig. 2.).

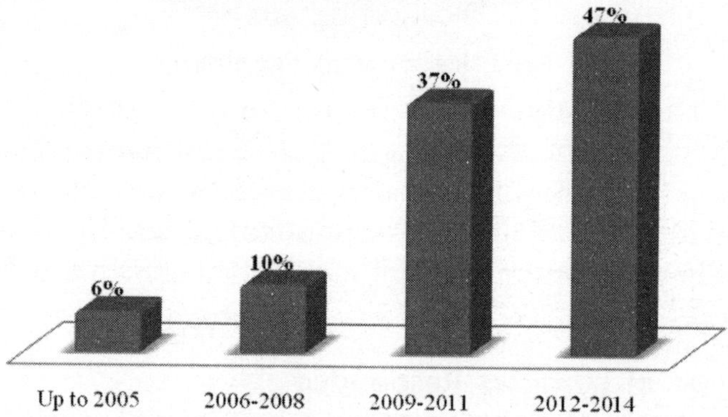

Fig. 2. Progression of OSILS adoption

The analysis shows that there was a drastic uplift in the rate of adoption of OSILS during the last decade among Indian libraries.

D. Justifications for the Adoption of Open Source ILS

Survey to measure the major reasons why the respondents adopted or migrated to OSILS from their legacy commercial system reveals that 14% of the respondents equally expressed the ability of OSILS to customize to fit the library's local requirements and also to reduce the cost associated with the adoption and maintenance appealed them to use. Freedom from maintenance, licensing fee and vendor lock, and wider adoption and support and presence of online community and the easiness in installing, maintaining and modifying the software are the other major reasons indicated equally (11%) by the respondents to adopt OSILS. The other reason indicated are availability of source code (8%), availability of quality documentations (7%), concerns about the suppliers of proprietary ILS (5), uncertainty due to merges and outside ownership of proprietary software (4%) and as a provision to become part of the consortium (4%). Few of the respondents indicated that they have adopted OSILS to improve their skills and promote the use of OSILS and their previous experience in using both commercial and OSLIS. The reasons for adoption indicated by the respondents are graphically represented in Fig. 3.

Analysis indicates that the major reasons for switching over to OSILS are its advantageous features viz. ability for customization,cost effectiveness, software control, ease of use, and community support from all over the world.

E. Measures to Enhance OSILS Growth and Sustainability

For any OSILS the growth and sustainability depends on its active community participation of developers, potential contributors and users. Sharing of knowledge, experience and expertise among the collaborators highly influence the growth and sustainability of the software. Library professionals can contribute and promote to the growth of OSILS through modifying its codes, solving bug problems, writing documentations, educating the users through training, workshops etc. If a person has knowledge on systems and programming languages he can contribute lot for the development of the software.

To measure the attitude of OSILS users on the growth and sustainability of the existing software, respondents were asked to indicate their level of agreement with a set of statements and characteristics in five point scale.

Following were the statements put to test.

1. Application of OSILS should be part of the academic curriculum
2. LIS professionals require frequent awareness and training programs on OSILS
3. High quality documentation on OSILS should be available on the public domain
4. Indian libraries should consider consortia model for wider adoption of OSILS
5. Indian Libraries should have customized and single OSILS for any type of library
6. Indian Libraries should have an OSILS to support various Indian scripts

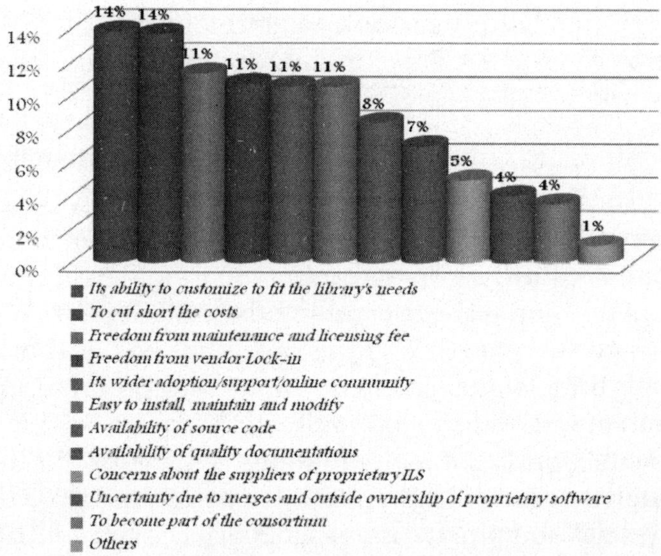

Fig. 3. Significance of OSILS

Higher majority of the respondents were either strongly agree or agree with all the above statement as a measure to keep sustain the development of OSILS.

Awareness on the issues and application of OSILS needs to be introduced in the LIS Course curriculum and the professionals are to be enabled to acquaint with these at the very beginning of their profession. When prompted a higher majority of the respondents either agreed (51%) or highly agreed (41%) with the statement. Lack of adequate training on implementation and maintenance is one of the main barriers in adoption and introduction of OSILS in Indian libraries. More than half (53%) of the respondent agreed and 43% of the respondents strongly agreed that they require frequent awareness and training programs. Another key factor to promote the use of OSILS is the availability of quality documentations. OSILS requires better and extensively available documentation to suit the needs of all type of Libraries. Respondents indicated 45%, 41%, 9% and 5% on Agree, Strongly agree, neither agree or disagree and disagree orderly with the statement. Consortia based adoption of the software which reduces the cost of implementation and maintenance and was highly supported by the respondents in 50% agree and 33% strongly agreed order. Software should have different customized versions to fulfill the requirements of all types of libraries. Majority of the respondents agreed (45%) with the need for customized version however comparatively higher percentage (20%) of respondents were unable to support the statements hence indicated they neither agree nor disagree with the statement. There is a need for single application in the software program that should be able to transform to a specific script. The rating revealed that overwhelming majority either agreed (45%) or strongly agreed (40%) the need for software which supports all the Indian scripts (Fig. 4.)

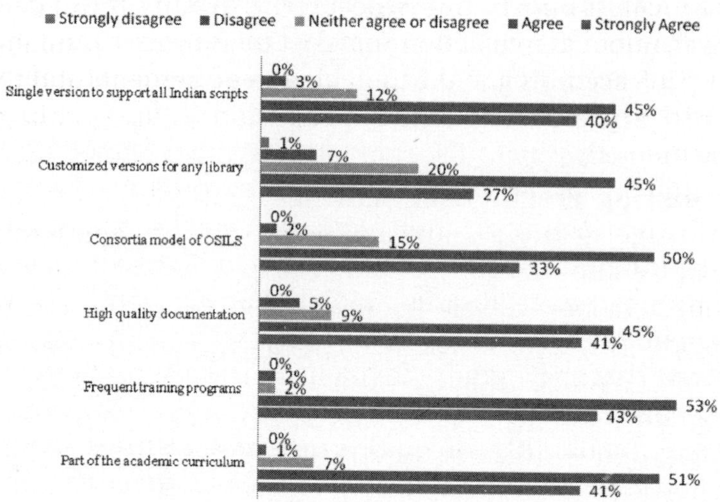

Fig. 4. Sustainability of OSILS.

F. Suggestions for Enhancing OSILS Implementation

Arranging Adequate Training Programs: Providing in-house technical expertise can promote OSILS which is highly economical and can give more opportunities to library professionals in enhancing their technical skills and provide them a sense of control and reduce their dependency on the vendors considerably. In-house training program to the working professionals should also be given consistently to practice and assimilate more on OSILS.

Formulating Organizational Policies : The importance of library automation in the technological era needs to be conveyed to higher authority in a proper manner. Appropriate changes in organizational policy to adopt OSILS need to be implemented

Evolving National Level Policies : The policy makers should recommend the strict usage of OSILS at least in Government organizations. There should be a strong technical supports from the expert groups formed by Government at free or nominal cost to improve the quality of OSILS according to the individual requirements and the group should customize and update the package continuously.

Organizing Promotional Activities : All libraries facing shrinkage in budget and current users of commercial software should consider migration to OSILS. Lack of interest in new developments should be eradicated by providing awareness. The library professional associations should conduct prolonged publicity campaigns, training programs, seminars, workshops etc to educate both library professionals and users. Universities and educational institutions should conduct regular training programs, conferences, workshops etc to train and make LIS professionals aware of OSILS. LIS professional experts of OSILS themselves should organize promotional activities for the benefit of the new entrants in library profession. Creating awareness and educating the professionals about the advantages of OSILS can rectify Issues associated with the rejection of open source software. Informal training program to other professional can also be extended within the library.

Cloud Based Applications and Services : Cloud based services to run the automation process need to be implemented to minimize the expenses of hardware and infrastructure.

Providing Technical Expertise : Library professionals should enhance their technical expertise by being involved with OSILS. Provision of sufficient skilled staff need to be provided

Developing Community Participation : Development of OSILS should be platform independent. Different versions of the same software should be made available for libraries according to their type like academic; public libraries etc or small, medium and large libraries etc. Equal consideration should be given in all aspects and functionalities of OSILS to accommodate both print and digital resources. While designing every module of the software, the development team should take the feedback and suggestion received from working professionals.

Exercising Consortium Approaches : Forming a council/ consortium to monitor quality control and share updates among the member libraries. OSILS requires much better and widely available documentation to suit needs of all type of Library professionals and users as well.

9. CONCLUSION

Open Source Integrated Library System offers libraries multidimensional functionality with limited cost to provide innovative library services. Many libraries in India have successfully implemented OSILS and there is a drastic increase in the rate of adoption of OSILS during the last decade among Indian libraries. Realizing the fact that OSILS are economical and low cost solutions for libraries the implementation of the software has been enhanced in Indian libraries and most of the library professionals are competent enough to adopt and implement OSILS. Library professionals must adapt to the technological changes and the use of existing software to manage library routine activities. Procurement of a software solution for library automation has been very crucial as the procedure includes financial involvements at one side and scope of keeping mission and goal of the library as well as the organization on the other side. Though there are number of software available as indigenous or adopted in both proprietary and open source streams for effective and efficient library automation, Libraries need to explore the use of OSILS to bring activities and services of libraries and user interfaces up to date. There are many companies in India offering paid services to OSILS. Regardless of the environment of the library, it is important that current generation library professionals need to acquire an adequate level of competency in automation processes, software models and architecture to sustain in the evolving technologies that are highly impacting on the nature of integrated library systems

As OSILS requires strong technical knowledge to maintain the server and the systems, support of technical expertise is required for successful implementation and management. OSILS shall enhance access to information and knowledge, collaborative research, innovations and communication at inter and intra institutions and shall also enable to meet the demands of the present and future generations for barrier-free information. Concerted efforts, intervention, orientation and path finding tools are to be implemented for the spread of OSILS and OSILS based information services in the Library and Information sector. Being an attractive alternative to costly commercial package for any type of libraries OSILS, which is free to experiment and easy to use and customize for local requirements needs to be promoted in Indian libraries using various methods, suggested in the study.

REFERENCES

1. A.K. Tyagi and V. Senthil, "Library automation in India: Assessment of library services platforms", DESIDOC Journal of Library & Information Technology, vol.35 (6), pp.408-416, November 2015
2. K. Allen and L. Harold, "Encyclopedia of library and information science, vol.8, pp.1-608, 1973
3. Kamila, Kanchan., "Koha: How open it is?. PLANNER 2008, Nagaland University, Nagaland, pp.286-304. Retrieved from http://ir.inflibnet.ac.in/bitstream/1944/1141/1/26.pdf
4. Kushwah, Shivpal Singh; Gautam, J N and Singh, Ritu, "Library automation and open source solutions major shifts & practices: A comparative case study of library automation systems in India.

6th International CALIBER -2008, University of Allahabad, Allahabad, 144-153.

5. S., Jasimudeen, Vimal Kumar V., and Biju V.V., "Open source software usage in Indian libraries: a survey",. In proceedings of Dravidian University National Conference, March 7-8, 2014
6. T.K., Gireesh Kumar, and M. Jayapradeep, "Perceptions of LIS professionals on open source integrated library system and adoptability of Koha over LibSys in India", International Journal of Information Dissemination and Technology, vol.5(2), pp.100-105, April-June 2015.
7. V. Kumar T. Abraham, "Development of library automation systems in open source software mode: opportunities and challenges for libraries in India. In Dr. Dineshan Koovakkai (Ed.). Library 2.0 and Information Management, Atlantic 2001.
8. V.T.,Kamble; Raj, Hans and Sangeeta, "Open source library management and digital library software", DESIDOC Journal of Library & Information Technology, vol.32(5), pp.388-392, September 2012.

2

Building Digital Libraries Using Greenstone

M.G. Sreekumar

ABSTRACT

Digital Libraries have been gaining increasing attention as well as academic interest over the years worldwide, owing to the growing demand for improved information and knowledge management solutions in universities, institutions as well as enterprises. Advancements in technology in recent years and its resultant diffusion into society are just the natural offshoots which propelled this movement. Digital Libraries (DL) are structured storage environments of digital data with a consistent format for index and content abstraction. DLs do enable the seamless integration of the scholarly electronic information, help in creating and maintaining local digital content, and strengthen the mechanisms and the capacity of the library's information systems and services. Considering the fact that currently the penetration of electronic content into our libraries and information centers is an unprecedented 70-80 percentage, it unequivocally prompts us to leverage on the latest digital technologies towards building practical digital libraries and in setting up dynamic electronic information systems. Without proper understanding of the complexities, procedures and practices involved in content building, content management, collection building, metadata harvesting as well as collaboration, and the long term preservation strategies, individual DLs will remain islands of structure in an unstructured Internet sea. Developing world standard digital libraries demand deployment of costly software solutions which are obviously beyond the reach of most of the universities/institutions and this is more so in the Asian and the African region. This paper therefore aims at portraying the unlimited potential of digital libraries in real world perspective by trying out open source solutions. It attempts to unleash and demystify the plethora of features and functionalities of the open source software 'Greenstone'. For the information professionals who subscribe to continuing education and to those who value and nurture the spirit of life long learning, Greenstone is close to their hearts, and needs no introduction. Greenstone is a top of the line and internationally renowned software system for developing digital libraries, promoted by the New Zealand Digital Library project research group at the University of Waikato. It is developed and distributed in cooperation with UNESCO and the Human Info NGO. The aim of the software is to empower users, particularly in universities, libraries, and other public service institutions, to build their own digital libraries. One of the key features of Greenstone is that it is quite easy to install, configure, customize and administer, even by the novice. It also facilitates seamless aggregation and integration of the digital content possessed by the library. More details of the software and example digital libraries built using the software are available at http://www.greenstone.org/.

Keywords : Digital Library, UNESCO, Archives, Software

0. INTRODUCTION

Libraries all over the world are in the constant business of providing their clientele nascent as well as legacy information and in the process they buy, subscribe, license and accumulate information in an unprecedented array of content categories or publication types, and in a rapidly proliferating mix of formats (digital as well as print). There is a great deal of cultural divide and philosophical deviation between the traditional information resources being handled by libraries for centuries now and the new genre of electronic and digital information being sourced and accessed. In the traditional paradigm, the books and journals bought and subscribed to by the libraries were naturally owned by them, allowing them to make the best use of the resources within the 'fair use' clause or principle. Whereas in the electronic publishing scenario all the traditional belief, approach and understanding about the digital documents that the library purchase / subscribe to, have a world of difference. Libraries get only a license to use the electronic information (books, journals, databases, softwares etc.) while purchasing, and even this license is issued only for a prescribed period of time. Librarians at same time, have the professional responsibility to assure uninterrupted as well as perpetual access to the information subscribed to by the library. Issues of copyright, intellectual property, and fair use are very much important to libraries [Orsdel, 2002].

In the current practical library setting there is an amazing penetration of digital information through a variety of publication forms such as books (published as such or issued as accompaniment), journals, portals, vortals, reports, CBTs, WBTs, cases, databases etc. The penetration level of electronic information in the special libraries and libraries belonging to centers of higher learning are supposed to be 70% as against their print counterparts. To make matters more complex the vast array of different formats, standards and platforms in which documents are published, pose a multiplicity of threats to the librarian who is supposed to be the custodian and service provider of these information products once it has found its way into the library. As librarians, we are sometimes the stewards of unique collections too.

1. DIGITAL LIBRARIES

Digital Libraries (DL) are now emerging as a crucial component of global information infrastructure, adopting the latest information and communication technology. Digital Libraries are networked collections of digital texts, documents, images, sounds, data, software, and many more that are the core of today's Internet and tomorrow's universally accessible digital repositories of all human knowledge. According to the Digital Library Federation (DLF, USA - http://www.dlf.org), "Digital libraries are organizations that provide the resources, including the specialized staff, to select, structure, offer intellectual access to, interpret, distribute, preserve the integrity of, and ensure the persistence over time of collections of digital works so that they are readily and economically available for use by a defined community or set of communities".

Currently in vast majority of instances, the concept 'Digital Library' is being practiced by and large loosely or even confused by many information systems. It is therefore imperative that the concept is properly understood so that there is no ambiguity while we progress with the work of designing or developing a digital library which is fully justified in the technical sense of the word. It is important that embarking on a digital library project is something which will take away substantial amount of time, energy, manpower and of course the hard earned money being pumped into it - be it for system development or towards development and maintenance of the collection, in a meaningful way. There is consensus all over that there exists a very large quantum of digital information, scholarly as well as trade, which are scattered and distributed throughout the Net and also being stored in numerous other databases and repositories spread across the world.

Also there is an unprecedented technology support and availability of infrastructure for digital libraries.

1.1. DL Features

Digital libraries offer new levels of access to broader audiences of users and new opportunities for library and information science field to advance both theory and practice [Marchionini, 1998]. They contain information collections predominantly in digital or electronic form. Electronic publications have some special management requirements as compared to printed document. They include infrastructure, acceptability, access restrictions, readability, standardization, authentication, preservation, copyright, user interface etc.

Digital libraries do enable the seamless integration of the scholarly electronic information, help in creating and maintaining local digital content, and strengthen the mechanisms and capacity of the library's information systems and services. They increase the portability, efficiency of access, flexibility, availability and preservation of digital objects. Digital Libraries can help move the nation towards realizing the enormously powerful vision of 'anytime, anywhere' access to the best and the latest of human thought and culture, so that no classroom, individual or a society is isolated from knowledge resources. Digital library brings the library to the user, overcoming all geographical barriers [ICDL, 2004].

1.2. DL Software

Undoubtedly it is essential to have a robust and flexible digital collections management and presentation software for creating and delivering digital collections. The preservation of digital objects is currently intimately tied to software that presents those objects. Complete preservation of complex digital objects, especially, is likely to require preservation of the software needed to use those objects. [Borgman, 1996]. The complexity of the situation is that digital library technologies and contents are not static. Continual evolution and investment are required to maintain the digital library. Commercial digital library products are comprehensive and extensible enough to support this evolution, but in many cases they are beyond the reach of most of the libraries in India. Some of the popular commercial DL software in the Indian libraries are VTLS (http://www.vtls.com) from the international market and ACADO (http://www.transversalnet.com/acado/index.htm) as an Indian initiative. The latter is definitely less costlier when compared but still striving its best to get a critical mass of users. The whole lot of associated issues include initial purchase fee, licensing fee, upgrade fee, annual maintenance contacts (AMCs) and so on. The best available choice for the librarian now is to turn to an Open Source Software (OSS). OSS has grown tremendously in scope and popularity over the last several years, and is now in widespread use. The growth of OSS has gained the attention of research librarians and created new opportunities for libraries [Frumkin, 2002]. OSS is close to our hearts primarily for their free (or almost free) availability and the broad rights it awards to the consumer. According to Stallman and others at OSS, 'Free Software' uses the 'free' from 'freedom', not the one from 'free beer' [http://www.opensource.org/docs/ definition_plain.html].

"OSS is software for which the source code is available to the end-user. The source code can be modified by the end-user. The licensing conditions are intended to facilitate continued re-use and wide availability of the software in both commercial and non-commercial contexts. The cost of acquisition to the end-user is often minimal. According to the proponents of OSS, 'Open source is a development methodology; free software is a social movement'. There are number of other notable features to OSS. Firstly, it has no secrets and the innards are available for anyone to inspect. It is not privately controlled and hence likely to promote open rather than proprietary formats. It is typically maintained by communities rather than corporations and hence bug fixes and enhancement are often frequent and free. It is usually distributed free of charge (developers make their money from support, training, and specialist add-ons; not marketing). It is also essential to clear up some of the misunderstandings about OSS. Open source software may or may not cost money. The cost of ownership often bears little relation to the cost of acquiring a piece of software. 'Public domain' is something different. Open source software has a copyright holder and conditions of legal use. Open source software does not mandate exclusivity. One can use open source programs under Windows. Also one should not choose software solely on the basis of open source. Interoperability and open standards for data are equally important" [OSS Watch, 2005].

According to Altman, for the library fraternity there are other set of reasons too for preferring OSS over commercial software. Long term preservation, assurance of privacy, provision for auditing, facilitating community resources, and conformity to open standards are hallmarks of OSS. Since commercial software is usually distributed only as a binary that will run only on a single hardware platform (and often only under a single version of a particular operating system) commercial software is very difficult to preserve over the long run without developing hardware emulation (and possibly OS 'emulation', as well). OSS, in contrast, can often be recompiled, or at least ported, to new hardware and operating systems [Altman, 2001]. In order to get a picture about the availability of OSS for digital library applications, it is encouraged to visit the directories of OSS projects, such as GNU [http://www.gnu.org/] and Sourceforge [http://www.sourceforge.net/] open source directory which lists over fifty-thousand projects, and the numbers continue to grow.

1.3. DL OBJECTIVES AND WORKFLOW

The primary objective of a digital library is to enhance the digital collection in a substantial way, by strategically sourcing digital materials, conforming to copyright permissions, in all possible standards/formats so that scalability and flexibility is guaranteed for the future and advanced information services are assured to the user community right from beginning. The digital library should also be able to integrate and aggregate the existing collections and services mentioned above with an outstanding client interface. This implies that the digital library system should also have a strong collection interface capable of embracing almost all the popular digital standards and formats and software platforms, in line with the underlying digital library technologies in vogue. This is crucial in the case of multimedia integration, which is again important as we planned to also host a digital audio and video library as part of the core library collection. Emphasis should also be given to maximise the efficiency and effectiveness of the information access and retrieval capabilities of the system by deploying Resource Description Framework [RDF] supplemented with popular descriptive metadata standards. The Internet also possesses, in addition to its mammoth proprietary information base, an invaluable wealth and a vast collection of public domain information products such as databases, books, journals, theses, technical reports, cases, standards, newsletters etc., scattered and distributed across the world. This treasure should also be explored to its maximum for collection building, based on the source and quality. Standard workflow patterns are to be identified for the system which include 'content selection', 'content acquisition', 'content publishing', 'content indexing and storage', and 'content accessing and delivery'. The system should also concern about such related issues, viz., preservation, usage monitoring, access management, interoperability, administration and management etc.

It is always desirable to have crosswalks between the digital catalogue of the library (OPAC) and the digital library, as the OPAC in most cases, acts as a stepping stone for effective information discovery in the library. It also facilitates a healthy bridging between the traditional and the digital library. MARC or any of its variant forms is the desired bibliographic standard recommended for the OPAC, for want of interoperability. Dublin Core [DCMI], MODS (Metadata Object Description Schema) or METS (Metadata Encoding and Transmission) are the recommended metadata format for the digital collection, and XML is the desired encoding scheme [XML]. The XML encoding schemas and the related DTDs (Document Type Definition) strengthen the digital library on strong footing and the XSL (Extensible Stylesheet Language) transformations acts as dynamic gateways between the diverse data streams and the HTML front-end.

1.4. Selection of the DL Software

The software selection based on set parameters is an uphill task, as the technology itself was still emerging only. In general, what is desirable is a system that is flexible enough to fit the current digital information system as above and to accommodate future migration. It should be robust in technical architecture as well as the content architecture. The system should address all major digital library related issues such as 'design criteria','collection building', 'content organisation', 'access', 'evaluation', 'policy and legal issues' including 'intellectual property rights'. That the system should be in a position to embrace almost all predominant and emerging digital object formats and capable of supporting the standard library technology platforms, should be the major focus. It should provide two important user interfaces: a public user interface for presentation and a metadata creation interface for administration. The system should also provide a powerful search engine and the interface should be easy to navigate and there should be provision for customisation.

There are many digital library softwares available, proprietary as well as open source, and most of them conform to international standards. As mentioned earlier, VTLS and ACADO are the commercial ones available and popular in the Indian market. Some of the popular Open Source Softwares for digital libraries, which are in use internationally, are 'DSpace', 'Dienst', 'Eprints', 'Fedora', 'Greenstone' etc. In line with the subject thrust of this paper, the Greenstone features are discussed in this paper.

1.5. Developing Digital Libraries using Open Source Software

Digital libraries do enable the creation of local content, strengthen the mechanisms and capacity of the library's information systems and services. They increase the portability, efficiency of access, flexibility, availability and preservation of content. A state-of-art Digital Library shall give a real boost to the library's modernization activities and its endeavours to launch innovative digital information services to the user community. Once the information is made digital, it could be stored, retrieved, shared, copied and transmitted across distances without having to invest any additional expenditure. Value added and pinpointed information at the click of the mouse will become a reality if there is a Library Portal to provide access to the invaluable collection hosted by the Digital Library.

World over there is increasing appreciation of the Open Access movement and the Open Source Software philosophies and for may a libraries it is a chosen decision, be it technical or financial reasons, not to go for a proprietary digital library software. One needs to evaluate some of the popular Open Source Software for digital libraries, which are in use internationally. 'Dienst', 'Eprints', 'Fedora', 'Greenstone' etc. are among the candidates for the preferred software. Obviously Greenstone outscores the group as a general purpose digital library software from the point of view of a multi-publication type, multi-format, multi-media and a multi-lingual practical digital library [Greenstone]. And once finalized, it could be formally adopted as the software for creating the digital library.

The Greenstone Digital Library Software (GSDL) is a top of the line and internationally renowned Open Source Software system for developing digital libraries, promoted by the New Zealand Digital Library project research group at the University of Waikato, led by Dr. Ian H. Witten, and is sponsored by the UNESCO. Greenstone software uses three more additional associated softwares namely, Java Run Time Environment (JRE), ImageMagick and Ghostscript. The software suite is available at the open source directory 'Sourceforge.Net'.

2. GREENSTONE FACT SHEET (WWW.GREENSTONE.ORG)

Greenstone is a suite of software for building and distributing digital library collections. It is not a digital library but a tool for building digital libraries. It provides a new way of organizing information and publishing it on the Internet in the form of a fully-searchable, metadata-driven digital library. It has been developed and distributed in cooperation with UNESCO and the Human Info NGO in Belgium. It is open-source, multilingual software, issued under the terms of the GNU General Public License. Its developers received the 2004 IFIP Namur award for "contributions to the awareness of social implications of information technology, and the need for an holistic approach in the use of information technology that takes account of social implications."

There are presently two versions of Greenstone going around, Version 2 and 3, and they are generally represented as Greenstone2 and Greenstone3. The latest in Greenstone2 as on June 2016 is V.2.86 and that of Greenstone3 is V.3.07. Greenstone2 will be there for some more years, but ultimately Waikato/Greenstone see that Geenstone3 will replace it.

3. TECHNICAL FEATURES

3.1. Platforms

Greenstone runs on all versions of Windows, and Unix, and Mac OS-X. It is very easy to install. For the default Windows installation absolutely no configuration is necessary, and end users routinely install Greenstone on their personal laptops or workstations. Institutional users run it on their main web server, where it interoperates with standard web server software (e.g. Apache).

3.2. Interoperability

Greenstone is highly interoperable using contemporary standards, It incorporates a server that can serve any collection over the Open Archives Protocol for Metadata Harvesting (OAI-PMH), and Greenstone can harvest documents over OAI-PMH and include them in a collection. Any collection can be exported to METS (in the Greenstone METS Profile, approved by the METS Editorial Board and published at http://www.loc.gov/standards/mets/mets-profiles.html), and Greenstone can ingest documents in METS form. Any collection can be exported to DSpace ready for DSpace's batch import program, and any DSpace collection can be imported into Greenstone.

3.3. Interfaces

Greenstone has two separate interactive interfaces, the Reader interface and the Librarian interface. End users access the digital library through the Reader interface, which operates within a web browser. The Librarian interface is a Java-based graphical user interface (also available as an applet) that makes it easy to gather material for a collection (downloading it from the web where necessary), enrich it by adding metadata, design the searching and browsing facilities that the collection will offer the user, and build and serve the collection.

3.4. Metadata formats

Users define metadata interactively within the Librarian interface. These metadata sets are predefined: Dublin Core (qualified and unqualified), RFC 1807, NZGLS (New Zealand Government Locator Service), AGLS (Australian Government Locator Service). New metadata sets can be defined using Greenstone's Metadata Set Editor. "Plug-ins" are used to ingest externally-prepared metadata in different forms, and plug-ins exist for XML, MARC, CDS/ ISIS, ProCite, BibTex, Refer, OAI, DSpace, METS.

3.5. Document formats

Greenstone basically supports all popular file formats and media. Plug-ins are also used to ingest documents. For textual documents, there are plug-ins for PDF, PostScript, Word, RTF, HTML, Plain text, Latex, ZIP archives, Excel, PPT, Email (various formats), source code. For multimedia documents, there are plug-ins for Images (any format, including GIF, JIF, JPEG, TIFF), MP3 audio, Ogg Vorbis audio, and a generic plug-in that can be configured for audio formats, MPEG, MIDI, etc.

4. USER BASE

4.1. Distribution

As with all open source projects, the user base for Greenstone is unknown. Tens of thousands of installations of Greenstone are estimated across world as is evidenced by the increasing volume of messages being exchanged in the various fora, especially the Greenstone E-lists. It is distributed on SourceForge, a leading distribution centre for open source software.

4.2. Greenstone Example Collections

Examples of public Greenstone collections (see http://www.greenstone.org for URLs) can be found at:

Association of Indian Labour Historians, Delhi	New York Botanical Garden
Auburn University, Alabama	Peking University Digital Library
California University at Riverside	Philippine Research Education and Government Information Network
Chicago University Library	Secretary of Human Rights of Argentina
Detroit Public Library	Slavonski Brod Public Library,
Gresham College, London	Slovenia State Library of Tasmania
Hawaiian Electronic Library Illinois	Stuttgart University of Applied Sciences
Wesleyan University	Texas A&M University Center for the Study of Digital Libraries
Indian Institute of Management Kozhikode (IIMK)	University of Illinois
Kyrgyz Republic National Library LeHigh University, Pennsylvania	University of North Carolina Bibiblio project
Mari El Republic, Russia	Vietnam National University
National Centre for Science Information, Bangalore, India	Vimercate Public Library, Milan, Italy
Netherlands Institute for Scientific Information Services	Washington Research Library Consortium
	Welsh Books Council

5. LANGUAGES

One of Greenstone's unique strengths is its multilingual nature. The reader's interface is available in the following languages: Arabic, Armenian, Bengali, Catalan, Croatian, Czech, Chinese (both simplified and traditional), Dutch, English, Farsi, Finnish, French, Galician, Georgian, German, Greek, Hebrew, Hindi, Indonesian, Italian, Japanese, Kannada, Kazakh, Kyrgyz, Latvian, Maori, Mongolian, Portuguese (BR and PT versions), Russian, Serbian, Spanish, Thai, Turkish, Ukrainian, Vietnamese.

The Librarian interface and the full Greenstone documentation (which is extensive) is in: English, French, Spanish, and Russian.

6. TRAINING AND SUPPORT

Training is a bottleneck for widespread adoption of any digital library software. Greenstone's Waikato site http://www.greenstone.org; the Greenstone Wiki http://greenstone.sourceforge.net/wiki/index.php/Greenstone Wiki, and the Greenstone Support for South Asia http://greenstonesupport.iimk.ac.in give many training materials and guidance on the software. It is observed that Greenstone training and workshops are quite common in digital library conferences and seminar all over the world and this itself speaks volumes the importance of Greenstone.

6.1. E-mail Support

There are many E-Lists and E-Groups available for Greenstone support. For subscribing to the main Greenstone lists, visit https://list.scms.waikato.ac.nz/mailman/listinfo/greenstone-users for User's List (greenstone-users-request@list.scms.waikato.ac.nz) and https://list.scms.waikato.ac.nz/mailman/listinfo/

greenstone-devel for Developer's list. There is also an E-List for supporting the South Asian Greenstone users greenstonesupport@iimk.ac.in. You can join the South Asia Support E-List by filling the form at http://eprints.iimk.ac.in/mailman/listinfo/greenstonesupport.

7. GREENSTONE : FEATURES

The salient features of Greenstone are basically taken from two of the official publications of the software development team appeared in D-Lib Magazine during the year 2001 [Witten, 2001] and 2003 [Witten, 2003]. Greenstone builds collections using almost popular and standard digital formats such as HTML, XML, Word, Post Script, PDF, RTF, JPG, GIF, JPEG, MPEG etc. and many other formats which include audio as well as video. It is provided with effective full-text searching and metadata-based browsing facilities that are attractive and easy to use. Moreover, they are easily maintained and can be augmented and rebuilt entirely automatically. The system is extensible: software "plug-ins" accommodate different document and metadata types. Greenstone incorporates an interface that makes it easy for people to create their own library collections. Collections may be built and served locally from the user's own web server, or (given appropriate permissions) remotely on a shared digital library host. End users can easily build new collections styled after existing ones from material on the Web or from their local files (or both), and collections can be updated and new ones brought on-line at any time. The Greenstone Librarian Interface (GLI) is a Java based GUI interface for easy collection building. Greenstone software runs on a wide variety of platforms such as Windows, Unix / Linux, Apple Mac etc. and provides full-text mirroring, indexing, searching, browsing and metadata extraction. It incorporates an interface that makes it easy for institutions to create their own library collections. Collections could be built and served locally from the user's own web server, or (given appropriate permissions) remotely on a shared digital library host. The other set of features include OAI plug-in (introduced since the 2.40 version) and DCMI compliance, UNICODE based multi-lingual capabilities and a user-friendly multimedia interfacing [Unicode]. Further more, it has a powerful search engine 'Managing Gigabyte' Plus-Plus ('MG' PP) and metadata-based browsing facilities. A very interesting feature of Greenstone is its exhaustive set of well documented and articulated manuals (http://www.greenstone.org/cgi-bin/library?e=p-en-docs-utfZz-8&a=p&p=docs) such as 'Installer's Guide', 'User's Guide', 'Developer's Guide', and 'From Paper to Collection' a document describing the entire process of creating a digital library collection from paper documents. This includes the scanning and OCR process and the use of the "Organizer". There is one more interesting documentation 'Inside Greenstone Collections' which clarifies most of the trickier parts of using Greenstone, especially dealing with configuration file for the collection in question.

The primary objective of any digital library will be to enhance the digital collection in a substantial way, by strategically sourcing digital materials, conforming to copyright permissions, in all possible standards / formats so that scalability and flexibility is guaranteed for the future and advanced information services and are assured to the user community right from beginning. The digital library has to be planned in such a way that it will integrate and aggregate the existing collections and services with an outstanding user interface. Accordingly, necessary strategies are to be adopted towards working out the digital library system. This implies that the digital library system should have a strong collection interface capable of embracing almost all the popular digital standards, digital formats and software platforms, in line with the underlying digital library technologies in vogue. This is crucial in the case of multimedia integration, which is again important as it is planned to host digital audio and video library as part of the core library collection.

8. GREENSTONE INSTALLATION

The GNU Public License version Greenstone can be downloaded from 'http://www.greenstone.org' or 'http://sourceforge.net/index.php'. You can download the binaries for Linux or Windows. The associated softwares such as Java Runtime Environment (JRE) and the Imagemagick also to be downloaded. A graphical tool is used for collection building and configurations and customization. This is called the Greenstone Librarian Interface (GLI) and it requires the Java Runtime Environment (JRE). The latest version pertaining to Volume 2 release of Greenstone as on June 2016 is V.2.86.

Installation

Here is what you need to do to install Greenstone.

Select the language for this installation. We choose English

Welcome to the Greenstone Digital Library Software Installer. It is recommended that you uninstall any previous installations of Greenstone2 before running this installer. Click <Next>

License Agreement. Click <Accept>

Choose location to install Greenstone. Leave at the default and click <Next>

Components. Click the question mark button on the right of each component will display the description of this component in a popup window. Leave at the default (all components are selected) and click <Next>

(For older installers you must now select collections. Leave at the default, Documented Example Collections, and click <Next>)

Enable administration pages. Read the description on this page, if you check to enable, click <Next> to set admin password. Choose a suitable password and click <Next> (If your computer will not be serving collections online, the password doesn't matter)

Click <Install> to start the installation. Click <Show Details> to show the details of this installation

Files are copied across

8.1. Collection Building and Configuration

Greenstone used to have three modes for collection building, viz., Command Line, Web Interface and the Greenstone Librarian Interface (GLI). Among these GLI is the one getting more prominence as far as the librarian / information professionals are concerned.

8.1.1. Greenstone Librarian Interface (GLI)

The GLI (Greenstone Librarian Interface) was introduced recently, progressing with the version 2.4x. Soon the GLI got strengthened as well as popularized, and the Web Interface mode has been withdrawn temporarily, while it could also be reinforced if one wishes so. The GLI based collection building is quite easy and simple a method. Collection developers can activate the GLI software and use the 'Gather', 'Enrich', 'Design', 'Create', and the 'Format' panels for making, configuring, customizing and managing collections.

8.1.2. The 'Gather' Panel facilitates putting the relevant files from the 'workspace' to the 'collection building' area. The 'Enrich' Panel explains how metadata is created, edited, assigned and retrieved, and how to use external metadata sources. Help for this is provided in the GLI Interface. The

'Design' Panel facilitates customising your interface, once your files are marked up with metadata. Using the Gather Panel, you can specify the fields that are searchable, allow browsing through the document, facilitate the languages that are supported, and provide the buttons that are to appear on the page. Help for this is provided in the GLI Interface. The Create Panel facilitates creation of your collection.

To build a typical collection, say 'MyTest' collection, first go to 'File' section, select 'New' and then give the collection name as 'MyTest'. Select OK from the panel and then you will get another panel popped up where you will select the appropriate Metadata Set. You may also give the description about the collection here. By default, the system will prompt Dublin Core metadata set. Click on OK button and you will get the collection create panel made ready for accepting the file(s).

The 'Gather' Panel is activated now. From the 'Workspace' provided, identify the document to be put in the collection by locating it in the local folder. Drag and drop the file to the Collection Area using the mouse. The necessary 'plugin' for the creation of the collection is to be tick marked and enabled in the 'Design' panel, which is the next step in the collection building process. If the collection has objects for which 'plugins' are not provided in the default set, a new dialog box for adding the required plugin will appear and it has to be the added to the default set.

2. Go to the 'Enrich' panel and give necessary values for the Dublin Core element sets.

   Manage Metadata Sets - This feature allows you to add, configure and remove the Metadata Sets in your collection and what Elements they contain.

3. Design Panel

The next step is to give necessary values and arguments for the 'Design' panel which include [Note: GLI Design Panel's own language is used below i. to x., for want of clarity and to avoid any ambiguity in usage]:

i. General Options : In this section, give the e-mail address of the 'collection creator', 'collection maintainer', 'collection title' (will be supplied by the system), collection folder (will be supplied by the system), Image file location for the Collection icon and the Image file location for the Document icon. Click on the Tick mark for making this collection publicly available.

ii. Document Plugins : This section facilitates adding, configuring or removing plugins from your collection. To add one, choose it from the combobox and click 'Add Plugin'. To configure or remove one, select it from the list of assigned plugins and then: i) Change its position in the plugin order by clicking on the arrow buttons. (Note: The position of RecPlug and ArcPlug are fixed). ii) Configure it by clicking 'Configure Plugin', iii) Remove it by clicking 'Remove Plugin'. Plugins are configured using a pop-up design area with a scrollable list of arguments. Enable arguments and enter or select values as necessary.

iii. Search Types : Defining the search type is an advanced feature, only available when enabled (by checking the 'Enable Advanced Searches' box). Once enabled, further controls for selecting and changing the order of search types become available. See the'Search Type Selection and Ordering' section of the 'Design' Panel for more information on this.

iv. Search Indexes : The required number of searchable indexes the collection must have, is to be selected here. To add a new index, enter a unique name for the index, select material/metadata is to be indexed, and click 'Add Index'. If you wish to add all of the available sources so as to have indexes built on them, then click 'Add All'.

v. Partition Indexes : This feature help to refine index creation. This facility is disabled in the GLI mode.

vi. Cross-Collection Search : This feature facilitates cross-collection searching, where a single search is performed over several collections, as if all the collections were one. Specify (Tick Mark) the collections to include in a search by clicking on the appropriate collection's name in the list below. The current collection will automatically be included. [Note : If the individual collections do not have the same indexes (including sub collection partitions and language partitions) as each other, cross-collection searching will not work properly. The user will only be able to search using indexes common to all collections].

vii. Browsing Classifiers : This feature allows the AtoZ browsing of the collection and by default if takes the 'Dublin Core. Title'. You can more data elements in the AtoZ classify list as deem fit for the collection using this feature.

viii. Format Features : The web pages you see when using Greenstone are not pre-stored, but are generated 'on the fly' as they are needed. Format commands are used to change the appearance of these generated pages. Some are switches that control the display of documents or parts of documents; others are more complex and require html code as an argument. To add a format command, choose it from the 'feature' list. If a True/False option panel appears, select the state by clicking on the appropriate button.

For example, to get the Cover Image displayed in the document while building the collection, go to the 'Choose Features' dropdown box and enable the 'DocumentIMages', i.e., make its value to True.

ix. Translate Text : Use this feature to review and assign translations of text fragments in your collection. The translated text will appear in a different box in the browser.

x. Metadata Sets : This feature allows you to add, configure and remove the Metadata Sets in your collection and what Elements they contain.

4. Now go to the 'Create' panel and click on the 'Build Collection'. Greenstone will start creating the collection. You can see the built collection by clicking on the 'Preview Collection'.

Please remember you have to save your collection development process from time to time. It is not mandatory that you need to comply with the entire set of formalities for a building a collection in a single stretch. You can do it in different sessions too. What is important is saving the sessions from time to time. In the GLI mode of collection building, the various panels to be used are illustrated in Figure 1.

5. Format Panel

i. General : This section explains how to review and alter the general settings associated with your collection. First, under the "Format" tab, click "General". Here some collection wide metadata can be set or modified, including the title and description entered when starting a new collection. First are the contact email addresses of the collection's creator and maintainer. The following field allows you to change the collection title. The folder that the collection is stored in is shown next, but this cannot be altered. Then comes the icon to show at the top left of the collection's "About" page (in the form of a URL), followed by the icon used in the Greenstone library page to link to the collection. Next is a checkbox that controls whether the collection should be publicly accessible. Finally comes the "Collection Description" text area as described in "Creating a New Collection".

ii. Search : This section explains how to set the display text for the drop down lists on the search page. Under the "Format" tab, click "Search". This pane contains a table listing each search index, index level (for MGPP or Lucene collections), and index or language partition. Here you can enter the text to be used for each item in the various drop-down lists on the search page. This pane only allows you to set the text for one language, the current language used by GLI. To translate these names for other languages, use the Translate Text part of the Format view (see "Translate Text" feature in the Format panel).

iii. Format Features : The web pages you see when using Greenstone are not pre-stored, but are generated 'on the fly' as they are needed. Format commands are used to change the appearance of these generated pages. Some are switches that control the display of documents or parts of documents; others are more complex and require html code as an argument. To add a format command, choose it from the 'feature' list. If a True/False option panel appears, select the state by clicking on the appropriate button.

For example, to get the Cover Image displayed in the document while building the collection, go to the 'Choose Features' dropdown box and enable the 'DocumentIMages', i.e., set its value to True.

iv. Translate Text : Use this feature to review and assign translations of text fragments in your collection. The translated text will appear in a different box in the browser.

v. Cross-Collection Search : This feature facilitates cross-collection searching, where a single search is performed over several collections, as if all the collections were one. Specify (Tick Mark) the collections to include in a search by clicking on the appropriate collection's name in the list below. The current collection will automatically be included. [Note : If the individual collections do not have the same indexes (including sub collection partitions and language partitions) as each other, cross-collection searching will not work properly. The user will only be able to search using indexes common to all collections].

vi. Collection Specific Macros : Under the "Format" tab, click "Collection Specific Macros". This view shows the contents of the collection's extra.dm macro file. This is where collection specific macros can be defined. To learn more about macros, see Chapter 3 of the Greenstone Developer's Guide.

8.2. Hierarchy Structure

To create indexes for section and sub-section, the pre-requisite is that the document should be in HTML format. Therefore your collection files in other formats like PDF, Word, etc. are first to be converted into HTML format. Also in the Collection Configuration file (for GLI, in the Design Panel, in the Document Plugin section, while configuring the Arguments in the HTML Plugin, click and enable the 'description_tags'), the HTML plugin has to be modified to 'plugin HTMLPlug -description_tags'. Corresponding changes have to be made in the 'indexes' and the 'collectionmeta' lines. Obviously now the Source File has to be edited as a HTML file structure. For the section and sub sections, you need to edit the source file as follows, giving XML tags as comments in the body of the HTML file. Fig. 1 below shows a hierarchy structured EBook.

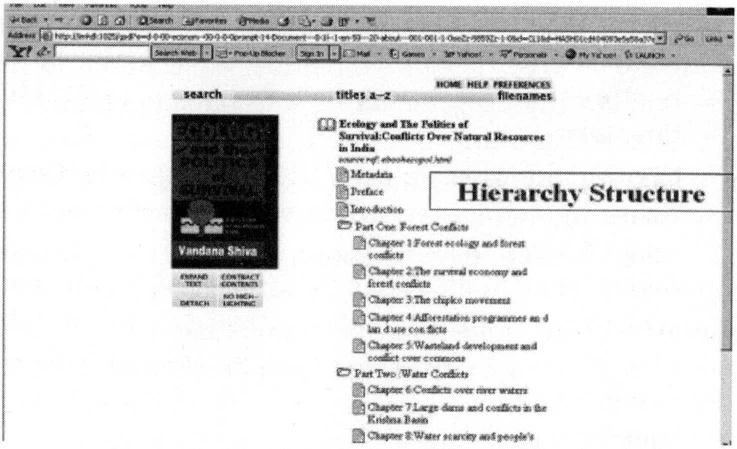

Fig. 1. An EBook with the Hierarchy Structure

8.3. Customization of User Interface (MyLibrary)

In order to change the look and feel of the Greenstone user interface, you need to work on the Collection Configuration (Collect.cfg) files. Customising the User Interface requires a certain degree of knowledge on HTML and some level of Web Designing skills are pre-requisites for this.

i. **Collect.cfg :** This is the collection configuration file. You can find this file in the "Program Files\Greenstone\collect\etc" directory. Details on how to create this file can be found in the Developer's Guide, "1.5 Collection configuration file" and "2.3 Formatting Greenstone output".

ii. **Macro files :** Macro files have an extension '.dm'. All macro files are stored in the "macros" directory. Details on how to create macros and macro files can be found in the Developer's Guide "2.4 controlling the Greenstone user interface".

iii. **Image files :** All images files can be found in the 'Program Files\Greenstone\images' directory.

iv. **Main.cfg :** This file contains a list of all macro files used for the User Interface. If you created a new '.dm' file, you need to add it to this file. The main.cfg file is stored in the "Program Files\Greenstone\etc" directory.

v. **Getting the Cover Image :** For you to get the Cover Image of your input document, you need to put the image file and the source file (document) into a single folder. They both should bear the same name also. While building the collection, Greenstone will take both the files to "Program Files\Greenstone\collect\<collection name>\archives\Hash". The collection thus built will display the Cover Image along with the document. Also in the Design Panel, in the Document Plugin section, while configuring the Arguments for the HTML Plugin, give the custom argument as 'cover_image'.

vi. **Getting the Collection Icon :** Click on Design panel ->General Option -> URL to home page icon (Browse for image and locate it).

vii. **Getting Header Image for the Digital Library :** To get the header image which says MyLibrary banner in the DL head, create the graphic file (preferably a GIF file), name it as 'gsdlhead.xxx' and then replace it with the file available in 'Program Files\Greenstone\images.'

viii. **Deep Level Customization :** By default, Greenstone's collection icon area is a matrix grid (the N X 3 format). You can change the collection icon area by editing the '_content_ macro' in 'home.dm'. You will need to remove the '_homeextra_ macro' (this is the N x 3 table that the Greenstone C++ code automatically creates for you) and can then put whatever design customization you want into this area. You will need to put the icons and links to the collection yourself.

You can also achieve high end customization by replacing the 'home.dm' with 'yourhome.dm' in the \greenstone\etc folder.

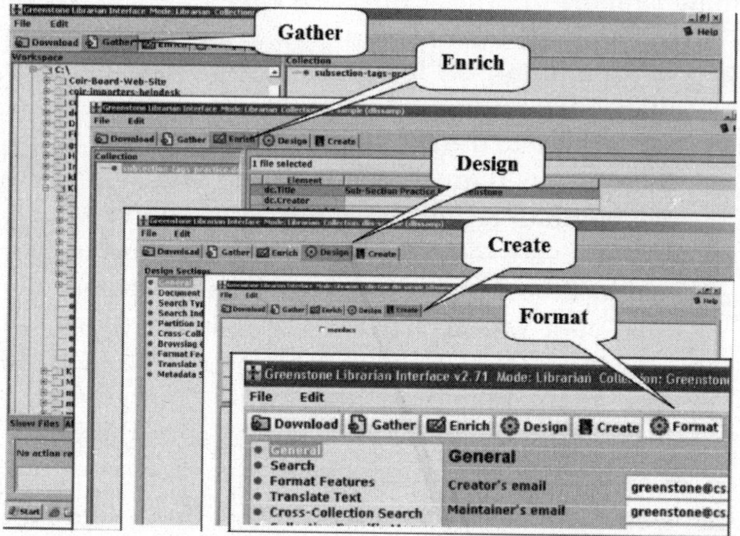

Fig. 2. GLI Panels for Gather, Enrich, Design, Create and Format

8.4. GSDL : Helpline, Archives

Greenstone's E-Mail list is a very useful and active listserv which shares and clarifies user experiences and stories dealing with real life situations. To subscribe or unsubscribe to the list via the World Wide Web, visit "https://list.scms.waikato.ac.nz/ mailman/listinfo/greenstone-users" or, via email, send a message with subject or body 'help' to "greenstone-users-request@list.scms.waikato.ac.nz". Greenstone has started one more List recently, for the Greenstone 3 Version (the latest Beta version) user group, and the details are avaiiable at "https://list.scms.waikato.ac.nz/mailman/listinfo/greenstone3".

UNESCO has initiated a Greenstone support organization for South Asia in 2006, supported by a group of experts in the region, and it is coordinated by IIM Kozhikode http://greenstonesupport.iimk.ac.in. The site is rich with many of the Greenstone support materials. In addition, an E-list greenstonesupport@iimk.ac.in offers online support to professionals on Greenstone.

For those looking for quick solutions for their real-time or on-the-job trouble shooting while using the software, 'Greenstone Archives' is a treasure house. It is a database of the email messages circulated in the List, and is searchable. The mails generated from the List and its threads are archived and made available for the user community. The archive is available at "http://www.sadl.uleth.ca/nz/cgi-bin/library?a=p&p=about&c=gsarch-e". This is the major list used worldwide for Greenstone and the content of the messages is usually global in nature. Developers and Greenstone users can avoid a great deal of unwanted labour by carefully going through the archive before they start working on problem solving, or before shooting a mail to the List.

9. CONCLUSION

The ever changing landscape of the information paradigm poses a host of new IT and information challenges not only to the library and information professionals, but to the users, patrons and scholars and the publishing community as well. Indeed the new environment throws up a host of unprecedented features and avenues, and interestingly enough, if we know how to tap them well, we find there is a plethora of opportunities, and most of them even for free. The 'free things', so belovedly called world wide the 'Open Source Softwares', many of them could even be compared against their commercial counterparts in terms of their strength, efficiency, power and the ever increasing user base. Among the major challenges include the information professionals' emergent need to acquire the necessary skill sets and working knowledge on the cutting-edge information science and information technology areas and in leveraging them in a contextually relevant manner.

Working on a Digital Library project in general, especially working with the Greenstone Digital Library Software in particular, has been highly exhilarating, enriching as well as rewarding. The treasure of knowledge, skills, experience, expertise, and exposure we have achieved and accomplished during the past four years have been extremely enjoying and simply terrific. It is also important sharing the real life experience of a particular software as a an application user, as there exist a great deal of difference in view points when it comes from the software developers themselves. Frankly, we also have grown with the software from strength to strength. We have every appreciation to Greenstone as far as its usability, extensibility and flexibility are concerned. We are also indeed pleased with its consistent technology catch-up strategies and their untiring extension activities. One should appreciate the dynamic Greenstone team for their selfless open source philosophy, and their relentless work in this regard just for the cause of science. We have been closely watching the world scenario in the area of digital library research and we are quite convinced that Greenstone is a fast growing community coupled with deep commitments from the developers in taking this software to further heights and making this an outstanding open source model for digital library development. The Wiki and the OAI features of Greenstone and the ambitious 'Greenstone 3', released already and running in its version 3.07, which draws its strength from the open source family of 'Web Services' technologies facilitating configurable, extensible and dynamic digital libraries are all testimony to their commitment to excellence in digital library software development. In the meanwhile UNESCO came forward to support them unconditionally and it is a proud privilege to announce that we have the Greenstone Support for South Asia already launched with their support, to take care of the DL needs of this region.

ACKNOWLEDGEMENT

This review article on digital libraries is for the promotion of open source softwares by information professionals.

REFERENCES

[1] Orsdel, Lee Van; Born, Kathleen. 2002 Doing the Digital Flip.Library Journal, 127 (7): 51-55.

[2] OCLC Report on Five-Year information format trends. 2003. http://www.oclc.org/reports/2003 format.htm

[3] Marchionini, G. 1998. Research and development in digital libraries. Allen Kent (Ed.)Encyclopedia of Library and Information Science, 63: 259-279.

[4] ICDL 2004. www.teriin.org/events/icdl/background.htm

[5] Sreekumar M.G. and Sunitha T. 2005. Essential Strategies and Skill Sets Towards Creating Digital Libraries Using Open Source Software. [Proceedings of NACLIN 2005, DELNET, Bangalore, India].

[6] Borgman, Christine L. 1996. Social Aspects of Digital Libraries,pp170. [Proceedings of the first ACM international conference on Digital libraries. Bethesda, Maryland, United State, March 20-23, Organised by Association of Computing Machinery]

[7] Frumkin, Jeremy (ED). 2002 Special Issue: Open Source Software. Information Technology and Libraries 21(1).

[8] Stallman, Richard. http://www.opensource.org/docs/definition_plain.html

[9] OSS Watch <http://www.oss-watch.ac.uk/talks/2003-09-24-csg/index.xml.ID=body. 1_div.37>

[10] Altman, M. 2001. Open Source Software for Libraries: from Greenstone to the Virtual Data Center and Beyond. IASSIST Quarterly. Winter : 1-7.

[11] GNU (GNU's Not Unix!) <http://www.gnu.org/ (13 June, 2005)>

[12] SourceForge.Net (world's largest Open Source software development website) http://www.sourceforge.net/.

[13] RDF (Resource Description Framework). <http://www.w3c.org/RDF>

[14] DCMI (Dublin Core Metadata Initiative) <http://dublincore.org>

[15] Greenstone Digital Library Software <htttp://www.greenstone.org>

[16] Witten, Ian H. et al. 2001. Greenstone : Open-Source Digital Library Software.D-Lib Magazine, 7 (10): 1-16.

[17] Witten, Ian H. 2003. Examples of Practical Digital Libraries : Collections Built Internationally Using Greenstone. D-Lib Magazine 9 (3): 1-15.

[18] Unicode Consortium <htttp://unicode.org>

[19] IIMK Digital Library <http://iimk.ac.in/gsdl/cgi-bin/library>

[20] Greenstone Support for South Asia <http://greenstonesupport.iimk.ac.in >

3

Achieving the Objectives of the Public Library Movement Using Information and Communication Technologies (ICT)

P.J. Joseph

ABSTRACT

Gives a bird's eye view of Kerala's library movement stressing the unique character which is a movement starting at the grass roots level later getting accepted and supported by Government. The author states that with the availability of numerous technologies for digitizing content and disseminating it through network any village library can offer services that earlier only large libraries like State Central Library or University library were able to offer. Gives suggestions for proper use of ICT to extend public library services of required quality and variety to all the people transcending economic, and geographical boundaries.

Keywords : public library, networking, state central library, library legislation, digitization, community information services, and library automation

1. INTRODUCTION

Kerala has a unique library movement, which attracted attention worldwide. Unlike in other countries and other regions of India, Kerala's library movement was initiated at the grassroots level and was not enforced from above. People, especially ordinary people living in remote villages from different strata of society understood the need for dissemination of information and they established a system by themselves. It later got organized and coordinated by stalwarts like Sri. PN Panikkar which opened the eyes of the authorities and later it was supported or taken up by government.

A democratic system of government implies equal right of all citizens to get information services from outlets near his home/workplace. This service should be free. It should be speedy and efficient. Information service of this nature cannot be provided by public libraries that exist as independent units or as separate groups under states or councils without provision for sharing or getting access to resources built up all along the state and the country. Only a nationwide network of public libraries catering to the information needs of the people, literate or illiterate, rich or poor, rural or urban, can provide the knowledge-based services required in a modern society. This service should be maintained wholly from public fund. There should be trained and experienced professionals to manage the services. The system should also be supported by legislation. The role of Public Library System (PLS) in supporting people to adjust to the continuous changes that result from developments in Science and Technology, in enabling government to achieve transparency in its actions to make democracy meaningful, in boosting economic and social development, and in providing facilities for non formal education and healthy entertainment cannot be done by any other agency. Government of India should consider the plans prepared by Ranganathan for adoption and a national level legislation for Public library systems which prescribes a model also for State level legislations, which is mandatory, should be enacted as a priority item if the public library movements are to become fruitful. Now the developments in Information and communication Technology which has provided digital libraries, online journals and the like give immense power to public libraries if we approach the system with an integrated vision.

Before thinking about modernization of the library systems it is essential to understand the history and objectives or the library movement of our regions.

2. HISTORICAL PERSPECTIVE

The first library in Kerala is the Trivandrum Public Library, which started functioning in 1835. Ernakulam Public Library started functioning in 1861. The Trichur Public Library came into existence in 1873 and the Kottayam Public Library in 1882. In British ruled Malabar area, three libraries were established at Tellichery (1901) Calicut (1924) and Cannannore (1927). An attempt to co-ordinate the functioning of the libraries started very early in this century. The first meeting for that purpose was held at Neyyattinkara in 1926. But there was no follow up activity after that. There was a second attempt towards this goal in the Malabar region in 1931. In the same year there was another meeting in Trichur and as a result of that a periodical called 'Grandha Vicharam' (Thoughts on books) was published. On 6th December 1943, an organization called Kerala Library Association was formed at Tellichery. In the Travancore State also there were a few similar attempts. At the initiative of Neyyoor Divan, Nanu Pillai Memorial Library, an organization was formed under the leadership of Malloor Govinda Pillai. At the initiative of Sri Chitra Thirunal Library, Trivandrum, a conference was held at Trivandrum. But none of these attempts succeeded in starting an organization that could stand the test of time.

It was on the initiative of P.N. Panikkar who was then the Secretary of P.K. Memorial Library at Ambalappuzha, that a meeting of the representatives of 47 libraries of the Travancore State was held on 14th September 1945 at Ambalappuzha. They formed an organization called All Travancore Library Union with P.N. Panikkar as its Secretary. All the 47 libraries of Travancore became members of the Union paying Rs.5/- as membership fees.

3. AIMS AND OBJECTIVES OF LIBRARY UNION

The following were the aims and objectives of the organization:

- to function as the Central Committee of all the libraries of the state,
- to support and develop the libraries that already exist,
- to promote adult education programme,
- to develop language ability among the neo-literates,
- to organize night classes for the adults,
- to persuade the Government to start a department for libraries,
- to organize programmes to train librarians
- to start periodicals to publish news activities of organizations which have reading libraries,
- to work for the development of the vernacular,
- to start a good library in every Taluk and
- to patronize and promote the similar purposes and aims as that of the libraries.

In August 1946 the executive committee of the Library Union made a representation to the government for financial support and the Government sanctioned a financial grant to employ four persons as organizers. On

27th May t947, the organization got itself registered under the Travancore Companies Act and thus it became a legal entity. By the time the association had nearly 500 member libraries and the government gave a grant of Rs. 100,000 to be distributed among the member Libraries for buying books and maintaining a staff. The office of the association was at Ambalappuzha in the beginning but a year later it was shifted to Trivandrum. Though the association was as non-governmental organization, the government entrusted them with the task of supervising and strengthening the libraries of the state. During this time, in the State of Cochin the affairs of the libraries were governed by a Government Department. After unification of Travancore and Cochin States, the libraries in Cochin area were also affiliated to the Association, which was renamed as the Travancore Cochin Library Union, in 1949. After the Kerala State was formed the Libraries in Malabar area were also affiliated to the Association, which was again renamed as Kerala Library Union in 1958.

The Government entrusted the Union with task of grading the libraries into different categories and giving annual grant for each category. On the basis of assets, the number of books and the number of books issued to the members the libraries were divided into eleven categories and the financial grant of each category and the salary of the librarians of each category were fixed and the government gave the required money to the Union which distributed the money to the libraries.

4. LITERACY PROGRAMME

In the 1970s the Library Union launched two literacy projects with the help of Central Education Department. One for the educationally backward district of Malappuram and another for the poor people of the costal region of Poovar and Vizhinjam. This further diversified the activities of the library association. The association started producing learning and reading materials for the adult illiterates and the neo-literates. A statewide campaign was launched for the purpose. In 1971, the Union launched the functional literacy project and in 1975 UNESCO gave the 'Literacy Award' to the Library Union.

5. GOVERNING OF THE COUNCIL

In the beginning the elections of the office bearers of the Library Union were almost unanimous. But as the union developed into an important movement, the elections were keenly contested. Political interests also came to be reflected in the contests. By 1977 the ruling party of Kerala found that most of the office bearers of the Union were persons belonging to the opposition parties. Further, there were disputes regarding the elections held in some 17 libraries. Those disputes were used as a pretext to dissolve ail the existing committees of the Union at the State and Taluk levels by an ordinance promulgated on 16th March 1977. By the ordinance the government entrusted the administrative control of the union with a Board consisting of members nominated by the Government. The nominated members were officials and the members of the ruling parties. There were strong protests from the public against this. But the government held that it was only an ad-hoc arrangement till the newly elected office bearers took charge. But since 1977 no election was held for quite a long time till 1994. It took more than a decade for the Government to present the bill in the Legislative Assembly laying down the rules of election and administration of the libraries. That legislation came into force in 1989. Once the Government took over the control of the union, it ceased to be a popular movement. As the arrangement was said to be ad-hoc, no innovative programmes were introduced and there were no new initiatives. The organization became stagnant. But since nineties elections have been held and stalwarts like Kadmmanitta Ramakrishnan headed the Library council. Recently also elections have been held recently and new office bearers have taken charge. Now there are more than 7600 libraries under Kerala State Library Council.

6. ICT DEVELOPMENT BY THE LIBRARY COUNCIL

The Council is automating thousands of libraries under it. This can be a multicrore project. But these projects are to be viewed seriously. Is it using technology that enables pooling resources and sharing resources at least at bibliographical level with State Central Library, National Library etc.? Is KSLC using apt technology? Is there Council's own expert staff to look after the projects? Can the technology used be scaled up if essential ? Are the terms and conditions under which work is outsourced safe and ensures proper utilization of public funds? As per my information there is no Senior ICT expert permanently associating with the Library Council. There is no permanent senior library staff also. In such a situation there is all possibility that the project going on can become unsustainable or obsolete at some time. The temporary experts who associate or recommend decisions are not responsible to the projects till it brings in result. They may be associates of the firms who undertake the work and can protect or support business interests. This will not occur if the Council is having its own senior Library and ICT Professionals. When Council has to look after 7000 libraries and ICT projects worth Rs. 50 or 100 Crore, it is very important to maintain permanent council's own technical personnel with specified duties and responsibilities to ensure quality of the work or at least minimum returns for the project undertaken using public fund. The cost of maintaining such staff will only be less than 0.55 of what is spent for library development but can ensure that the 99% of money spend is used fruitful and Council gets the quality returns.

7. SCL AS CENTRAL HUB

State Central Library is State's largest collection of books. It has been developed and maintained from public funds, even the money paid by the farmer from remote villages of Idukki or Kasaragod. So it needs to be accessible to the remote villager also through the village library. Is it possible now? Technology can make this possible. But our complexes are hindrances. Building up the resource built up by public library in quantity and quality at a District level Library or village level library is impossible, not practical and is not necessary. There is no need for duplicating that resource if it can be made accessible through the public library system. To make this possible the State Central Library should become the Central hub of our public library system. This will enable the State Library Council to get a Senior Professional Manager to advice or look after the technical affairs of libraries under the system. This will also enable the Council to get senior ICT people from State Central Library to give advice or look after projects of Library automation networking etc of Kerala State Library Council. Without using ICT Council cannot maintain libraries under it as useful knowledge dissemination centers.

8. NETWORKING AND KNOWLEDGE DISSEMINATION

So my suggestion is that State Central Library should form the Central Hub of public library system managed by the Library Council. State Librarian should involve in the technical management of public library system under the council and develop the libraries in a scientific way according to the vision of the State and Library Council. All libraries should be networked. The catalogue of State

Central Library and other major libraries under the council should be accessible online in all village libraries. The digital resources developed by State Central Library also should be made accessible to all village libraries through the public library network managed by the State Central Library. The State Central Library should develop a common collection in digital form, which can be used by all village libraries. This can enable avoiding duplication of work, resources and achieve cost effectiveness and efficiency.

9. CONCLUSIONS AND RECOMMENDATIONS

When we consider introducing new technology or systems in regard to libraries we have to make things fool proof. We have to consider people like P N Panikkar who walked from Kasaragod to Kaliyikkavilai spending days at each and every village influencing people to establish libraries, sustain existing libraries or improve their system and services ~~with~~ without wasting a single pai and using meagre salary provided by government. ICT projects are at present wasting huge amount from public funds without results. There is also duplication of efforts. Unless the council is having expertise to evaluate projects and extract proper work from outsourced agencies, the huge sums of public funds will go waste. But if ICT systems can be properly developed in Library networks, each and every village library will have resources equal to that of State Central library accessible online and various services expected from a community information center can be provided in villages at no cost.

The Kerala Public Library Act needs to be amended to make the public library system efficient to fulfill its role in managing public knowledge. The State Central Library existing at present under Government should become the State Central Library of the public library system of the

State. The provision for establishing more than one State Central Library should be removed. It will be unnecessary duplication in the present digital age and the more staff to be recruited and costly resources to be duplicated will end in wastage of substantial amount from public funds. A Directorate of Public Libraries needs to be created as per the Act. State Librarian can act as Director Public Libraries to look after the execution of the decisions of the State Library Council. There should be sufficient provisions in the Library Act to use current technologies and share resources with National Library and other specialized systems and organizations for mutual benefit. The whole information resources of the State and country should be made accessible in each and every village through the information infrastructures developed by State, NIC, etc.

REFERENCES

[1] Govi, K. M. Public Library. Trivandrum, CSIS, 2010.

[2] Govi, K.M. Library and Information Science. Tvpm. CIRD, 2011.

[3] Jayakrishnan, J S *Kerala Public Library Network: A Project Report.*, 2013 Post Graduate Diploma Project Report thesis, Indian Institute of Information Technology and Management - Kerala. [Thesis]

[4] John, PA and V. K. G. Nair. Public Library Movement in Kerala. Twenty Fifth All India Library Conference Souvenir. 14 -18, May 1979, Trivandrum.

[5] R. Raman Nair. Peoples Library Movement in Kerala. New Delhi, Concept, 2010.

[6] Raman Nair, R. Public Library System: A modem outlook on its principles and practice. National Seminar on National Information System: Policies and programs. Indian Institute of Technology, Madras, 1991.

[7] Ranjith. Rural libraries of Kerala. Trivandrum, Centre for Development studies, 2004. Seek possible matches

4

Access to IEEE Transactions, Journals and Conference Proceedings: Challenges to Self Financing Institutions

Preethi Thekkath

ABSTRACT

The paper highlights the financial challenges faced by self financing engineering colleges in Kerala in procuring the required IEEE journals, transactions and conference proceedings which are essential for postgraduate students and researchers to keep pace with the latest developments in the field of science and technology. Even though AICTE mandatory list contains only IEEE All Society Periodical Package, conference proceedings which are not included in the package have to be purchased by the users. The support offered to self supporting colleges by INDEST – AICTE Consortium ended in the year 2012 and institutes were compelled to make huge payment to concerned publishers through private agencies for enjoying the benefits. IEL Growth Plan which emerged in the year 2014 added financial burden to self financing institutions whose subscription cost increased from eleven lakhs in the year 2014 to twenty one lakhs in the year 2016 with little additions in the package offered. The paper also presents some of the attractive offers from IEEE to increase the number of subscriptions.

Keywords : Higher Education, Research, Technology, Engineering, Journals, Consortia, Cost- Benefit Analysis, INDEST

1. INTRODUCTION

The state of Kerala has given a lot of importance to science, engineering, technology and research. Among the institutions that provide engineering education in the state, there are nearly 160 self financing institutions. Initially many of the self financing institutions had only undergraduate level courses but since 2006 many of them started providing masters programme in specialised fields of different engineering disciplines. There are also faculty pursuing their doctoral studies in these institutes. This necessitated subscriptions from international online digital libraries like IEEE, Elsevier, ACM, Springer etc which provides technical magazines, journals, transactions and conference proceedings that keeps pace with the latest developments in the field of engineering and technology. It became mandatory that a library should have all the journals and transactions as prescribed by AICTE.

The paper presents the financial challenges faced by self supporting colleges in procuring the required journal/ transaction package. It highlights the support provided by INDEST-AICTE Consortium from its inception in 2003 [1]. Even though it was an excellent package with less financial burden, it literally ended in the year 2012 when they passed the burden of making the payment directly to the publishers through private agencies like Global Information Technology(GIST). In the year 2013 IEEE offered All Society Periodicals Package (ASPP) package which was affordable but provided no access to conference proceedings which are also equally important to keep pace with the current advances in respective fields [2].

2014 saw the advent of IEEE Electronic Library (IEL) growth plan offered by IEEE [2]. It offered a very good package comprising of journals, transactions and conference proceedings. But this involved being a member of the plan for a continuous stretch of three years with the cost of the package tremendously increasing over the years. There are also new options like IEEE ASSP and Proceedings Order Plans (POP) combo package offered since 2016 [2], but the institutions with IEEE IEL growth plan has to continue with the same till the tenure of three years is over. Several offers which were put forward by IEEE for the renewal of subscriptions by self supporting institutions are also highlighted in this paper.

2. INDEST-AICTE CONSORTIUM

National Digital Library in Engineering Services and Technology (INDEST) was a government funded library consortia which provided electronic accessibility to international journals in Indian universities and technical institutions which was previously restricted to premier institutions like IISCs , IITs ,IIMs etc. The consortium was set up in 2003 by the Ministry of Human Research Development(MHRD).There were thirty eight centrally funded institutions whose funds for e-resources were met by the consortium centred at IIT Delhi. INDEST - CONSORTIUM was renamed as INDEST –AICTE consortium in 2005 and had three category of institutions namely Core, AICTE supported and self supported type. This offered full text of twelve thousand e-journals, conference proceedings, standards , chapters of books etc and had six bibliographic data bases. It is reported that there were 820 self supporting members in the consortium in 2009 [3-6]. The consortium provided IEEE Electronic Library (IEL) online single user facility at an annual payment of nearly three lakh eighty three thousand to self supporting institutions. Table 1 shows the amount paid for IEL online single user license in the years 2010-2011. It can be noticed that there is only a nominal increase in annual subscription rates.

Year	*Annual payment made for IEL online single user*
2010	Rs. 383390
2011	Rs. 386750

3. IEEE ASPP PACKAGE

In 2011 December it was informed by INDEST- AICTE consortium that all future payments by the subscribing institutions have to be made directly to the publishers after logging on to the AICTE website. GIST was the private agency between the publisher and IEEE. IEEE-ASPP provides access to the 169 IEEE online society-sponsored journals, transactions, and magazines in specialized fields of engineering like Electrical, Electronics, and Computer science. This also provides back files to 2005, abstracts and bibliographic records. The subscription amount accounted to Rs. 276390 in the year 2012. But this package does not support conference proceedings which are also essential for researchers and student members. ASPP subscription cost for the year 2016 is between 6000-8000 dollars.

4. IEEE IEL GROWTH PLAN: COST ANALYSIS OVER THE YEARS 2014-2016

IEL provided access to nearly 174 journals along with 26 IET journals, conference proceedings, back files till1988, 2800 standards and four million articles. Table 2 shows the subscription rates for the years 2014-2016.

Year	*Subscription Rates*
2014	Rs. 11,62516
2015	Rs. 17,54472
2016	Rs. 21,59600

It is evident from Table 2 that there is an approximate increase of four and half lakhs every year without any proportionate increase in the services provided. This growth plan is valid for three years and the institutions who have entered the growth plan are not allowed to change it until the contract period is over. This imposes lot of financial burden on the institute and they find it difficult to renew their subscription. At this juncture it is high time to think whether the motive of IEEE was to increase the number of members who utilise the facility or to increase their profit.

5. ATTRACTIVE OFFERS IN THE YEAR 2016

When the number of self supporting institutions subscribing IEL online decreased substantially some attractive offers were also put forward by IEEE. A special IEL price of 7500 dollars/institution was offered to engineering colleges in Kerala if 160 colleges could join together and make a one- time payment of1200000 dollars. The IEEE subscription period was specified as November 2015 to December 2016. But this did not work out since many colleges refused to join hands owing to drastic decrease in Post graduate admissions.

Yet another attractive offer put forward by IEEE was the IEEE anniversary offer in which the subscription amount would be calculated only from the month it is renewed.

6. IEEE ASPP AND PROCEEDINGS ORDER PLANS (POP) COMBO PACKAGE

This is yet another package offered by IEEE to self supporting institutions. This provides research papers from IEEE conferences in addition to ASPP package. The subscription cost for the year 2016 is Rs. 7,23486. An excess amount of nearly fourteen lakhs has to be paid by the institutions who are under IEEE- IEL growth plan to enjoy the same facility as offered by the Combo package or they have to wait till the contract period of three years is completed.

7. CONCLUSIONS

IEEE is an international organization who have helped many researchers and student members attain their goals and keep themselves in touch with the latest innovations and developments in the field of engineering and technology. It would be extremely helpful if IEEE could device some means so that self supporting colleges also can enjoy the benefits offered without much financial burden.

REFERENCES

[1] Jagdish Arora and Kruti Trivedi INDEST-AICTE Consortium: Present Services and Future Endeavours, DESIDOC Journal of Library & Information Technology, Vol. 30, No. 2, March 2010, pp. 79-91.

[2] ieeexplore.ieee.org/, IEEE Explore Digital Library

[3] INDEST-AICTE Consortium. INDEST Consortium Annual Report, April 2008 to March 2009. INDEST Consortium, New Delhi, 2009.

[4] Bibhuti.B. Sahoo and Gopal .P.Agarwal, INDEST-AICTE Consortium: A Decade of Service for Engineering,Science and Technology Community of the country, Annals of library and Information Studies,Vol.59,September 2012,pp.170-180.

[5] Arora, Jagdish & Agarwal, Pawan. In Indian National Digital Library in Engineering Sciences and Technology (INDEST) Consortium: Consortia-based subscription to electronic resources for technical education system in India, edited by S.M. Salgar, et al. In Proceedings of CALIBER 2003, Ahmedabad, 2003. pp. 271-90.

5

Consortium for E-Journals: An Imperative for Self Financing Engineering Colleges

M Jayapradeep

ABSTRACT

The paper discusses the need of library e-journal consortium for resource sharing among Self Financing Engineering Institutions in Geographical groups of Kerala State. The need for consortium stands same as historically evolved such as diminishing library budget vs variety of information services, increasing subscription rates, etc. AICTE-INDEST consortium categorizes private engineering colleges as "Self supported institutions" and deprives them with only "lower subscription rates and better terms of agreement with publishers". Price of e-resources being prohibitive, it has become inevitable among the Engineering Institutions to practice resource sharing and cooperation through library consortia in the networked information environment. The issues such as bias, need for and benefits of consortium, operability, pre-requisites and services are discussed and a consortium model is suggested. The author concludes that the experiences, trust and understanding build by the consortium shall benefit the self financing colleges on a long term basis and also equip the libraries and library professionals to the new realms and responsibilities in the technology driven information environment.

Key words : Library consortium, E-resource consortium; e-journal consortium; self financing engineering institutions.

1. INTRODUCTION

Library cooperation started long ago. Inter-library loan, document delivery, library networks, etc., are its variants. Presently, library consortium is the more accepted system of resource sharing. Consortium approach is one of the many ways of maintaining cooperation and coordination among the libraries. A Library Consortium is an association of a group of libraries and may be formed on geographical or on functional or on format or on a subject basis or on a combination of all these. The terms library cooperation, library networking, library resource sharing, library consortium, etc., are used interchangeably to denote formal and informal cooperation, partnership and resource sharing activities in libraries.

Library consortium concepts came first time from academic libraries and was formed for the purpose of sharing printed materials. The real drive for cooperation and resource sharing is Information Technology, which enabled cooperation in a much broader and deeper level than ever before. The traditional role of library cooperation has been changed significantly by the advent of electronic resources and the capabilities for networking among institutions. (Chandra Prabha and Dannelly, 1997). Cost sharing library consortium is decisive now as access to electronic resources across the Internet is very costly for a single library to attain due to rising cost of publications and databases. Allen and Hirshon observe it as one of the most important development for academic libraries during the decade that has moved from organizational self-sufficiency to a collaborative survival mode, personified by the growth of library consortia (Allen and Hirshon, 1998).

Library consortium provides for physical and electronic delivery of materials, integrates the collection development process, aid in exploring the features of e-resources and effects savings by making it possible to purchase information in discounted and reasonable prices. Friend FJ opines that the formation of consortium has given librarians the strength that few libraries can exercise individually but all libraries can exercise collectively. (Friend, Frederick J)

Formal library consortium share common interests based upon certain missions. The driving force is resource sharing or to reduce some common costs. By working together, libraries are enabled to do more than what they could do alone. The fundamental functions of a library in terms of collecting, accessing, and archiving information does not change in spite of technological advancements but the concerns facing the libraries are the challenges related to electronic information market place, high costs of entry that no one library can afford to face the technical or economic hurdles alone. By joining a consortium, libraries integrate access to resources by sharing virtual resources via technology.

2. ENGINEERING EDUCATION

Education including technical education is on the Concurrent List of the Indian Constitution, which means both the centre and state have jurisdiction over various aspects. With the mission of developing and promoting quality technical education in a coordinated and integrated manner, the engineering education institutions are placed under the aegis of two agencies, the All India Council for Technical Education (AICTE), the national level Apex

Advisory Body which accredits the institute and its courses. Another is the university affiliating the courses. Both these agencies fix quality assurance norms, standards, controls and checks in providing a proper impetus to Institutions in generating competent engineers. Higher technical education in the state is under the aegis of Kerala Technological University named after Dr AJP Abdul Kalam, in Kerala.

The State government has opened up the sector to the private enterprises to start and run engineering colleges under self financing scheme in order to provide opportunity to the students of the State to pursue engineering courses in Kerala itself. This has revolutionized the sector and engineering has now become the de facto course for attaining graduation. There are 120 self financing colleges in Kerala, affiliated to the Technical University of Kerala. Norms and standards governing them have helped in building libraries in engineering colleges. But that alone does not ensure library and information management in these institutions. There are also instances that the regulatory agencies have gone wayward in emphasizing e-governance, e-resources, journals, etc., to the system. Regulation or no regulation, many prestigious private institutions in Kerala have built library system with strong information bases including online resources. The antithesis is that many of the private institutions have established libraries because of the norms laid by the regulatory agencies concerned.

3. CRITICAL ISSUES

AICTE proposes a number of e-journal packages for the colleges for mandatory purchase depending on the courses offered by each college. However, Delnet/INDEST members are granted certain exemptions in subscribing to the packages prescribed by AICTE. In 2005, AICTE joined hand with INDEST (Indian National Digital Library in Engineering Science and Technology) Consortium and got renamed the consortium as INDEST-AICTE Consortium helping the engineering colleges to afford e-resources. The move acknowledges the financial burden that e-resources inflict now. Nevertheless, the consortium considers the self-financing colleges as self supporting members and e-resources of the consortium are not accessible to them. On becoming member by paying membership fee to INDEST-AICTE, they are discounted by publisher/vendor on subscription made through the consortium. State owned consortium - INDEST AICTE – makes sense for public institutions but the private institutions are deprived from accessing consortium resources though they are part of the State and contribute towards progress of engineering education. The critical areas of this set-up can be summarized as follows:-

- Bias: Clear bias between Level 1, 2 and 3 institutions and Self supported members of consortium. Students are the ultimate sufferers.
- Colleges need to subscribe each resource individually.
- Financial burden – 15 to 20 lakhs per year, finally to be borne by the students
- Library collection building suffers as major share of money diverted for e-resources
- No perpetual access for subscribed e-resources. No effective bargain for cost reduction.
- Procedural delays at intermediary levels.
- Costly e-resources under used.
- Commercial preferences are evident in the listing of E-resources by the regulatory agencies.
- Often, libraries are de-linked from Consortium operations especially in Government and aided colleges.

The rapid growth of e-journals and other e-resources which are currently seem more as an add-on expense rather than a replacement for the print journal has greatly affected stable library budget. Libraries are also compelled to purchase traditional print resources against the burgeoning pressure for electronic information.

Proposing costly international e-journals for undergraduate courses by AICTE is only out of fashionable trend. Generally, the undergraduate students do not consult journals and Post graduate students may consult these resources during their project preparation only. Number of students in the Level 1, 2 and 3 institutional members of INDEST-AICTE are more and their curriculum compel for proper utilization of the resources.

Number of students for various courses in private engineering colleges is very low. Many times, the intake capacity of post-graduate students are not filled in private colleges. Observance of norms becomes economically viable and management becomes cost effective for private universities with large number of students. The State of Kerala does not permit private universities to form and administer engineering courses in the State.

Though AICTE fixes the norms for library and library resources, it has not conducted scientific studies on usage of information resources suggested for engineering colleges nor recommended activities that encourage use of library resources by the students. AICTE has not ensured inclusion of OA resources, online tutorials, etc as mandatory e-resources in engineering college libraries. Financial implications are hardly studied.

4. NEED OF THE CONSORTIUM

Under these circumstances, engineering colleges should look to library consortium, not only to reduce the library costs but also to tap into a wider range of expertise, to share resources, and even to share the rising prices on e-journals that are larger than any one institution can afford. Cost reduction is a desirable short-term goal. The true value of a consortium comes from helping the library to learn, understand and articulate trends as they are emerging and to create standardized methodologies that individual libraries can employ and customize at their own institutions.

As national level library consortia such as INDEST-AICTE cannot fully address the issues relating to the self supporting engineering colleges, it shall be the stepping time for a micro level consortium of Self Financing Colleges against the backdrop of AICTE regulatory norms operational for mandatory purchase of e-resources, e-journals and print journals (international and national). As e-resource consolidation and publishing is monopolistic, bargaining for cost reduction even by national level Consortium may not be effective in the near future. In such a case the members should have a broad understanding on how to cope with these issues and thereby have an ideal opportunity to explore these issues objectively.

Therefore, it is imperative to propose a positive model or a warning example on forming a consortium for providing electronic delivery of information and integrating the collection development process, especially e-journals for libraries in self-financing engineering colleges of Kerala. Team work, trust, openness and honesty are the foundation stone of the consortium. It also requires an open dialogue between libraries and between libraries and publishers/vendors/aggregators, in a spirit of partnership to help the end users. The requisites for the formation of the proposed consortium are:-

- Interactions between institutions, brain storming sessions and discussions towards reaching consensus for evolving Library Consortium of Self Financing Engineering Colleges of Kerala.

- Formation of Expert Group for suggesting organization of the Consortium, member responsibilities, office bearers, suitable consortium model, services, structure, Lead Library, and other modalities.
- Formation of Consortium HQs at the Lead Library.
- Entering into MOUs, fund mobilization, choosing resources, fixing purchasing options, engaging consultants/experts for negotiations with publishers/ vendors/aggregators, etc.
- Incorporation of mutual objectives in the consortium agreement/charter.
- Ensuring joint decision making process to jointly own and resolve the problems by the team.

5. MODEL

Consortia models are still in an evolving phase, constantly affected by technological changes. Nevertheless, the conceptual model suggested for Library Consortium of Self Financing Engineering Colleges of Kerala which is not being seriously thought or attempted by any of the association/federation/group of self-financing engineering colleges is outlined in succeeding paragraphs. The proposed consortium is named Kerala Engineering Library Consortium of E-resources (KELCER). It shall be based on resource sharing and cooperation among the self-financing engineering colleges in Kerala. The schema of the proposed consortium is given below:-

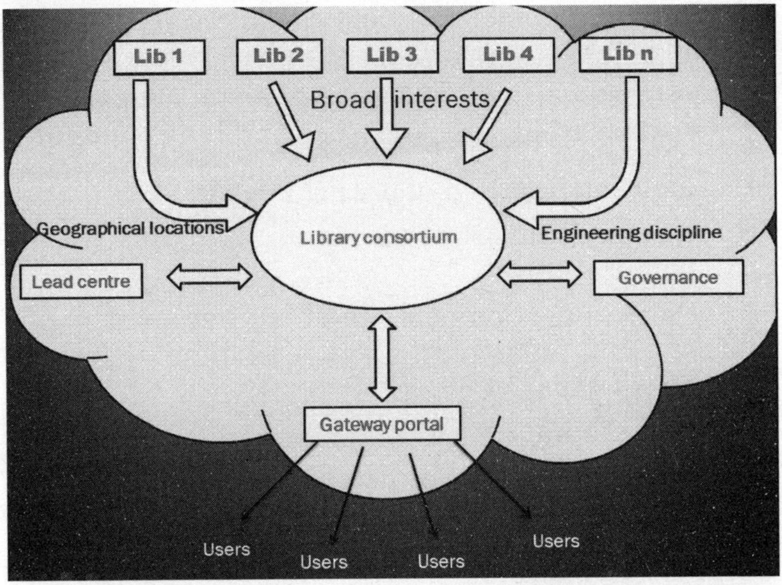

The State level licensing of information products could be achieved by the consortium for Self Financing Engineering Colleges of Kerala which push quality engineering education, abiding by the norms of regulatory agencies and universities. The model suggested is a combination of Geographical location linked Libraries in the same discipline (Engineering) for the purpose of accessing e-resources. The objectives can be widened to make them efficient instruments of sharing of all types of library resources. The goals of the proposed consortium are discussed below.

- Create and increase the access base with e-resources, e-journals, e-databases suggested by AICTE, University etc.
- Savings by negotiating for joint licensing for use of e-resources, avoiding duplication, etc.
- Develop experience of negotiating licenses with publishers/vendors/ aggregators and to raise awareness of the importance of paying careful

attention to the terms and conditions of licenses.

- Ensure comprehensive collection, continuous subscription, perpetual access, etc.
- Qualitative resource sharing.
- Judicious selection of pricing models.
- Enhanced image of the library including smaller libraries.
- Harness developments in IT for improved library services, infrastructure for access and delivery of information.
- Cost sharing.
- Increase user base by developing collection, access tools etc as per user demand.

6. LEAD CENTRE

The lead centre shall perform strategic missions of lobbying, fund raising, purchasing, etc; tactical programmes of e-resource subscription, access, creation of union catalogue, digital libraries, archiving, and the practical governance aspects such as governing body, council, task forces, coordination etc.

7. CONSORTIUM SERVICES

Library consortium is based on the tenets of library resource sharing, networking and cooperation. Therefore the evolutionary tools of library cooperation such as Union catalogue that is applicable for effective and efficient resource sharing among consortium shall be created and implemented.

- Developing common interface to consortium services.
- Union catalogues of e-resources, Books, Journals, Technical Reports and Conference Proceedings.

- Portal by Lead Library; Shared library systems-Hardware, Software and other infrastructure.
- Creating inter-operability among member systems, databases and services.
- Shared professional expertise.
- Develop and realize consortia goals.
- Human resource development-Training the staff and the users. Conduct of Seminar/ Conferences.
- Electronic contents licensing for providing access to Bibliographic databases, e-Journals, Full test reports, Conference Proceedings etc.
- Inter Library Lending and Document Delivery.
- Electronic content generation, loading and access.
- Archival of digital information, back volumes and less used documents.
- Development of enabling technologies, IR systems, etc.
- Evolve standards for techniques, hardware, software and services

8. CONSORTIUM GATEWAY

Consortia are using the Internet as a global way to offer their services. KELCER shall use Internet as back bone for connectivity. As Portals are the tool of interface and communication, KELCER shall have portal for gateway consortium services and delivery of information in member log-in mode. The study suggests Library and Information resource Network (LIRN) at *https://www.lirn.net/* as a model for KELCER portal. LIRN is a consortium of educational institutions which have joined to share access to information resources. The home page is given below:-

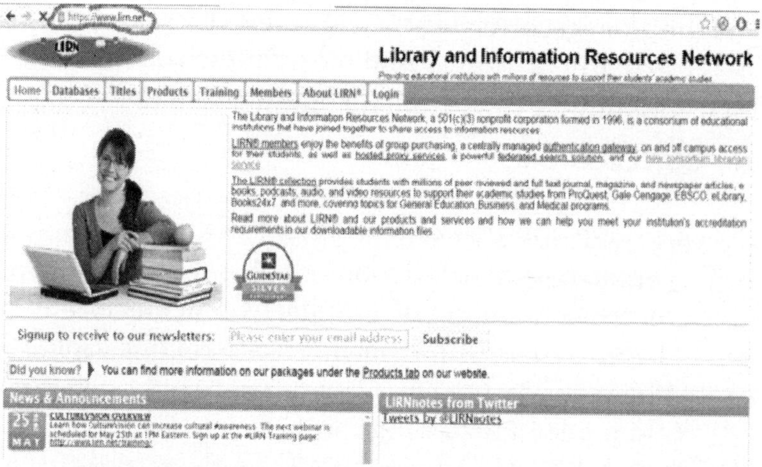

KELCER Portal shall provide gateway services for Union catalogue, Directories, Document Delivery services, Newsletters, training etc. Member Consultation Cards can also be introduced in KELCER so as to enable users of the member institutes to consult the facilities and resources available in consortium libraries.

9. SUGGESTIONS AND RECOMMENDATIONS

Only seminal ideas on consortium of self financing engineering colleges in Kerala are discussed in the article. It needs further brainstorming and discussions for shaping it to a reality. Out of 152 engineering colleges in Kerala, 120 are in self financing sector. The contributions of self financing colleges in engineering education are very significant. Kerala Technological University Library and Information System may or may not happen. Such lack-luster attitude shall continue indefinitely but norms on self financing engineering colleges shall come heavily. It shall become arbitrary to build knowledge base in self-financing engineering colleges. It is better done in a resource sharing and cooperative mode. As self financing engineering colleges play major role in higher education in Kerala, the professional image has to be boosted by them and the efforts shall not go un-noticed in the State. KELCER suggested in the study shall foster technology-driven information revolution which is imperative.

10. CONCLUSION

Higher education system shall undergo changes in the very near future. Curriculum and other credentials of higher education shall be unbundled with the launch of massive open online courses (MOOCs) with dozens of global institutions and millions of learners participating. As an industry, the self financing engineering colleges in Kerala have so much more to learn and do in shaping the electronic future in ways that serve the goals of research, scholarship and teaching. Regulatory bodies shall, in near future, start pressure on not only commercial e-resources but also print collections, authenticated online engineering resources and services, online tutorials, etc. in the library system. The benefits of Library consortium, as said earlier, shall be far reaching than being short-term. Library consortium will become even more important in the future by assisting institutions in implementing and managing the process of changes in knowledge sector that is poised for leaps in India.

The new means of information access and delivery is redefining the major functions of the libraries that are dramatically different from the way they acquired and provided access to information in the past. The combined buying power of the consortium has a better chance than do individual college libraries of persuading e-resources providers to change unacceptable terms in addition to lowering the prices. Library consortium shall help in reinventing the libraries and librarians themselves in meeting the new demands and challenges collectively, unitedly and economically.

REFERENCES

1. Lynch, Cliffort A. Building the Infrastructure of Resource Sharing: Union catalogs, Distributed Search, and Cross-Database Linkage, *Library Trends*, Vol. 45, No. 3, Winter 1997, pp. 448-461.
2. Kingman, Bruce R. Interlibrary Loan and resource Sharing: The Economics of the SUNY Express Consortium. *Library Trends*, Vol. 45, No. 3, Winter 1997, pp. 518-530.
3. Kopp, James J. Library Consortia and Information Technology: The Past, the Present, the Promise. Library Consortia and Information Technology.
4. Potter, William Gray. Recent Trends in Statewide Academic Library Consortia. *Library Trends*, Vol. 45, No. 3, Winter 1997, pp. 416-434.
5. Kohl, David F. Resource Sharing in a Changing Ohio Environment, *Library Trends*, Vol. 45, No. 3, Winter 1997, pp. 435-447.
6. Chandra Prabha and Dannelly, N Gay. *Library Trends* Vol. 45, No. 3 Winter 1997, pp 367-372.
7. Allen, Barbara McFadden and Hirshon, Arnold. Hanging Together to Avoid hanging Separately: Opportunities for Academic Libraries and Consortia. *Information Technology and Libraries*, Mar 1998.
8. Hirshon, Arnold. Libraries, Consortia, and Change Management. *The J of Academic Librarianship*, Vol 25 No. 2, pp. 124-126.
9. Archana, S.N. and Humayoon Kabir, S. E-Resources in the Engineering College Libraries of Kerala: Problems towards Sustainable Collection Development. [Online at] dyuthi.cusat.ac.in/.../E-resources%20in%20the%20engineering%20college %20libraries
10. Friend, Frederick J. New Wine in a New Bottle: Purchasing by Library Consortia in the United Kingdom.

6

Knowledge Based Library and Information Services in R & D Organisations

Letha M M
Wilson K Cherukulath
T Mukundan

ABSTRACT

In this era of knowledge economy, possession of relevant knowledge is highly essential for an organization to gain competitive edge. Knowledge management (KM) activities are now being practiced in Government and research organizations as well as from business organisations. In this context, librarians have to play a major role in collecting, organizing, leveraging, archiving and disseminating knowledge. This paper briefs on knowledge management, and role of librarians and information professionals in knowledge management in a niche area. It also discusses the steps taken by information professionals to create, collect, store and disseminate knowledge in Naval Physical & Oceanographic Laboratory (NPOL), a DRDO unit in detail. Also illustrate a study conducted to know the usefulness and publication pattern of the technical journal published as part of KM.

Keywords : Knowledge Management; KM; Knowledge Website; Knowledge Repositories

1. INTRODUCTION

The thrust of knowledge management is to create a process of valuing the organization's intangible assets in order to best leverage knowledge internally and externally. [1]. Knowledge management is essentially about getting the right knowledge to the right person at the right time. This in itself may not seem so complex, but it implies a strong tie to corporate strategy, understanding of where and in what form knowledge exists, creating processes that span organizational functions, and ensuring that initiatives are accepted and supported by organizational members. Knowledge management may also include new knowledge creation, or it may solely focus on knowledge sharing, storage, and refinement. The overall objective is to create value and to leverage, improve, and refine the firm's competences and knowledge assets to meet organizational goals and targets[2].In order to enhance organisational knowledge, KM has to be involved across the entire knowledge spectrum. It must help knowledge development at all levels and facilitate & promote its diffusion to individuals, groups, and/or across the entire firm, in accordance with the organization's requirements. KM must manage organizational knowledge storage and retrieval capabilities, and create an environment conducive to learning and knowledge sharing. Similarly it must be involved in tapping external sources of knowledge whenever these are necessary for the development of the organizational knowledge resources.

To a large degree, KM is therefore dependent on the understanding and management of organizational learning, organizational memory, knowledge sharing, knowledge creation, and organizational culture.

2. KNOWLEDGE MANAGEMENT IMPLEMENTATION

The overall objective of KM is to create value and to

leverage, improve and refine the firm competences and knowledge assets to meet organizational goals and targets. Implementing knowledge management has several dimensions including [3]:

KM Strategy : Knowledge management strategy must be dependent on corporate strategy. The objective is to manage, share, and create relevant knowledge assets that will help meet tactical and strategic requirements.

Organizational Culture : The organizational culture influences the way people interact, the context within which knowledge is created, the resistance they will have towards certain changes, and ultimately the way they share (or the way they do not share) knowledge.

Organizational Processes : The right processes, environments, and systems that enable KM to be implemented in the organization.

Management & Leadership : KM requires competent and experienced leadership at all levels. There are a wide variety of KM-related roles that an organization may or may not need to implement, including a CKO, knowledge managers, knowledge brokers and so on.

Technology : The systems, tools, and technologies that fit the organization's requirements - properly designed and implemented.

Politics : The long-term support to implement and sustain initiatives that involve virtually all organizational functions, which may be costly to implement (both from the perspective of time and money), and which often do not have a directly visible return on investment.

3. ROLE OF LIBRARIANS IN KM

The key professionals involved in knowledge management programs are information technologists and human resource managers but the librarians/information professionals also have a role to play as they are traditionally known as good managers of explicit knowledge. First and foremost, librarians are experts in all aspects of information—finding it, authenticating it, distilling it, and organizing it. The skills that librarians possess in these areas can be very beneficial to KM.

Librarians and information professionals have significant advantages as KM players and they are both effective and customer-oriented. Secondly, they understand the ways in which people communicate information needs. Librarians have knowledge of subject formation in the universe of knowledge. Some of the qualities of a librarian to become a knowledge manager are providing services to the user community, sharing the information and understanding the user needs, theoretical and practical experience in designing and implementing information systems, analysing the documents, classifying and indexing them for easy retrieval thereby having meta knowledge i.e. knowledge about knowledge. The one quote, "one good librarian is worth a hundred databases" from Tindall [4] clearly reflects this. Knowledge of current advances in information technologies and their application in libraries will help these information scientists to convert their information centres to a knowledge repository.

4. KNOWLEDGE BASED LIBRARY SERVICES

Naval Physical and Oceanographic Laboratory (NPOL) is a well-known establishment of the Defence Research and Development Organisation (DRDO) under the Ministry of Defence. Over the years, NPOL scientists have acquired a wealth of knowledge in naval surveillance systems and allied technologies. Being the only R&D establishment in India dealing with such naval technologies, NPOL is a knowledge-intensive organisation and therefore efforts on KM acquire significance. The origin of NPOL dates back to 1952 when it was started as as an in-house laboratory of Indian Navy, then called as Indian Naval Physical Laboratory (INPL), for providing scientific support to Navy. NPOL has grown from a fleet support laboratory of the Indian Navy to sonar systems developer during the last six decades. When the Defense Research and Development Organization (DRDO) formed in 1958, INPL was absorbed into the new organization. Later, when Oceanography assumed a principal role in the research interests of the Laboratory, INPL was rechristened NPOL in 1969. NPOL now is a matured System Laboratory handling more than 10 defence projects at a time, which include S&T, technology demonstration and the mission mode projects [5].

The laboratory has recognized the importance of knowledge management especially collecting and sharing knowledge created within the organization. NPOL has a special library, Technical Information Resource Centre (TIRC). TIRC has a vast collection of print and digital documents. All the digital documents are made accessible to all users through TIRC portal. Thus librarians (scientists in TIRC) are playing their role in managing explicit knowledge effectively.

In addition to this TIRC made the knowledge management initiatives in NPOL way back in 2003. Now also TIRC is managing both explicit as well as tacit knowledge of the organization efficiently and effectively. The KM activities for managing tacit as well as explicit knowledge in NPOL by TIRC follow:

4.1. Tacit knowledge Mobilization

Knowledge residing in the minds of people is tacit/ non tangible Knowledge and it is very difficult to manage. We can capture the K if only the knowledge holder is willing to share. Even if they, it is very difficult to capture skills and expertise. However some methods were adopted to capture tacit knowledge from NPOL scientists.

4.1.1. KM Tutorials

The initiative of tutorials is only an attempt to sort, disseminate and leverage the acquired knowledge in a presentable and palatable manner. The effort of technical tutorial is in enthusing ourselves, to collect, collate, compile and disseminate knowledge in an organised manner. The individuals can serve NPOL better by sharing what we know, thus enriching our own fellow colleagues. With more people becoming more knowledgeable in the laboratory, NPOL can become learning organization [6].As a small initiative, KM awareness provided to employees. Experts in specialized areas of interests were identified and ask them to prepare tutorials in PowerPoint with footnotes in their areas of specialization. All the tutorials were collected and made available through intranet to users. These tutorials helped a lot new entrants to the organization to understand the varied and narrow fields of work at NPOL. This also helped to train the staff during their assessment for promotions. Thus before an expert leaves the organization a small portion of their tacit knowledge is captured.

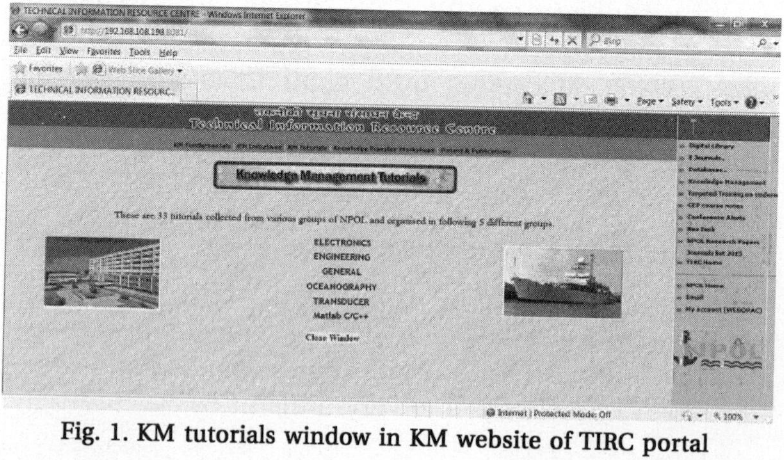

Fig. 1. KM tutorials window in KM website of TIRC portal

4.1.2. Publications

Publications are containing the tacit knowledge converted to explicit knowledge. NPOL is bringing out publications like departmental research reports, project documents, technical journal, in-house bulletins, etc. which codifies the knowledge generated by NPOL scientists during research. These documents help to avoid reinventing the wheel.

4.1.2.1. Coffee Table Book

During the Diamond jubilee year of NPOL 'Diamond Octaves' a photo essay of NPOL @ 60 was published that maps the contours of technological and infrastructural growth attained by NPOL. The volume contains photo essay on technological achievements, technical facilities, milestones achieved, brief on sonar technology and the story of development of sonar systems starting from APSOH to the latest HUMSA NG in ship sonar category, fist indigenous submarine sonar PANCHENDRIYA to latest USHUS and airborne sonars, torpedo defence system. Knowledge collection and codification were done by librarians and others from archives of 60 years of data for the publication of the book. This document now acts as a good reference on NPOL.

Another book on diamond jubilee celebrations also published with various events conducted during the year. A series of events with photographs were depicted in the book which will serve as a guideline to other DRDO labs while conducting celebrations in their respective labs and to NPOL in future.

4.1.2.2. Monographs

Several Monographs were published by NPOL scientists and retired stalwarts on their areas of expertise. For this librarians have role in conducting literature research to provide precise literature for authors.

4.1.2.3. Special issues of Technology Focus

Information professionals of TIRC is also the correspondent for 'Technology Focus' a journal published by DESIDOC.TIRC brought out two special issues of Technology Focus on 'Sonar system technologies' by consolidating all the new products developed by technical groups of NPOL. These documents are a very good compilation which helps in image building of the organization. NPOL brought out two special issues within a gap of 3 years i.e.in 2010 and 2013. This publication is an open access one and is circulated among most of the academic and special libraries.

Technology Focus

टैक्नोलॉजी फोकस

SONAR SYSTEM TECHNOLOGIES

Technology Focus

टैक्नोलॉजी फोकस

ISSN : 0971-4413

BULLETIN OF DEFENCE RESEARCH AND DEVELOPMENT ORGANISATION

TECHNOLOGIES FOR SONAR SYSTEMS

Sonar systems have undergone evolutionary changes from unitary systems to composite systems where fusion of data from multiple sensors makes sonar displays highly user-friendly. Over the last three decades, DRDO has designed, developed and inducted several sonar systems for the warships and submarines of the Indian Navy to enhance its capabilities.

4.1.2.4. Technical Journal

In NPOL more than 200 Scientists and an equal number of Technical Officers are working in various science and technology areas. Mostly the work is project based and time bound. Hence scientists of pure science groups are writing more papers to journals and conferences. TIRC took a lead role in enthusing the scientists from projects and other technical groups to write research articles with maximum help provided to the in the form of literature search. TIRC has decided to publish a technical journal from NPOL namely 'Sea Tech'. With keen interest from top management we could publish Volume 1 issue 1 of our technical journal in the year 2005.From 2011 onwards it has been a practice in NPOL to publish the journal biannual-one general issue and one special issue. This journal helped the scientists to increase their capability in writing research articles and other employees of NPOL will get an opportunity to read the article based on the area of work of the authors. All the journal issues were made online through intranet.

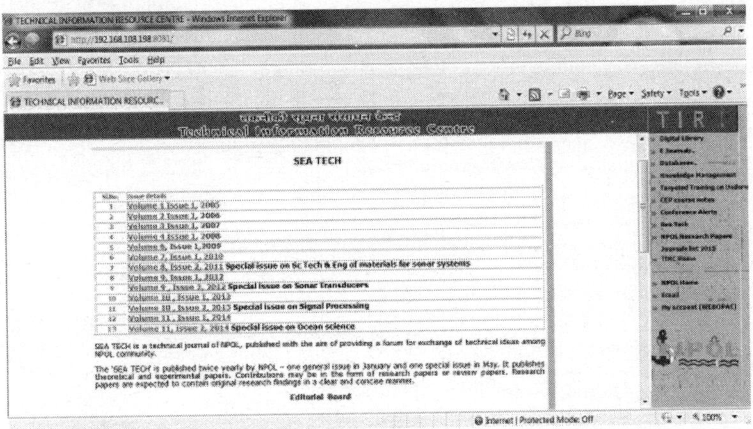

4.1.2.4.1. Publication Pattern in Technical Journal

Study has been conducted to know the usefulness of SEA TECH. For this a questionnaire was distributed among scientists. Survey was conducted mainly among scientists and authors of papers. The survey results showed that the preferred way of reading Sea Tech is hard copy for 80% of the respondents even though 90% know that 'Sea Tech' is available in TIRC portal. 70% of the respondents are aware of the impact of publishing their articles in 'Sea Tech' on their career prospects. But survey shows that about 30% of the respondents were published their articles in sea tech and 70% not yet published. Study shows that most of the articles are written by more than one author which reflects the team work. The analysis also showed that special issues contain more papers than general issues.

4.1.3. Knowledge Transfer Workshops

NPOL has its history of 60 years. Many stalwarts with deep subject knowledge in core areas of NPOL are available. We thought of capturing their knowledge for the benefit of future generation. Finally with the top managements support we have arranged workshops and recorded their lecture series to the youngsters. Newly joined scientists were the participants and they could get enough chances to interact with the experts during this lecture series thereby understood their knowledge in many sonar projects of the lab. All the recordings and PowerPoint presentations with footnotes were made available to all through TIRC portal.

4.2. Explicit Knowledge Management

Knowledge residing in the form of documents or digital is explicit/tangible K and it is easy to acquire process, store and disseminate. Mainly information professionals are managing explicit K by means of knowledge repository and disseminating the same through K website, a window in TIRC portal.

4.2.1. Knowledge Repository

A knowledge repository is a computerized system that systematically captures, organizes and categorises an organisation's knowledge. The repository can be searched and can be quickly referred. Knowledge repositories help organisations to connect people with information and expertise [7]. Explicit knowledge in the form of research reports, project documents, research papers, photographs, etc. constitutes the knowledge repository. Both document repository as well as photo repository were created and embedded in TIRC portal for web based access across the campus.

4.2.1.1. Role of K Repository in KM

What is a knowledge repository and how does it support a knowledge management strategy? Well-designed and used knowledge repositories are small but key elements of an overall strategy to manage knowledge as an asset. A repository is not a large database to satisfy Freedom of Information purposes. Rather, it houses organizational doctrine from which people can access critical, reasonably stable information. Repositories can complement other document and content management work, such as policy or procedures.

Research organizations are themselves knowledge reservoirs. These highly valued intellectual assets, regardless of whether they are explicit or tacit, should be inventoried, archived, indexed, frequently updated, and made accessible in digital form. These repositories can fall into four categories [1]:

- To create knowledge repositories, which store both knowledge and information, often in documentary form.
- Those which include external knowledge, such as competitive intelligence.
- Those that include structured internal knowledge, such as research reports and product oriented marketing materials, such as techniques and methods.
- Those that embrace informal, internal or tacit knowledge, such as discussion databases that store "know how".

- To improve knowledge access and transfer. Here the emphasis is on connectivity, access and transfer.
- Technologies such as video conferencing systems, document scanning and sharing tools and telecommunications networks are central.
- To enhance the knowledge environment so that the environment is conductive to more effective knowledge creation, transfer and use. This involves tackling organizational norms and values as they relate to knowledge.
- Increase awareness on sharing knowledge embedded in client relationship and engagements.
- Provide awards for contributions to the organization's structured knowledge base.
- Implement decision audit programs in order to assess whether and how employees were applying knowledge in key decisions.
- Recognize that successful knowledge management is dependent upon structures and cultures.
- To manage knowledge as an asset and to recognize the value of knowledge to an organization.

4.2.1.2. Document Repository

Digital library was set up in 2005 which holds the Institutional repository. These documents are organized as databases and can be retrieved as and when needed. Digital library with a collection called 'Institutional repositories', holds the project documents, departmental research reports and research papers of scientists of NPOL. Due to defence policies, the knowledge is secret, restricted, classified and unclassified. Open access is provided to all unclassified documents. Restricted and classified documents like research reports and project documents are accessible only through login and password. The knowledge base is more tacit than explicit because the knowledge available through experience, intuition and skill is more. Knowledge base of documents, tutorials, FAQs, glossaries, etc are collated and kept for ready reference in the knowledge portal.

4.2.1.3. Photo Repository

Photographs form an integral part of NPOL in all its technical and non-technical activities. These photographs were archived year wise and event wise. For getting a photograph from this huge collection is not so easy task. Also photographs exist in the form of print, negatives as well as digital. The first task carried out by TIRC is to convert the negatives to digital. Then the issue of creating a searchable database came. This was solved by creating a database using open source software. Now adding up of photographs to this database is going on. Further access will be provided through TIRC portal.

4.3. Information Consolidation Packages

NPOL, as told earlier, is an intensive research organisation in the area of sonar technology, oceanography, ocean engineering, materials and underwater communication. Scientist will be always busy with design and development and project completion before probable date of completion So TIRC decided to provide information after leveraging by doing Literature search and consolidation of information. For example in project formulation stage lots of literature has to do and NPOL is the only organisation in India doing sonar technology. During development of indegenised sonars also information is needed in time. What the scientists of TIRC are doing is conducting extensive literature survey and consolidating the results category wise like journal articles, patents, standards, etc. and create a hypertext linking of all these to get user a feel of web search and in their busy schedule the users may go through only the articles required to them.

5. KNOWLEDGE WEBSITE

The knowledge website provides a gateway to databases, institutional repositories, and internal web content even if users from remote places will be able to access the same. Knowledge Portal will offer the capability to create, transfer, deliver and access information. The web site of each library should serve as a portal for all sources of selective and relevant knowledge and information whether explicit or tacit, whether on site or remote, and in all formats. To facilitate the implementation of knowledge management, a well-designed and operational knowledge management system should be in place. Latest information technology should be used as an enabler. In this regard, the library director should consider him/her self as the chief knowledge officer of the entire organization and should work together with the CIO, heads of the planning department, the computer and information technology center, the human resources management department, the finance department, etc. to design and develop such a system. Such a knowledge management system should be built on existing computer and information technology infrastructures, including upgraded intranet, extranet, and Internet, and available software programs to facilitate the capture, analysis, organization, storage, and sharing of internal and external information resources for effective knowledge exchange among users, resource persons (faculty, researchers, and subjects specialists, etc.), publishers, government agencies, businesses and industries, and other organizations via multiple channels and layers. In recent years, many of the newly developed information technologies for database and information/ document management can be utilized in knowledge management; such as, data warehousing, data mining, text mining, content management, knowledge extraction, knowledge mapping, groupware, and information visualization, etc [1].

The utmost goal of knowledge management is to provide users with a variety of quality services in order to improve the communication, use and creation of knowledge. As much as possible these services should be tailored to the interest and needs of each user.

An organizational culture for sharing of knowledge and expertise should be established with appropriate rewards and incentives. Those staff members who share their tacit knowledge and experiences through writing, publishing, lecturing, tutoring, or mentoring should be appropriately recognized and rewarded. An organizational culture which emphasizes cooperation, sharing, and innovation can only be established by strong leadership and commitment from the library director and a shared vision by the library staff.

Libraries should also encourage the transfer of knowledge and experience from experienced staff to new staff members. A mentoring system should be in place to help newcomers to learn from experienced library staff. Informal seminars and brownbag sessions where staff can interact and exchange "lessons learned", "best practices" and other specific experience and knowledge should be scheduled at regular intervals and at convenient times. Special interest groups and chat rooms can be created through intranet [1].

TIRC portal contains a window for KM which holds the knowledge assets of NPOL. The idea is to create a knowledge sharing environment. The website provides basics of knowledge management for beginners. This write up will provide a bird's eye view on KM to a fresher in the area of KM. What are all practices being carried out at

NPOL as part of KM is explained in this website so that new scientists also may play their role in KM of the organisation by means of KM tutorials, publications, journal papers, etc.

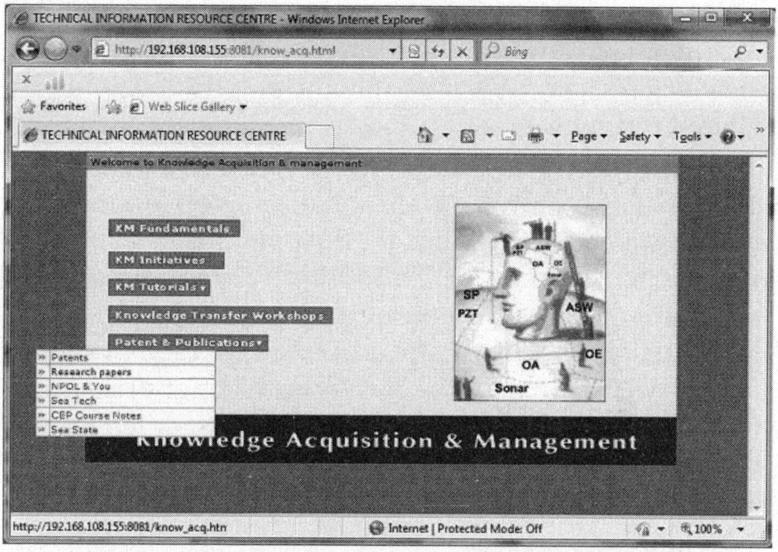

As mentioned earlier, KM website provides the access to KM tutorials, KM workshops and institutional repositories.

Knowledge management requires more useful effective methods are information services, speedy transfer of information and linking of information with individuals and their activities. Libraries have thought as being expert at collecting and organizing published information.

5. CONCLUSION

In an era where knowledge is power, librarians should have the responsibility to provide knowledge itself rather than information or mere data alone. Librarian suits more for KM than computer technologies since Knowledge sharing basically depends on human attitude rather than computer tools and techniques to extract Knowledge from experts. In order to promote knowledge sharing habit, TIRC used to display the research articles of NPOL scientists published in journals and proceedings in TIRC notice board, portal and DESIDOC website.

New methods such as data mining, text mining, content management, search engines, spidering programs, natural language searching, linguistic analysis, semantic networks, knowledge extraction, concept yellow pages, and such techniques in information visualization as two-dimensional or three-dimensional knowledge mapping, etc. have been a part of recent developments in knowledge management systems [1]. The best practices or procedures followed in the organization may be uploaded for future reference. Now we are in the process of creation of subject gateways. Now buzz words like Performance Management and talent management are started in foreign organisations and slowly coming to India to which librarians also has to step in.

ACKNOWLEDGEMENT

The authors express their deep gratitude to Shri S Kedarnath Shenoy, Director, NPOL, for motivating them to work in this area and for permitting to publish this paper.

REFERENCES

[1] Hwa-Wei Lee, Knowledge Management and the Role of Libraries. Available: http://www.white-clouds.com/iclc/cliej/cl19lee.htm

[2] Introducing Organizational Knowledge. Available: http://www.knowledge-management-tools.net/introducing-organizational-knowledge.html

[3] KMT:an educational KM site.Available:www.knowledge-management-tools.net

[4] Tindall, C. (1997): "Profiting from a Groupwide Knowledge Management Program"

[5] Letha M.M, et al. "Specialities of Knowledge Management in a Defence Research Organisation: Naval Physical and Oceanographic Laboratory" *Proceedings of the first National*

Conferenece on Knowledge Management-NCRTKM. Kochi:CUSAT, 2014

[6] R.M. R. Vishnubhatla and M. M. Letha, Managing Knowledge Markets in Research Organisations, *R & D Management Conference* Delhi:CSIR, 2003

[7] Sunita Sijwal, Knowledge Repositories.Available: http://www.slideshare.net/soniya302/knowledge-repository-and-knowledge-management

7

Library Space: The Means to Bridge the Gap Between the Recorded Knowledge and the Living Knowledge

John N. V.
S. Ally Sornam

ABSTRACT

The growing gap between the recorded knowledge has attracted the attention of academicians all over the world. This article is focusing on the widening gap between the recorded knowledge and living knowledge. The key solution to this problem is promoting library space – research ecology. The library and information science played a great role to spread the knowledge around the world and to create a knowledgeable and networked society. The same LIS have to take the initiative to cure the problems of the horizon of knowledge. The researchers are speculating many reasons for this phenomenon like: information explosion, information overload, and limited capacity of human brain. They are wondering about few consequences of the same such as: data mines, skill gap, knowledge monopoly, stagnancy of knowledge, knowledge filtering and unmanageable amount of information waste.

The "... university libraries are symbolically considered as the heart that pumps knowledge to every part of its constituent bodies."[22] So the universities have to take special initiative to the bridging of recorded knowledge and the living knowledge to protect and promote quality knowledge by good research.

Key words : Research ecology, Data mined, Skill gap, Knowledge monopoly, Stagnancy of knowledge, Knowledge filtering, Information waste, Information explosion, Information overloaded

1. INTRODUCTION

When we are analyzing the growth of humanity and evaluate the role of the following areas like: library, library service, knowledge, information and communication technology, etc., we can see many positive notes. The same way there are areas to improve and require regulations for the integrated development of the humanity. The researchers are highlighting some internal problems related to the above mentioned areas like: information explosion, information overloaded and limited capacity of human brain. They are wondering about few consequences of the same such as: data mined, skill gap, knowledge monopoly, stagnancy of knowledge, knowledge filtering and unmanageable amount of information waste. The library and information science (LIS) professionals have to pay special attention to modulate the developments to the sustainable manner. The existence and purpose of library and its services become more confusing and complicated now. So we have to reformulate the life and mission of library with wider canvas. All the additions, deletions and modifications should have to be properly planned. The "... university libraries are symbolically considered as the heart that pumps knowledge to every part of its constituent bodies."[22] So the universities have to take special initiative to the bridging of recorded knowledge and the living knowledge by providing inspiring space for library to protect and promote quality knowledge by good research.

2. BACKGROUND

If we closely observe we can see a large gap between the recorded knowledge and the living knowledge. From a layman's point of view, it can be argued that there are fewer readers for the records at the library. Here the researchers are analyzing this issue in different ways. They are observing that, the history of knowledge and the history of library and information science have a healthy and progressive blending in the last century. In the recent past they detect that, both the knowledge and the LIS are diminishing by several aspects.

The researchers are alarming us to reawaken the mission which was handed over by our father of Indian library and information science Dr. S. R. Ranganathan. Horizon of Knowledge is the patrimony given by our LIS ancestors. So the library has the responsibility to bridge the gap between the recorded knowledge and the living knowledge. To live, to flow, to keep quality, to produce the KNOWLEDGE, it must exist in human person instead of in records.

2.1. Museum to Library

The ColinWight explain the history 'The Museum's Department of Printed Books was founded in 1753, the year of the foundation of the Museum itself. Over the intervening two hundred years, the library of the British Museum had grown into one of the largest in the world.' [2] Library was an exhibiting part of museum. The materials were exhibits. After two centuries of growth the concept of library became a reality in the 'British Library'. The ancient spirit was a 'museum spirit' i.e. collects, preserve and exhibit.

2.2. Collection, Organization and Retrieval

The founding fathers of library science broadened the objective of library to: "A collection of materials organized to provide physical, bibliographic and intellectual access to a target group, with a staff that is trained to provide services and programs related to the information needs of the target group. A building or structure that houses such a collection... " American Library Association (ALA) has defined "library" in its Glossary of Library and Information Science. [14] It is a place for collecting, storing, organizing, preserving and providing the documents to the users. At the same time, a library is an environment for enlightenment or research. The priority of material become little down and user become almost equal.

2.3. Five Laws

The 5 laws openly made it as a law that 'the availability of recorded knowledge is a right of humanity'. Dr. Ranganathan presented his Five laws of library science for the first time in 1928 in a conference of teachers held in the Meenakshi College, Annamalainagar.

1. Books are for Use
2. Every Reader His Book
3. Every Book Its Reader
4. Save the Time of the Reader
5. A Library is a Growing Organism.

The revolutionary act of Dr. Ranganathan starts from the first law onwards. It constitutes the basis for the library services. Dr. Ranganathan observed that books were often chained to prevent their removal and that the emphasis was on storage and preservation rather than use. He did not reject the notion that preservation and storage were important, but he asserted that the purpose of such activities was to promote use. Without user access to materials, there is little value in these items. By emphasizing use, Dr. Ranganathan refocused the attention of the field to access-related issues, such as the library's location, loan policies, hours and days of operation, as well as the quality of staffing and mundane matters like library furniture, temperature control and lighting. [20]

2.4. New Horizon for Knowledge

The awareness as well as a thirst for knowledge was a new paradigm shift in the last two centuries. The quest for knowledge increased among the people and the society. Education for all was one of the dreams for them. The primary education opened the door to a large number of people to enter in to the horizon of knowledge.

2.5. Library as an Instrument for Awakening the Society

The new consciousness of people, emergence of the education institutions and the different social reformation movements made lots of changes in the society. The revolutionary philosophy of Dr. Ranganathan's five laws became the energy for library movements. These library movements helped to widely spread the right of knowledge among the society.

2.6. Library and Information Science Played a Vital Role for Knowledgeable Society

One of the greatest changes that happened during the last decades in the humanity was that a good number of people became educated and society became knowledgeable. In this process of becoming knowledgeable society, the library and information science education and service, and the library movements have played an extremely large role.

3. ICT IMPACT ON CONTENT

Space and Content are interdependent and existential requirements of library. The drastic changes in the Content demand systematic and creative modification of Space. Managing the Space and content in library for the networked society is a challenge for librarians, institutions and library makers. [5]

3.1. Production of Knowledge

Impact of ICT had changed the scenario of the knowledge production. ICT is helping the information to reach out maximum. As an instrument, ICT is providing highest bandwidth for the dissemination of information. This impact helped the people to produce huge amount of information. Quantity vice, this progress is a great achievement but the quality of the bulk production of information is still challenging.

4. INFORMATION EXPLOSION

Katz reported that the invention of printing in the mid-15th century, the wide distribution of books by the 16th century, the growth of literacy among the middle classes in the 17th and 18th centuries, and mass education movement in the 19th century increased both the amount and the demand for information. The invention of electronic media, especially the Internet, has contributed immensely to the information explosion. Information and communication technology (ICT) has played a key role for the emergence of information explosion. If the invention of printing has promoted an increase in information generation, ICT has multiplied it. [15]

4.1. Information Overloaded

There is overload information in the world "The flood of information that swamps us daily seems to produce more pain than gain. And it is not just the incoming tidal wave of e-mail messages and RSS feeds that causes me grief. It is also the vast ocean of information I feel compelled to go out and explore in order to keep up in my job" [1] Paul Hemp a renowned writer expressed this idea in Harvard Business Review under the title 'Death by Information Overload'.

4.2. Capacity of Human Brain

Thad McIlroy in the article 'The Information Explosion and its implications to the Future of Publishing' observed that "The Internet easily defeats advanced filters, delivering millions of words per second to brains that can process only 10 words per second" [7] from Peter J. Denning, Director of the Cebrowski Institute for Information and Innovation and Superiority at the Naval Postgraduate School in Monterey, CA.

5. CONSEQUENCES

A lot of consequences are there for the new impact of the ICT applied information system. Few of them are listed below:

5.1. Data Mind

Most of the students are tuning their brain as a data or information storage or carrier. Brain will gather the information from classroom, reading materials and other ways of collecting information. Without much personalization or assimilation, students will deliver this gathered information in the exam. Many students are not able to remember, recollect and apply the information which they learned during the course time in practical life. Two important reasons for these phenomena may be: 1) Information overload and 2) Easy accessibility of information at anytime and anywhere. A number of students are keeping their heads empty after the downloading process at exam time. Impact of using brain as 'random memory' for data storing the human mind is knowingly or unknowingly becoming 'data mind[1]'.

We can observe some habits or culture of 'data mind' as follows: 1) Always people keep the data, information and knowledge out and keep mind free and clean. 2) Outsourcing the memory for personal data, information and knowledge. 3) Depending upon quick search and its tool at the time of application.

5.2. Skill Gap

"Skill Gap is the difference in the skills required on the job and the actual skills possessed by the employees is called as skill-gap." [9] It is a gap between qualification and quality. The society is expecting something from the qualified people. But their capacity is exceptionally different from the expectation. This is a common phenomenon of the present day education. "While more than 11 million Americans are unemployed and millions more are underemployed or have dropped out of the workforce, businesses routinely says they can't find the skilled workers they need." [8]

5.3. Knowledge Monopoly[2]

The habits and culture of 'data mind' will cause to overdependence on data, information and knowledge providers. Lack of personal knowledge will lead to over dependency on knowledge banks and information providers. The other end of this phenomenon will promote the knowledge monopoly and the clients will be the people of networked society.

5.4. Stagnancy of knowledge

By very nature of the knowledge, after the production it may flow to other. This other may be one or many. According to Indian tradition *vidiya danam* (the flow or providing of knowledge to other as a donation) *is* considered as a *mahadanam* (great donation). In the article, the term *'jnanadara'* is explained by K. Ramakrishna Rao as follows 'In the native Indian tradition there is another step called *nididhyasana*, meditation on the truth learnt through *sravana* and *manana*. *Nididhyasana*, involving an unceasing flow of knowledge (*Jnanadhara*), takes one beyond understanding the truth. It gives one realization of truth in his/her being'. [12] This flow of knowledge from person to person(s) is very essential. But in the present scenario, the flow is affected by many other agencies. The knowledge becomes stored at its storage place or space. If the knowledge flow[3] is not take place, knowledge will become stagnant. The stagnancy of knowledge will pollute the knowledge and create problems.

5.6. Knowledge Filtering[4]

Filtering is a very soothing word to hear. But huge danger is hidden behind the filtering culture. Normally we do filtering or fix filter at the user end or at the taping point. We believe that the things after the filtering become pure. That means the source may not be pure. The best example for this filtering culture is water filtering system and its culture. To get more clarity, we can take the impact of water filtering culture in Kerala, a southern state of India. The people of Kerala were blessed with natural mineral water in almost all the areas of the state. Around 50 years back water filtering, machine for water filtering and filtered bottle water for drinking etc. were not understood among the people of the Kerala. Entire water sources were clean and good for drink. Those days the people never do any filtering before drinking. There was no possibility to buy filtered water bottle for drinking also. In those days, people were very vigilant about the source of the water to be pure and protect it away from pollution. That was a common custom. After 50 years, now filtering culture is very common and most of the people are using filtered water for drinking. This filtering culture teaches us to forget about the source and be careful about the using water after the filter point. The same problem may happen in the case of the horizon of knowledge within few decades. Some of the problems regarding the filtering culture that can be expected in the future are: 1) Source of the knowledge may keep always polluted 2) Over dependency on filtering agency 3) Indirect slavery to the knowledge filtering agencies 4) May lose confidence in one's own knowledge / self-knowledge. Today or tomorrow all of us will become directly or indirectly the client's of this California inventors to filter the knowledge.

5.7. Unmanageable amount of information waste

These phenomena like information exploration, knowledge filtering, knowledge monopoly, etc. may be a burden for ordinary people. They cannot handle the enormous amount of information. It will create a kind of 'information numbness'. This stage will lead to generation without balanced information or knowledge. That means a kind of ignorance becomes common to the majority of the society. This state of life will create another set of problems like: it affects the value system; utility may assess the value of information and knowledge; decline of human dignity; abandoned records; information slavery; etc.

6. LIBRARY SPACE AS A BRIDGING FORCE

Library space is the source for bridging the recorded knowledge and the living knowledge. Information and knowledge should live in the human person instead of in record storages. The librarian, the library space and the university have to be alert to realize this mission.

6.1. Research Ecology: Inspiring Space for Production and Protection of Quality Knowledge

It is an extreme level concept of space for the

university library, to create 'research ecology'. Neelankavil, J. observed that "... university libraries are symbolically considered as the heart that pumps knowledge to every part of its constituent bodies." [22] It is not a simple physical space, but it is an atmosphere of research with many unseen components to inspire the scholars. If the university is giving paramount importance to the research then only the research environment may actualize in a classical way. By this innovation, the higher education should become qualitative, library centred and research oriented. If the high quality universities and institutions start to think about this qualitative space - research ecology – definitely it will reflect in the horizon of knowledge.

7. REAWAKENING ROLE OF LIBRARY

The patrimony of Dr. Ranganathan is not a building (library), not a set of books, not the technology, etc. but the horizon of knowledge. Now the knowledge is in a dangerous situation. We have to own it and cure it. Among you there is a RENGANATHAN, he/she can come and lead us.

8. CONCLUSION

This article is a call for reawakening the real mission of librarianship. When we look into the history of knowledge and evolution of library and information science, we can observe a few realities like: 1) both horizon of knowledge and LIS had a healthy and energetic blending in the past century 2) now both the horizon of knowledge and LIS are going through an unbalanced situation 3) this situation is leading to a kind of information numbness. This numbness may be expanding the gap between the recorded knowledge and living knowledge. This is a serious issue which the library has to address. It is the right time to interact with the knowledge: in its production; flow; quality and the life; with the capacity of library and information science profession.

LIS had a great role in the process of making people knowledgeable and networked society. Now the libraries have to reawaken to protect the horizon of knowledge, because it is our patrimony which the LIS ancestors have handed over to us. We have to bridge the gap between the recoded knowledge and the living knowledge. So let the knowledge live; let the knowledge flow; let the knowledge grow; let the knowledge be pure; let the knowledge be constructive.

REFERENCES

1. P. Hemp, "Death by information overload," in *IT*, Harvard Business Review, 2009. [Online]. Available: https://hbr.org/2009/09/death-by-information-overload. Accessed: Apr. 23, 2016.
2. P. Hemp, "Death by information overload," in *IT*, Harvard Business Review, 2009. [Online]. Available: https://hbr.org/2009/09/death-by-information-overload. Accessed: Apr. 23, 2016.
3. C. Wight, "History of the British library," The British Library, 2015. [Online]. Available: http://www.bl.uk/aboutus/quickinfo/facts/history/. Accessed: Apr. 24, 2016.
4. B. S. Kademani, V. L. Kalyane, and V. Kumar, "BOSALA One day seminar: Resource management 2003 preservation of information resources in libraries: New challenges," 2003. [Online]. Available: http://eprints.rclis.org/4927/1/preservation.PDF. Accessed: Apr. 24, 2016.
5. J. Reed-Scott, "Collection management strategies for Archivists," *The American Archivist*, vol. 47, no. 1, pp. 23–29, 1984. [Online]. Available: http://www.jstor.org/stable/pdf/40292633.pdf?_=1461475151539. Accessed: Apr. 24, 2016.
6. DVK Central Library, "International conference on library space & content management for Networked society," in *IC-LISCOM-2014*, 2014. [Online]. Available: http://www.liscom.org/. Accessed: Apr. 28, 2016.
7. B. Thomas, "We are the Information Multiplication Generation," 2014. [Online]. Available: https://www.linkedin.com/pulse/20140620201810-19895279-we-are-the-information-multiplication-generation. Accessed: Apr. 28, 2016.

8. T. McIlroy, "The information explosion (and its implic ations to the Future of Publishing)," in *hitpages.com*, 2009. [Online]. Available: https://www.hitpages.com/doc/5056095630393344/1/ . Accessed: May 6, 2016.

9. JP Morgan Chase &Co., "Skill Gap,". [Online]. Available: file:///C:/Users/john/Downloads/EMSI-SkillsGap-Brief.pdf. Accessed: May 6, 2016.

10. Human Resources (HR) Dictionary, "Skill gap definition," in *mbaskool.com*, MBA Skool-Study.Learn.Share., 2008. [Online]. Available: http://www.mbaskool.com/business-concepts/human-resources-hr-terms/2134-skill-gap.html. Accessed: May 6, 2016.

11. Malaspina University-College, "Harold Adams Innis: The bias of communications & monopolies of power," in *Dr. Marshall Soules, Malaspina University-College*, 2007. [Online]. Available: http://www.media-studies.ca/articles/innis.htm. Accessed: May 6, 2016.

12. G. Peri, "KNOWLEDGE FLOWS AND INNOVATION," California, 2002. [Online]. Available: http://eml.berkeley.edu//~obstfeld/e281_sp03/peri.pdf. Accessed: May 6, 2016.

13. K. R. RAO, "The Hindu: Learning, understanding and realisation," in *Online edition of India's National Newspaper*, 2001. [Online]. Available: http://www.thehindu.com/2001/08/28/stories/13280377.htm. Accessed: May 3, 2016.

14. J. M. Reitz, "Online Dictionary for Library and Information Science," in *abc-clio.com*, 2014. [Online]. Available: http://www.abc-clio.com/ODLIS/odlis_l.aspx. Accessed: May 7, 2016.

15. M. Levine-Clark and T. M. Carter, *ALA glossary of library and information science, fourth edition*. American Library Association, 2013. [Online]. Available: https://books.google.co.in/books?id=QQObAwAAQBAJ&pg=PA151&lpg=PA151&dq=library+is+a+A+collection+ of+materials+organized+to+provide+physical, +bibliographic +and +intellectual+ access+to+a +target+group &source=bl&ots=KVci5IrKAi&sig= q79vqdLBBMdVwCr55cNo3n6HPXI&hl=en&sa=X&ved=0ahUKEwj26Luf6cbMAhXOSo4KHR2JAH8Q6AEIITAC #v=onepage&q=library%20is%20a%20A%20collection%20of%20materials%20organized%20to%20provide%20physical %2C%20bibliographic%20and%20intellectual%20access%20to%20a %20target%20group&f=false. Accessed: May 7, 2016.

16. W. A. Katz, *Introduction to reference work*, 8th ed. New York:

McGraw-Hill, 2002.

17. Data Mind, "Home | data mining," 2013. [Online]. Available: http://www.datamind.cz/en/. Accessed: May 7, 2016.

18. R. R. Nair, "Library Space from Prehistoric Caves to the Cloud," in *Library Space and Content Management for a Networked Society*, B. Ramesha, S. A. Sornam, and J. Neelankavil, Eds., 1st ed. Bengaluru: Dharmaram Publication, 2014, pp. 17–23.

19. J. Neelankavil, A. Sornam, and B. Ramesha, "Transforming Library Space: An Environment for Enlightenment," in *Library Space and Content Management for a Networked Society*, B. Ramesha, S. A. Sornam, and J. Neelankavil, Eds., 1st ed. Bengaluru: Dharmaram Publications, 2014, pp. 33–39.

20. S. A. Sornam, "Green Library Buildings: A mission to Accomplish!," in *Library Space and Content Management for a Networked Society*, B. Ramesha, S. A. Sornam, and J. Neelankavil, Eds., 1st ed. Bengaluru: Dharmaram Publications, 2014, pp. 41–43.

21. B. K. Sen, "Ranganathan's five laws," *Annals of Library and Information Studies (ALIS)*, vol. 55, no. 2, pp. 87–90, Jun. 2008. [Online]. Available: http://nopr.niscair.res.in/bitstream/123456789/1769/1/ALIS%2055%282%29%2087-90.pdf. Accessed: Jun. 5, 2016.

22. R. E. Rubin and N. Y. London, "Foundations of library and information science THIRD EDITION Neal-Schuman publishers," Neal-Schuman Publishers, New York, London, 2011. [Online]. Available: http://www.alastore.ala.org/pdf/0424-foundations-of-library-and-information-science—third-edition.pdf. Accessed: Jun. 5, 2016.

23. J. Neelankavil, "Transcendental Aspect of University Library : Space , Knowledge and Librarian," in *Global Conference on Emerging Trends in Business Librarianship*, presented at the ETBL - 2015, IIM Ahmedabad, 2015. [Online]. Available: http://www.iimahd.ernet.in/library/conference/programme.html. Accessed: May 3, 2016.

24. Patent US8943069 - knowledge filter, by M. C. Heumann, K. Cooley, and K. I. Applications. (2009, Sep. 14). [Online]. Available: https://www.google.com/patents/US8943069. Accessed: Jun. 5, 2016.

8

Open Source Software Tools and Services for Academic and Research Process

Sainul Abideen P

ABSTRACT

Information and Communication Technology (ICT) can help to realize the dream of universal access to high-quality education. ICT would be a key enabling technology for making this dream a reality by providing the ability to produce compelling and individualized content, the means for delivering it, and effective feedback and assessment mechanisms. Numerous innovative software for accessing information, organizing information, processing it for presentation or storage, retrieval, dissemination through time and space etc. have become available. This paper introduces a few open source software tools and free online services that can be used for managing academic content, presentation of content, organization of content in digital and traditional media, making content accessible to the academic community as well as checking and evaluating the quality and originality of the content.

Keywords : ICT, Software Tools, Teaching, Research, Piracy Checking, Evergreen, ABCD, GreenStone, DSpace, Mendeley, Eprints, Joomla, Droopal, LaTeX, Plagiarism, Viper.

1. INTRODUCTION

Exponential developments in computer and communication technology during the last two decades have resulted in the availability of numerous compelling and engaging software tools for education and research than we could have dreamed of earlier.

Now information and communication technology is playing a crucial role in education. It provides numerous tools that encourage and support different processes and functions in education and research. Teachers and research supervisors needs to be trained in the use of these ICT based tools to take harness these new capabilities.

There are hundreds of software tools used for different processes in higher education and research. This paper introduces some of the packages selected from different functions in academic & research processes. It also discusses a few free online services, which will support academicians and researchers. The software discussed is related to the processes given in the following figure related to the interaction in academic and research system.

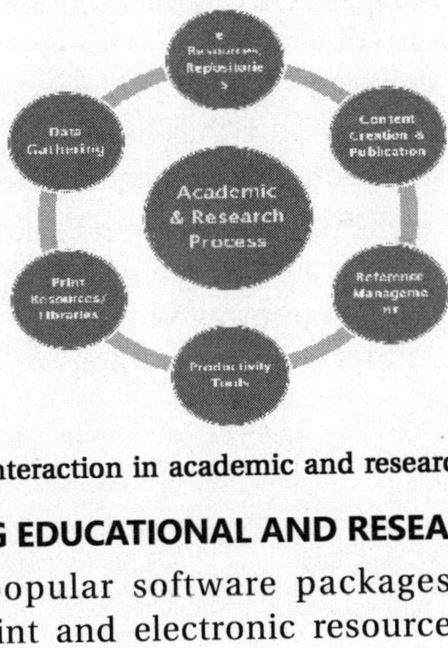

Fig. 1. Interaction in academic and research system

2. MANAGING EDUCATIONAL AND RESEARCH CONTENT

Some popular software packages available for managing print and electronic resources in academic libraries are Evergreen ILS, Koha and ABCD. These packages can look after most of the house keeping activities of the library like acquisition, cataloguing, circulation, periodical management etc. Their search engines, which replace our traditional catalogue, do most important function and an important addition is their module for Online Public Catalogue (OPAC).

Koha : Koha is an Integrated Library Management System. Koha is a fully featured, open source, scalable system. Libraries of varying types and sizes, volunteers, and support companies worldwide sponsor its development.

Evergreen : Evergreen is an open source Integrated Library System (ILS), initially developed by Georgia PINES consortium for use as their automation system, and now includes contributions from around the world. Designed for large-scale deployment in very large libraries and statewide consortium environments with tens of millions of records and hundreds of libraries, but can also be scaled down to the smallest of single-branch libraries. It is written in C, JavaScript and Perl, is GPLed, runs on Linux with Apache, uses a Postgre SQL database, Jabber for messaging and XUL as client-side software. The system allows easy clustering and is based entirely on open protocols. IISER Thiruvananthapuram library has been using Evergreen ILS since 2009 for complete library automation.

ABCD: ABCD is web-based integrated library management software. Its development was promoted and coordinated by BIREME, with the support of VLIR. Its development and maintenance is under the methodology of Free and Open Source Software.

Fig. 2. Evergreen Integrated Library System at IISER, Thiruvananthapuram

Digital Library Packages

Like books and other documents in shelves and the card catalogue to retrieve them, in digital libraries we find documents in digital form in digital storage mechanisms and the database management system at its front-end which connects catalogue record instantly to the document which opens in computer screen if we require. Prominent software for managing such digital resources and institutional repositories are DSpace, Greenstone and E-Prints.

DSpace : DSpace is used for digital object management systems. It is developed jointly by the MIT Libraries and Hewlett-Packard Labs. Being open source software, it facilitates open access and digital archiving. It is used mainly for building institutional repositories

Greenstone : Greenstone is software suited for building, maintaining, and distributing digital library collections. It is open-source software developed by New Zealand Digital

Library Project at the University of Waikato.

Eprints : Eprints is a free and open-source software package for building open access repositories that are compliant with the Open Archives Initiative Protocol for Metadata Harvesting (OAI-PMH).

NityaDArch : NityaDArch is a digital library software that can process all Indian languages. It also has facility to search inside the full text files in all local scripts. It is used in the Mahatma Gandhi University Ph.D Theses online library, Kerala Gazette Archives and Rare Books Digital Library of State Central Library of Kerala.

Content Management Systems

There are numerous content management systems, which can help academic systems to manage their content in digital libraries as well as web pages. A few such packages are discussed below.

Joomla : Joomla is a free and open-source content management system (CMS) for publishing web content. The software can be downloaded from https://www.joomla.org/

Drupal : Drupal is a free and open-source content-management framework written in PHP. The software can be downloaded from https://www.drupal.org

E-Learning

Numerous E-learning system packages are available in commercial and Open Source streams. Some examples are the following.

Moodle : Moodle is a free and open-source software for learning management system written in PHP and distributed under the GNU General Public License. Further details can be had from https://moodle.org/

ATutor : ATutor is an open source web-based learning

management system, with variety of useful features, ranging from email notifications to file storage. It is very user-friendly and suitable for those who may be new to the world of eLearning design and development. More details about this can be had from http://www.atutor.ca

Reference Management

Reference management software is used by scholars and authors for recording and utilising bibliographic citations (references). There are numerous software for reference management. Some examples are given below.

Zotero : Zotero is free and open-source reference management software to manage bibliographic data and related research materials including PDF files. The software can be obtained from https://www.zotero.org/. Features of Zotera are web browser integration, online synchronization, generation of in-text citations, footnotes and bibliographies, integration with the word-processors like Microsoft Word, LibreOffice, OpenOffice.org etc.

Mendeley : Mendeley is a reference management system. It is a desktop and web program for managing and sharing research papers, discovering research data and collaborating online. It combines Mendeley Desktop, a PDF and reference management application. Free and Paid versions of the package are available from the website: https://www.mendeley.com/. One can search and sort his/her references, documents and notes in one place. It can be used online or offline to access PDFs on the move. It can publicly or privately share reading lists, references or full-text articles. It can generate citations and bibliographies in the style of our choice quickly. The software is compatible with Microsoft Word, LibreOffice and BibTeX. It can also create groups to tackle research assignments, share feedback and write papers with collaborators. This tool helps to showcase published research to millions around the world. Mendeley has mobile apps for iPad, iPhone and Android, allowing access to Mendeley library, read and annotates PDFs, and keeps everything synchronized across devices.

Word Processors

Word processors are software for document preparation and type setting. There are packages like Open Office and other free suites that provide word processing. One very advanced and widely used text processing software, which has facilities for typesetting scientific papers and documents, is LaTeX.

LaTeX

LaTeX is a high-quality typesetting system; it includes features designed for the production of technical and scientific documentation. LaTeX is the de facto standard for the communication and publication of scientific documents. Details and the package is available at https://www.latex-project.org

Features of LaTex

- Typesetting journal articles, technical reports, books, and slide presentations.
- Control over large documents containing sectioning, cross-references, tables and figures.
- Typesetting of complex mathematical formulas.
- Advanced typesetting of mathematics with AMS-LaTeX.
- Automatic generation of bibliographies and indexes.
- Multi-lingual typesetting.

Collaborating Service

There are numerous collaborating services for research content maintained by commercial firms as well as international organizations as free service. Some examples are discussed below.

ResearchGate : ResearchGate is a social networking site for scientists and researchers to share papers, ask and answer questions, and find collaborators. The service can be accessed at https://www.researchgate.net/. It currently has more than 12 million members.

E-LIS : E-LIS is world's largest collaborating service and open archive in Library and Information Science and related areas. It can be accessed at http://eprints.rclis.org/

Plagiarism Checking

Plagiarism is the "wrongful appropriation" and "stealing and publication" of another author's "language, thoughts, ideas, or expressions" and the representation of them as one's own original work. There are numerous software in Commercial and Open streams for plagiarism checking. They are online tools and some examples are provided below.

Viper : is a plagiarism checker that scans over 10 billion resources. It has an easy-to-use interface and highlights areas of plagiarism. It scans against documents on our computer and scan against essays published on the Internet. It gives easy side-by-side highlighted comparison. It is freely available from the website http://www.scanmyessay.com/

Quetext : Quetext is another free plagiarism checking tool. It is 100% free. It has an easy to use interface. It permits unlimited usage without having to create an account or download software. But cannot upload files, one can only copy and paste text. It is available from http://www.quetext.com/

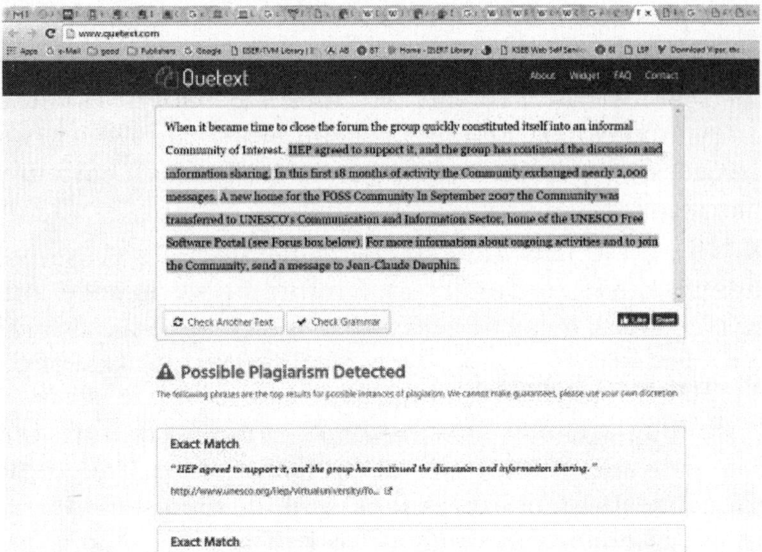

Fig. 3. Quetext

Duplichecker : Duplichecke is also another free antiplagarism service. It is also 100% free, extremely easy to use and has the options of copy-pasting the text, entering the URL of the content destination required to be checked, or uploading a text file. Registered users can perform 50 free plagiarism searches per day. Unregistered users can perform only one free plagiarism search per day. It is available from the website www.duplichecker.com/

CONCLUSION

Availability of free/open source software helps in academic and research activities. Several time consuming academic and research processes can easily be managed using freely available software and services without any financial burden. The teachers, research guides and students need to be familiarized in software tools for education and research, which can improve the quality of academic process.

REFERENCES

[1] Bainbridge, W. The scientific research potential of virtual worlds. Science, 317, 27, 2007. 471-476

[2] John Seely Brown, "Growing Up Digital: How the Web Changes Work, Education, and the Ways People Learn," Change, March/April 2000, http://www.aahe.org/change/ digital.pdf.

[3] Jerome S. Bruner, The Process of Education (Cambridge: Harvard University Press), 1960, 33.

[4] Kung, April. The Case for Educational Software in the Life Sciences (2004). http://ramsites.net/~kungae/deck.pdf

[5] Raman Nair, R. Content Management for Agricultural Research and Development in India., 2001 . In 23rd IASLIC Conference, Thiruvananthapuram (India), December, 2001. [Conference paper]. http://eprints.rclis.org/7639/

[6] ResearchGate, https://www.researchgate.net/about

[7] Wikipedia. Educational Software. https://en.wikipedia.org/wiki/Educational_software

9

Digital Library Software for Managing Collections in Indian Languages: A Case Study of Nitya D Arch

Bino Jose

ABSTRACT

Defines Digital Library software. Presents the digital Library solutions available. Discusses them in the context of Indian library and archive environment. Opines that all the library software promoted in India are developed outside India apt only for international languages. Discusses in detail and indigenous digital library package developed in India, which has compatibility with Indian languages and scripts. Examines its features citing major projects having multilingual documents in Indian scripts that used the package.

Keywords : Digital Library, Nitya D Arch, Mahatma Gandhi University; Trivandrum Public Library; Institutional Repository; Software

1. DIGITAL LIBRARY/ARCHIVE

A digital library is a library in which collections are stored in digital formats (as opposed to print, microform, or other media) and the digital content may be stored locally, or accessed remotely via computer networks. A digital library is a type of information retrieval system. A distinction is often made between content that was created in a digital format, known as born-digital, and information that has been converted from a physical medium, e.g., paper, by digitizing. The term hybrid library is sometimes used for libraries that have both physical collections and digital collections.

The main objective of digital library is to collect, organize, preserve and disseminate documents transferred to digital media, which are also termed as digital objects. Digital objects may be in the form of text, images, audio and video. Digital content has become crucial in education and research. It is also important in all other sectors of human activity. Digital libraries facilitate dissemination/ access of scholarly output available in electronic form. So digital library systems can be considered to be supporting effective collection, organization and dissemination of knowledge. By this it supports generation of new knowledge.

2. FEATURES OF DIGITAL ARCHIVING SYSTEMS

The following are the important features of the digital library system

- Digital library systems incorporate the features and components, which increase the portability and preservation of digital content. Following are considered to be the essential features required in a digital library system.
- Searching capability: good digital archival software should have the capability to search both Meta data and full text of the documents.
- Browsing: Browsing through list of authors, keywords and titles are convenient for users to find the desired

digital document.

- Character representation: Ability to store and retrieve documents in different languages is an added advantage of a good digital library system. In India, which uses more than 20 regional languages, compatibility to these languages is very important. A Unicode compliant digital library can accommodate digital documents in Hindi and other Indic languages.
- Document representation: Ability to handle documents in various formats like plain text, post script, PDF, word processor documents etc, is an essential feature of any digital archiving system.
- Multimedia representation: Ensure the capacity to support compressed multimedia formats while selecting digital archiving software for your library. Users can access streaming audio and video even in low bandwidth Internet connection.
- Metadata: Metadata is important for locating digital resources in archival systems. MARC, Dublin Core, BibTex, and Refer are popular metadata standard for representing bibliographic information. Metadata for images and multimedia is also important.
- Standards and protocols: Open Archives Initiative Protocol for Metadata Harvesting (OAI-PMH) is a standard for communication between open access digital archiving systems.
- Web 2.0/3.0 features: Personalization, tagging (folksonomies), book marking, and authoring features in digital archiving system can enhance the user interaction capabilities.

3. DIGITAL LIBRARY PACKAGES

Developing Digital Libraries requires use of a Digital

Library package. Digital library packages contain a database at front end to upload and connect a digital object to the concerned record in the database. Digital Library packages are available under the category of commercial and Open Source streams. Open source digital library systems are more popular than proprietary systems due to its free availability. The following are the popular digital library packages available.

Alfresco is digital library package for Microsoft Windows and Unix-like operating systems. It can be used for content management for documents, web, records, images and collaborative content development. It is developed using java Technology. It was developed by John Newton John Powell.

DSpace is open-source digital library software developed by MIT for managing electronic documents and other objects especially of academic interest. It supports a wide variety of data, including books, theses, 3D digital scans of objects, photographs, film, video, research data sets and other forms of content. The data can be arranged as community collections of items.

Eprints is a digital library packages, which is primarily used for institutional repositories and scientific journals. Eprints was developed at the University of Southampton School of Electronics and Computer Science UK and one of the largest collections in Library and information science and related are meant for Open Access is E-LISis hosted using E-Prints.

Fedora is a general-purpose, open-source digital object repository system. Fedora (Flexible Extensible Digital Object Repository Architecture) was originally developed by researchers at Cornell University as architecture for storing, managing, and accessing digital content.

Greenstone is a package for building and distributing

digital library collections on the Internet or CD-ROM. Greenstone is produced by the New Zealand Digital Library Project at the University of Waikato, and has been developed and distributed in cooperation with UNESCO.

Hydra is an open-source digital repository software product. Hydra's main components are Fedora Commons, Solr, Blacklight, and HydraHead. The software was developed as collaboration between Stanford University, the University of Virginia, the University of Hull, and Fedora Commons.

Invenio is an open source software package that provides the tools for management of digital assets in an institutional repository. The CERN Document Server Software Consortium developed Invenio.

Kete is open source software, developed by Katipo Communications for Horowhenua Library Trust, that can be used to create online areas for collaboration for community. It is software that combines aspects of Digital Libraries/Repositories, Knowledge and Content Management Systems, and collaboration tools to make it easy to add and relate content.

Nitya D'Arch is a bibliographic information system applied to digital library management. It is capable of search and retrieval using any Indian Script. Nitya is a procedure as well as a programme. Nitya can retrieve specific pages where the information user sought for occurs. It is developed by Beehive digital concepts, India.

OPUS is an open source software package under the GNU General Public License used for creating Open Access repositories that are compliant with the OAI-PMH. It provides tools for creating collections of digital resources, as well as for their storage and dissemination. OPUS, originally an acronym for the Online Publikationsverbund der Universität Stuttgart, was developed with the support of the Deutsches Forschungsnetz at the University of Stuttgart.

Most of the above software are used in different organizations and networks at national level state level and institutional level. DSpace is promoted by the multinational company HP with customized versions and supporting hardware. It is used in many projects like Shod Ganga of UGC INFLIBNET, Kerala State government repository projects, and institutional repository attempts of most of the universities in India. Other packages are also used in many institutions but installations are very less for each package. But among these less popular packages even though installations of Nitya was less it was found to be the only software that was successful tested for Indian languages.

4. NITYA D' ARCH: AN INDIGENOUS DL PACKAGE

Nitya D'Arch is an online digital archiving system specializing in Indian regional languages for digital library development. Nitya D'Arch facilitates for developing and hosting e-documents collections and has multilingual search facility, multilingual online keyboard and it satisfies UNICODE standards. Presently it has been used to host digital libraries with documents in English, Malayalam, Hindi, Tamil and Kannada the languages. The specificity in search and retrieval offered by Nitya is not available in any other digital library packages available at present. Its metadata format is OAI-PMH (Open Access initiative – Protocol for Metadata Harvest) compliant. The main advantages of Nitya are:

5. FEATURES OF NITYA D'ARCH PACKAGE

Regional Language Book-marking : Nitya can support a wide range of regional languages like Malayalam, Tamil, Hindi, etc. Bookmarks of a regional language book are stored in that language itself. Nitya also provides support for searching in regional languages.

Deep indexing : Nitya implements the technique of deep indexing, wherein even the bookmarks stored internally within the documents (for example in pdf documents) are harvested and are made available for searching. This allows users to pinpoint and retrieve the exact pages in documents rather than retrieving the whole large documents which can contain hundreds or thousands of pages

Speed : For normal digital archives, even with a 2 Mbps broadband connection loading a digital book with around 300 pages takes a lot of time because such a book will have a size of around 16-20 MB. This problem is particularly serious when the searching is done on bookmarks because the page to be loaded might be near the end of the book and the user will have to wait for the full book to load. But Nitya uses a special algorithm that loads only the page in focus and the 2 pages before and after it. So the user will feel that the full book is loaded even though only 3 pages are loaded.

6. MGU THESES ARCHIVE IN NITYA D'ARCH

The first successful and important use of Nitya package was for developing Online Digital Library of PhD These of Mahatma Gandhi University, Kottayam, Kerala. Assessing its capabilities and launching the Archive in 9th November 2008 HE Dr. A P J Abdul Kalam, the Former President of India stated that the project is an important step towards democratization of knowledge and that he was sure the model of digital archives created by MG University will be emulated by other Indian universities leading to transparency in the education system. Afterwards the package was used in many other important projects like Trivandrum Public Library Rare Books Online Archive, Travancore Cochin Gazettes Archive etc.

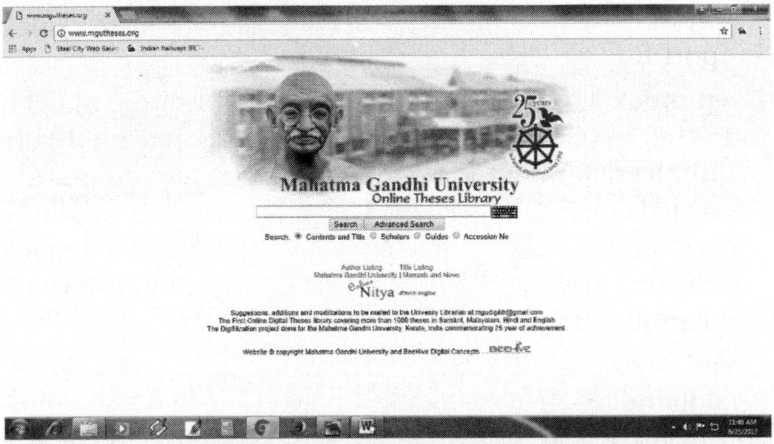

Home page of MGU Theses Library: http://www.mgutheses.org

7. NITYA D' ARCHIVE CUSTOMIZATIONS

In Mahatma Gandhi University Online Theses Digital Library the software was customized as per the requirement of MG University by Beehive DC a group providing solutions for digital library and content management. The groups has conceived and implemented many complex digital archiving projects since 2002 and are proficient in content management and indexing methods. They are also involved in the project Malayalam Granthavivarm a web based searchable archive of metadata for Malayalam books published from 1772. Their development team, which associated with MGU in the project, consisted of experts in documentation and linguistics. Nitya is a procedure as well as a programme. Search and retrieval of individual pages is a unique feature. While other programmes like Greenstone, DSpace etc retrieve whole documents, which contain the subject or key term of users search. Nitya can retrieve specific pages where the information user sought for occurs and from there user can navigate to other pages of the document. It is Unicode compliant and multilingual.

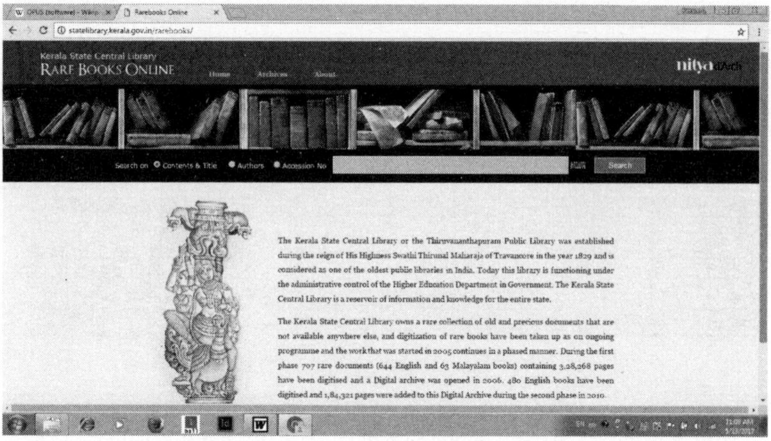

Home Page of Trivandrum Public Library Rare Books Online

7.1. Unique Features Nitya D'Arch

- Archiving and managing exhaustive collection of documents
- General retrieval of the whole documents as well as specific retrieval of pages/sections
- Open database allowing future migration to OAI-PMH compliant packages
- Continuous updating of the digital library

7.2. User Friendliness of Nitya D'Arch

The user Interface Nitya'D Arch is very simple and is similar to Google Search Engine. Subject keywords are to be entered in the search form given in the Home page. Then we have to click the 'Search' button

7.3. Getting List of Relevant Document

When the 'Search' button is clicked a list of relevant documents is displayed. All the titles of the retrieved documents having the search term in title, as well as highly relevant to search topic are first displayed. After that in continuation all the sections in other documents related to the query are listed in continuation. The list of documents generated by a query can be printed for future reference if essential.

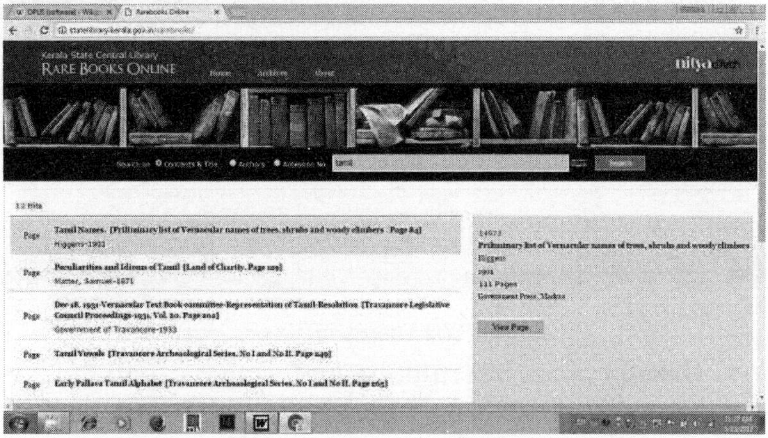

Retrieved List of Relevant Documents in Nitya

From this list user can chose the required title or document or the section of any document. For this the user has to check at the concerned item in the list. This opens the concerned full text and user can go to the full text of the document or concerned section.

7.4. Navigating Through Full Text

Once the full text is opened user can navigate through entire thesis back and forth. Bookmarks provided on the right side of the screen help the user to go to the relevant chapters instantly if needed.

7.5. Advanced Search

Searches can be made specific to categories like Author, Title, publisher, subject etc. is essential. 'Advanced Search' option permits the user to build complex Boolean queries in single steps.

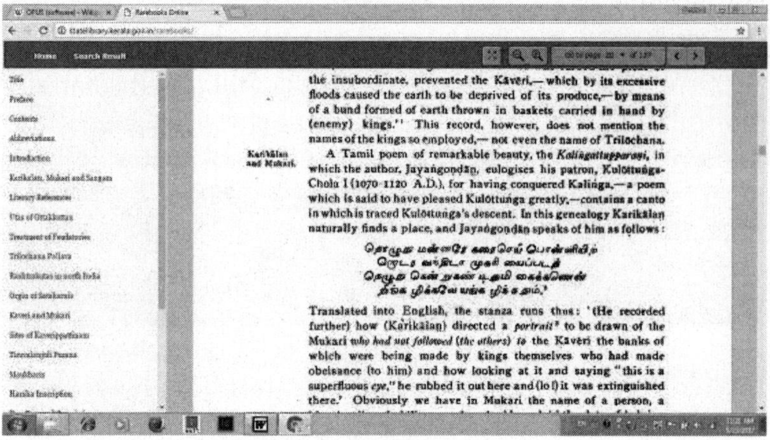

Full Text Opens in Nitya

Nitya D'Arch has multilingual, search capability (i.e. for searching Malayalam, Tamil, Kannada, Teleugu, Hindi and English etc). Mahatma Gandhi University Online Theses Digital Library is the best example for a Digital Library with multilingual search facility.

If user is not very familiar with the Malayalam, Tamil or other local language typing or any key board user can click on the key board symbol in the home page near the search form and get the Malayalam online key board in the screen. By clicking on the letters user can type the query in the search form.

7.6. Multi Lingual Search Facility: Hindi, Tamil and Kannada

By clicking on the TAB at the left side of the keyboard user can select Hindi. Even though Tamil and Kannada Theses are not available in the collection, facilities for those scripts are also available and those language documents can also be uploaded and searched through using concerned language provision in this archive.

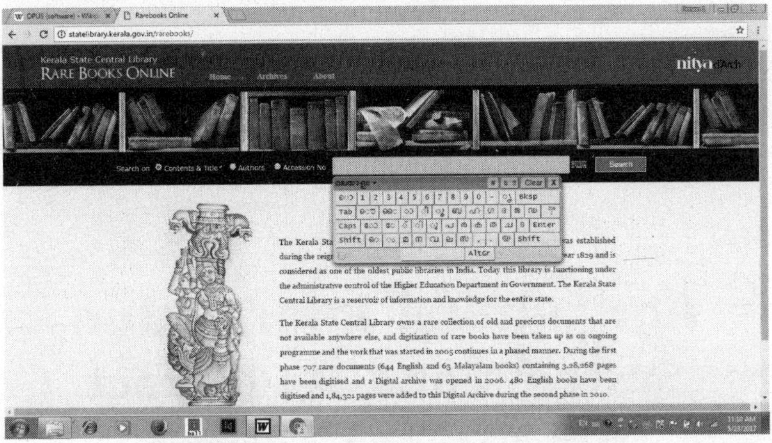

Multi Lingual Search Facility: Eg. Malayalam

7.8. Getting Bibliographical Data of a Theses

At any time while scanning through the documents by Clicking the tab 'Document Details', user gets full bibliographical data of the Documents.

REFERENCES

[1] Hussain K H, Vijayakumaran Nair P, Chitrajakumar R, Ravindran Asari K, Raman Nair R. Creation of Digital Archives in Indian Languages Using CDS/ISIS: Development of M-ISIS (Malayalam ISIS) and 'Nitya'. Information Studies 2005, 11(1), 59-68.

[2] Raman Nair, R. Developing Digital Libraries: Need For Proper Strategies. Advances in Library and Information Science. V5. Ed by D C Ojha and D V Kothari. Jodhpur, Scientific Publishers, 2005. Ch 21, P 259-271.

[3] Shalini R. Urs, N. S. Harinarayana, and Mallinath Kumbar. A multilingual multi-script database of Indian theses: Implementation of Unicode at Vidyanidhi. In ICADL '02:Proceedings of the 5th International Conference on Asian Digital Libraries, pages 305–314, London, UK, 2002. Springer-Verlag.

[4] Suber, Peter and Raman Nair, R. and Hussain, K. H. *Open Access to public funded research: a discussion in the context of Mahatma Gandhi University digital archives of doctoral dissertations.*, 2009. In CALIBER 2009, Pondicherry (India), 25-27 February 2009.

10

Agricultural Information Systems and Its Impact Among the Farmer Community: A Study With Special Reference to Kerala

Laila T Abraham
P Ganesan

ABSTRACT

Transfer and use of Agricultural information is very essential for sustainable agricultural development. The knowledge accumulated in different parts of the nation need to be coordinated and transmitted effectively so that it is utilized by farmer community for enhancing crop production. Hence the process of knowledge generation alone is not sufficient, its management and dissemination is equally important. The paper scrutinizes the services provided by some of the Agricultural Information Systems (AISs) of Central and State Governments. It is found that these AISs play an important role in the development of rural community. The activities of these systems and their impact among farmers in rural development have been examined and suggestions have been put forward to increase the utility of these Information systems.

Key words : Agricultural Information Systems, AISs, AgRIS, Krishi Bhavans, Krishi Vigyan Kendras, Kerala Agricultural University, KISSAN, mKissan.

1. INTRODUCTION

An information source is a knowledge enhancing or learning material for somebody, i.e. anything that might inform a person about something or provide knowledge about it. Different types of questions require different sources of information. Information sources may be observations, people, speeches, documents, pictures, organizations, websites, etc. There are primary, secondary and tertiary sources [1].

Information sources relating to Agricultural activities can be referred as Agricultural Information Sources. Agricultural related Books, Magazines, Television Programmes, Exhibitions, Extension Classes, Research Centres and Institutions both governmental and non-governmental, E-governance projects of Central and State governments, Databases, Websites etc. These types of information sources are utilized mainly by three groups of users like Scientists, Experts and Farmers. Hence Agricultural Information System is a system in which agricultural information is generated, transformed, consolidated, transmitted and feedback received to underpin knowledge utilization by agricultural producers [2]. Hence "an Agricultural Information System consists of components (subsystems), information related processes (generation, transformation, storage, retrieval, integration, diffusion and utilization), system mechanisms (interfaces and networks) and system operations (control and management). Analysis of an AIS will reveal the identification of basic components and structure of the system, various information sources used by different components in the system, the successful functioning of the system and the means to improve the performance of the system(system management) [3].

The paper examines the role of some of the Agricultural Information Systems (AISs) like AgRIS, Krishi Vigyan Kendras, Krishi Bhavans, Kerala Agricultural University and E-governance projects like mKissan and KISSAN in enhancing agricultural production and their impact in the development of rural community.

2. DEPARTMENT OF AGRICULTURE, GOVERNMENT OF INDIA

Ministry of Agriculture, Government of India, consists of major departments like Department of Agricultural Research and Education (DARE), Department of Agriculture and Cooperation (DAC), Indian Council of Agricultural Research (ICAR) and Krishi Vigyan Kendras (KVKs) come under DARE. Major divisions like Directorate of Extension and Directorate of Marketing and Inspection (DMI) are grouped under DAC [4].

Agriculture, with its allied sectors, is without doubt the resourceful income provider of farmers in the rural areas of India. It also contributes considerably to the Gross Domestic Product (GDP). Sustainable agriculture, in terms of food security, rural employment, and environmentally sustainable technologies such as soil conservation, sustainable natural resource management and biodiversity protection, are essential for holistic rural development. Indian agriculture and allied activities have witnessed a green revolution, a white revolution, a yellow revolution and a blue revolution. This department provides the information on agriculture produces; machineries, research etc. Detailed information on the government policies, schemes, agriculture loans, market prices, animal husbandry, fisheries, horticulture, loans & credit, sericulture etc. is also available.

3. DEPARTMENT OF AGRICULTURE, GOVERNMENT OF KERALA

The department deals with the planning, designing and implementation of a variety of programmes that focus on food and cash crop production in Kerala. Its activities includes encouraging scientific methods of cultivation, protection of plants from damages, supply of good quality seeds, seedlings, plant protection chemicals etc. It is responsible for framing policies and programmes for the benefits of farmer community. The three main functions of the department are conducting Research, Education and Extension in Agriculture and allied sectors. The department is headed by Director of Agriculture with offices at regional, district and panchayat levels in the State. There are Agricultural offices in every district with Joint Director as the head. Under district offices, Block offices are there with Assistant Directors as the head. Under each Block office, there will be 6-7 panchayats. Under each panchayat there is a Krishi Bhavan with Agricultural Officer as its head [5].

A. Agriculture in Kerala

In the present scenario, Kerala depends mostly on neighboring States for food grains and vegetables, at the same time it is a producer of major commercial and cash crops like coconut, cardamom, pepper, ginger, turmeric, tea, coffee, rubber and cashew. Due to its contribution in the commercial sector, Kerala is a major source for foreign exchange income of our nation. But it is found that in spite of the hardships encountered by the farmers for increasing agricultural production of the nation, they are not getting an income proportionate income for leading a comfortable life from their cultivation. To overcome this situation, farmers should be well informed of the modern developments in agricultural sector and means to improve his livelihood [6].

4. AGRICULTURAL INFORMATION SYSTEMS (AIS)

This paper examines some of the existing AISs such as Agricultural Information System (Agris), Krishi Vigyan Kendras, Krishi Bhavans and Kerala Agricultural University and E-governance projects namely mKissan and KISSAN of Central and State Governments[7].

A. Agricultural Resources Information System (AgRIS)

For promoting growth of agriculture, reduction of poverty and continuous utility of resources at the grass root level of farmer population, Department of Agriculture and Cooperation (DAC) has developed an e-governance programme namely Agricultural Resources Information System (AgRIS). The aim of the project is to help the users to access agricultural information on National Spatial Data Infrastructure (NSDI), guidelines on standard methodologies, best practices to be used and the Decision Support Systems (DSS) on Production practices and systems. Web portals belonging to livestock, commodity, buffalo's portal, Planning Commission's report, Agreement between NIC and DAC, extension activities in the field of agriculture, capacity creation and project reports are also included as part of their services [8].

B. Krishi Vigyan Kendras

Krishi Vigyan Kendras were established in 1992 by ICAR as part of providing support to agricultural related activities. KVKs have been strongly supported by an NGO Pravara Institute of Research and Education in Natural and Social Sciences (PIRENS) so as to provide better services for rural development especially to women and rural youths.

The objectives of KVKs include: the improvement of agricultural productivity, empowerment and energy utilization of rural youth and farm women, creation of employment in both farm and non-farm sector, enhancement of socio-economic conditions of rural community, planning and conducting survey to find out the training needs of rural farmers, developing and organizing in-formal education programmes, follow up of training programmes like visit to farms, farmers fair, radio talk, farm science clubs etc, conducting "On-Farm Testing" to find out the appropriate technologies for sustainable land use systems, conducting "Front Line Demonstrations (FLDs)" on different crops to create production data and feedback information, providing practical training to faculty and students of Vocational Higher Secondary Schools and general education to illiterates and school drop-outs and to support all schemes of ICAR for strengthening the training programmes of KVKs.

The mandates of KVKs are to conduct trainings: for developing farming skill to farmers and rural youths, exhibiting oil seeds, pulses and other important commodities, technology based On-Farm-Testing, for publicizing technologies in the districts by giving trainings to extension workers of the different line departments, for enhancing the production of good quality seeds, seedlings and different bio-agents.

Hence KVKs are the most effective institutions committed to rural development which provides vocational training, teaching latest technologies relating to Farm research. The activities of which enables evaluation of technology and to bridge the time gap between the technology created at the research stations and its implementation in the field. As per the report of NIC, there is one KVK in each district of the country. Due to its many fold activities like the use of Applied Biotechnology in agriculture, Promotion and development of Group Organization, use of IT in agriculture and 'Technology backstopping' using important inputs and services, KVKs are considered as one of the most effective agricultural institutions[9].

In Kerala, there are KVKs established in every districts, so there are a total of 14 KVKs in Kerala hosted by State Agricultural University(SAU), ICAR and by NGOs at Kumarakom (Kottayam), Panniyur, Kanhirangad & Thaliparamba in Kannur, Tavanur, (Malappuram,District), Kellappaji College of Agriculture Engineering & Technology, Vellanikara (Thrissur District), CPCRI Regional Station, Kayamkulam (Allappuzha District), Sadanandapuram (Kollam District), Santhanpara (Idukki District), Kolabhagon, Thadiyoor (Pathanamthitta District), Kudlu (Kasaragode District), Peruvannamuzhi (Kozhikode District), Ambalavayal (Wayanad District), Pattambi, (Palaghat District), Mitraniketan, Vellanad (Thiruvananthapuram District) [10].

C. Krishi Bhavans in Kerala

Under the Department of Agriculture, Krishi Bhavans form the lower end functionary in providing information to farmers. Each Panchayat has one Krishi Bhavan each. Following facilities are provided in Krishi Bhavans.

Direct access to information : Farmers can directly go the Krishi Bhavans and collect information relating to agriculture and related activities.

Subsidies to all types of cultivation in the panchayat: For all types of cultivation like paddy, plantain, vegetables, fish farming etc subsidies are given to those farmers under the Panchayat.

Pension scheme for farmers : Those farmers who have crossed the age of 60 are eligible for getting pension from Krishi Bhavan on the basis of one time registration in the office.

50% of the amount spent by farmers on cultivation and fertilizers will be refunded : The amount refunded will be about Rs.5000-6000/- , which is a great help to the farmers.

Demonstration classes : Classes will be given for modern methods of cultivation relating to each type of cultivation. One class each will be given to each type of cultivation.

Beneficial scheme : Farmers will be provided with one beneficial scheme in a financial year.

Kerala Karshakan : The magazine namely 'Kerala Karshakan' will be provided to farmers under Annual subscription basis Rs.100/- per year [11].

D. Kerala Agricultural University

Kerala Agricultural University (KAU) situated at Vellanikkara, Trissur forms the major institution that provides human resources, skills and technology necessary for the agricultural development in the State. Agricultural crop production and forestry are the main functions which involves integrating education, research and extension activities.

The services like establishment of Agro-clinic and Agro-Diagnostic team, Commercialization of Pseudomonads, the microbial inoculant, introduction of edible mushroom cultivation methods suitable to Kerala's ecological conditions are provided by the university for the benefit of farmers [12].

E. mKisan Portal

mKisan is a SMS portal of Central Department of Agriculture and Cooperation and Farmers Welfare created for providing information/services/advisories to farmers through SMS alerts in their own regional language under the National e-Governance Plan-Agriculture (NeGP-A) as part of agricultural extension activities. It was launched by the Hon. President of India on July 16, 2013. Among various other features of mKisan, it is found that mobile messaging is the most effective tool for transferring information to the farmer community [13].

Various modes of information delivery services have been introduced through mKisan. These are Internet, Touch screen kiosks, Agri-clinics, Private kiosks, Mass media, Common Service Centres and Integrated platforms in the Agricultural Offices where there are access to extension personnel with pico-projectors and hand-held devices to provide adequate information. Scientists, experts and government officers posted in the Block level are responsible to provide information and advisories to farmers through their mobile phones. Government offices both central and state relating to Agriculture and allied sectors including Agricultural Universities in the State, Krishi Vigyan Kendras, Agromet Forecasts Units of Indian Meteorological Department, ICAR Institutes, and Organizations in Animal Husbandry, Dairying and Fisheries etc.) are responsible to provide information/ services/advisories in the form of SMS to the farmers in their preferred language.

Services like Unstructured Supplementary Service Data (USSD), Interactive Voice Response System (IVRS) and Pull SMS of mKisan help the farmers and other stakeholders to receive broadcast messages and access to web based services on their mobile even without internet. Voice Message Service implemented can help semi-literate and even illiterate farmers to access information.

Buyer Seller Platform, KSEWA, Kissan Knowledge Management System (KKMS) are other services of mKisan which provides information and advisories to farmers in the State and Centre.

F. KISSAN Project

KISSAN is an e-governance project of Government of Kerala which provides various beneficial information and extension services to the rural farmers in Kerala. The project has been developed and managed by a team of experts from Information Technology, Agriculture, Scientists and Researchers and Visual media etc. with technological support from IIITM-K for the Department of Agriculture, Govt. of Kerala.

The aim of the project is to provide right information to the right person in the right place and in the right context using various integrated technologies for the effective information utilization by the farmer community in Kerala.

Important services of KISSAN include:

Portal based agri-advisory service : The online Kissan portal www.kissankerala.net helps the farmers to directly communicate with agricultural experts and extension workers regarding Information on weather conditions, market products and prices, advisory services on varieties of crop and fertilizers to be used are available.

Kissan Krishideepam : This is a 30 minutes weekly television programme undertaken by the State Government since 2010 which is telecasted 3 times in a week in Asianet channel.

Online Agri Video Channel : Kissan is the first project to introduce an online video channel in agriculture. It has the practice to telecast 100 selected videos.

Tele-Advisory Services : Agri-advisory services for the farmers are provided through a located telephone number (0471-2700965).

SMS Based agri-advisory services : Advisories and alert services to farmers are provided through their mobile.

Mobile Based Agri Information Services : Agricultural information services are provided to farmers through their mobile. [7].

5. IMPACT OF THE SERVICES PROVIDED BY AIS

For finding the impact of the above AISs among rural farmer community in Kerala, both personal and telephonic interviews were conducted among twenty farmers using random sampling method from four districts of Kerala such as Thiruvananthapuram, Idukki, Kottayam & Palakkad. Their responses relating to various AISs are tabulated below.

Table 1. Usage Statistics

Sl. No.	*Different AISs*	*No. of Farmers availing the facility*	*Response %*
1	Agricultural Resources Information System (AgRIS) by DAC	1	5%
2	KrishiVigyanKendras (KVKs)	7	35%
3	Krishi Bhavans	11	55%
4	Kerala Agricultural University (KAU)	4	20%
5	mKisaan	5	25%
6	KISSAN	8	40%

As the services of more AISs are used by the farmers, the usage percentage has exceeded 100%.

Table 2. Impact of Aiss for Rural Development

Sl. No.	*Information System/Project*	*Services provided*	*Impact according to the respondents*
1	Agricultural Resources Information System (AgRIS) by DAC	Providing information for agricultural growth, decreasing poverty and resources utility by rural farmers, Production practices, on various systems' portals and project documents.	Helps farmers to take effective decision regarding production practices, access to various information systems that help them to improve their Cultivation and livelihood.
2.	Krishi Vigyan Kendras (KVKs)	To conduct Trainings to achieve farming technology	Its activities enable farmers to evaluate innovative agricultural

		and skills to farmers and rural youths, Commodity exhibitions, On-Farm-Testing.	technologies and to bridge the time gap between the technologies created at the research stations and its implementation in the field.
3	Krishi Bhavans	**1.** Direct access to information. **2.** Subsidies to all types of cultivation in the Panchayat. **3.** Pension scheme for farmers. **4.** 50% of the amount spent on cultivation and fertilizers will be refunded. **5.** Demonstration classes on modern methods of cultivation. **6.** One beneficial scheme in a financial year. **7.** Provide 'Kerala Karshakan' magazine farmers @Rs.100/- per year.	(1-4). As these services deals with farmers' day to day activities, Krishi Bhavans have become a part of the life and income of farmers.(5-6). Farmers have become more confident by attending classes provided and are able to produce better yield through the modern technologies introduced. 7. "Kerala Karshakan" is a very useful information source and act as a solution to many of their problems.
4.	Kerala Agricultural University (KAU)	To provide a single window system for delivering agricultural information, technologies and products like seeds, planting ingredients, organic manures, bio-fertilizers, bio-control agents, value added crops, milk, meat and dairy related products.	Helps farmers to use quality seeds, adopt the modern technology in cultivation and to use organic manures and to increase quality and quantity in agricultural productivity.
5	mKisaan	**1.** Unstructured Supplementary	These services help the farmers and other

		Service Data (USSD). **2.** Interactive Voice Response System (IVRS) **3.**Pull SMS	stakeholders to receive broadcast messages and to access web based services on their mobile even without internet connection. Voice messages implemented can help semi-literate and even illiterate farmers to access information.
6	KISSAN	**1.** Portal based agri-advisory service **2.** Kissan Krishi-deepam Programme **3.** Online Agri Video Channel **4.** Tele-Advisory Services **5.** SMS Based agri-advisory sevices.	**1.** Through the online query management and fertilizer recommendation systems about 75% of solutions are provided in local languages. **2.** Study shows that about 30% of farmers see the program regularly and apply practically. **3.** This channel helps to access information on all agricultural related activities for the purpose of continuous learning. **4.** The farmers can directly communicate with agricultural scientists to seek expert advice regarding the use of crops etc. The extensive crop database developed as part of this service is very helpful for taking effective decisions in farm related activities. **5.** This helps the farmers to get to get precise and specific information very fast and also alert services.

From the responses received, it is found that even though several Agricultural Information Systems are existing in the country, only a very few are aware of these systems. Only 5% of the farmers are aware of AgRIS. Only 35% of the farmers are utilizing the services of KVKs. 55% of the farmers are using the services of Krishi Bhavans. Only 20% of the farmers are utilizing the services of KAU. 25% of the farmers are utilizing the services of mKisaan. 40% of the farmers are utilizing the services of KISSAN. This variation in awareness level and information seeking behavior mainly depend upon the farmers' educational background. Those farmers who are making use of the services of various AISs agreed that they have attained self confidence and are able to enhance their farm productivity and income due to the application of modern technology in their cultivation.

6. SUGGESTIONS FOR INCREASING UTILITY OF AIS

From the study it is found that in spite of the availability of various Agricultural Information Systems for providing information to the rural farmers, a proportionate increase in agricultural productivity is not found. This is due to the unawareness about these AISs among the farmer community. If these information systems have been utilized to a maximum level, India could have produced better crop yields resulting in an enhanced GDP rate. Hence some measures have been suggested to increase the utility of the above Agricultural Information Systems. They are:

- To establish channels of communication between farmers, coordinators, Experts, Scientists, Research Centres, Krishi Bhavans, Krishi Vigyan Kendras and other Governmental and Non-Governmental Information Centres.
- Information provided should be based on the needs

of farmers and Internet should be used as the transmission media.

- Government should take steps to create agricultural awareness among rural community and for that Public Information Agricultural Kiosks may be established in every village.
- Training in the use of information kiosks may be provided area-wise to all farmers in a periodic manner.
- More funding should be provided to support knowledge access among the public.
- Complexity of the Agricultural Information Systems and E-governance projects may lead to an underestimation among the farmers and its lack of utility. Hence simple process may be adopted at the user interface for such projects [14].

7. CONCLUSION

Due to globalization and liberalization, agricultural sector has encountered with several types of crises. To help the farmers to overcome the problems faced by them and to enhance agricultural productivity, various governmental and non-governmental knowledge management systems and e-governance projects like AgRIS, KrishiVigyan Kendras, mKisaan, KISSAN, Krishi Bhavans and Kerala Agricultural University have contributed considerably. The paper has discussed the various services offered by the above sources and their impact on the rural community. From the experience of those farmers who utilize the services of some of the AISs, it is found that through the use of the above systems the gap between innovative agricultural technology and its implementation in the field has been reduced and is helping to eradicate information illiteracy among farmers to a certain extent.

REFERENCES

[1] Wikipedia, "Information source," *Wikipedia, the free encyclopedia.* 04-May-2016.

[2] N.G.Roling, Extension Science: Information System in agricultural development, Cambridge:Cambridge University Press, 1988

[3] Demiyurek.,K, H. Erdem, V. Ceyhan, S. Atasever, and O. Uysal, "Agricultural Information Systems and Communication Networks: the case of diary farmers in the Samsung Province of Turkey", Information Research, vol 13,no.2, 2008. [Online]. Available: http://www.informationr.net/ir/13-2/paper343.html [Accessed: 15- May-2016]

[4] Raman Nair, R. Priorities in information management systems for agricultural research and development in India. *National Conference on Role of Libraries in National Development,* University of Calicut, 1996.

[5] Govt. of India, "mKisan: A Portal of Government of India for Farmer Centric Mobile Based Services." [Online]. Available: http://mkisan.gov.in/. [Accessed: 15-Jan-2016].

[6] Laila T Abraham, "Agricultural content dissemination: a study among farmers in Kottayam district of Kerala."

[7] Dept. of Agriculture, Kerala, "Kissan-Kerala Project." [Online]. Available: http://www.kissankerala.net/home.jsp. [Accessed: 15-Jan-2016].

[8] Ministry of Agriculture, India, "AgRIS Portal." [Online]. Available: http://www.agris.nic.in/. [Accessed: 15-Jan-2016].

[9] PIRENS, "Pravara Institute of Research and Education in Natural and Social Sciences." [Online]. Available: http://www.kvk.pravara.com/pages/about%20us/about%20us.htm. [Accessed: 15-Jan-2016].

[10] ICAR, "Krishi Vigyan Kendras in Kerala," 2010. [Online]. Available: http://www.icar.org.in/en/node/222. [Accessed: 18-Jan-2016].

[11] Jinraj P. V., "Performance Evaluation of Krishi Bahvan Set-up in Kerala." [Online]. Available: http://www.cds.ac.in/krpcds/publication/jinraj.html. [Accessed: 15-Jan-2016].

[12] Kerala Agricultural University, "Agricultural Technology Information Centre, Mannuthy," 2015. [Online]. Available: http://www.kau.in/institution/agricultural-technology-information-centre-mannuthy. [Accessed: 15-Jan-2016].

[13] Govt. of India, "National Portal of India." [Online]. Available: http://india.gov.in/topics/agriculture. [Accessed: 15-Jan-2016].

[14] Vidanapathirana, N. P. "Agricultural information systems and their applications for development of agriculture and rural community, a review study," in *The 35th Information Systems Research Seminar in Scandinavia–IRIS*, 2012.

11

Poorvanivasanusmrithi: Developing a Web Portal for Managing National Collection of Manuscripts

Nayana Nair

ABSTRACT

Manuscripts are the most valuable treasures of our heritage. In them are recorded our ancient literature, history, arts, knowledge on sciences and technologies and the like. They contain subjects like traditional medicine, architecture, astronomy, alchemy, and many are not having more than one copy. Now all over the world it is accepted that 'Traditional knowledge' contains sustainable methods. So the content of manuscripts are important for our healthy existence and so they are to be conserved and managed in a way in which the content is retrievable in time of need. If they any are lost, invaluable knowledge is lost forever to the humanity. The paper describes Poorvanivasanusmrithi - the design and functions of a prototype of the web portal developed by the author to manage the manuscript collections of the country.

Keywords : Digital Archiving, Manuscripts, Heritage Conservation, Traditional Sciences

1. RECODED KNOWLEDGE

It is human nature to seek, learn and explore new things. Information is increasing at a great momentum and is progressing to an altogether different dimension. Information is a key factor in decision making in all disciplines whether it is economical, scientific and political and what not. It has become an inevitable part of human lives and it is very important to use it wisely.

Now that information is growing at a great pace, so are the techniques and approaches for organizing and managing them. Information management has become a major challenge. Information explosion is one of the problems being faced now by the information scientists and hence to use it effectively, new methods are being implemented.

2. MANUSCRIPTS

Talking about the times of yore, the main sources of information were manuscripts. Manuscripts are nothing but handwritten documents. Past has played an important role molding the present and hence it is very important to acknowledge the past and maintain it in the best possible way. Manuscripts, as the name says, are nothing but handwritten documents. The etymology of the word is from the Latin language during the medieval period. In other words, it is from the Medieval Latin that the word has derived. The word 'manu' in Medieval Latin means 'by hand' and the word 'scribe' was developed into 'scriptus' which meant 'written'. And thus the word 'manuscriptus' developed, which in the late 16th century was improvised to 'manuscripts'.

3. PURPOSE OF MANUSCRIPTS

Coming over to the function of manuscripts, it roughly did the same thing, viz., storage and dissemination of information. The word spoken by the monks were generally written down by hand or sometimes it was written by self. When we hear about manuscripts the first thing that comes to our mind will be connected to religion. But on the contrary, manuscripts then covered a wide range of subjects, which included herbals, medicine, architecture, astronomy, bestiary etc. We know a few of them while a lot are not. The medieval manuscript culture is believed to have been started in the late tenth century. These were manuscripts that were traded into the markets. This eventually led to the growth of educational organizations. 'Traditional knowledge' is now understood to be that which helps sustainable development and so has gained importance in the recent years. Traditional knowledge is mainly recorded in manuscripts and other earlier formats for recording knowledge like leather, clay tablets, parchments etc. So the content recorded in these ancient records are important for our healthy existence and these records needs to be conserved and managed in a way in which the content it retrievable in time of need. As mentioned before, the major challenge when it comes to managing information in such media is storage and dissemination.

4. POORVANIVASANUSMRITHI

Poorvanivasanusmrithi is the prototype for a web portal designed and developed by the author exclusively for managing manuscripts. The etymology of the word Poorvanivasanusmrithi is from Sanskrit where it means, "remembering the past" or "reminiscences". Much like the name, the function of the portal is to create a gateway to the planet of manuscripts. The idea is to create a real time database that helps retrieving data on manuscripts from different member libraries across the nation implementing strict access controls.

It is said, 'time and tide waits for none.' Hence it is important for us as library and information professionals or archivists to meet the needs of the users. By making all the manuscripts available, in a single platform, the job of retrieval and dissemination of information from manuscripts is made much easier. Also the services will be based on maximum resources and will be more reliable also.

4.1. Coverage of Poorvanivasanusmrithi

There are lots of manuscript libraries throughout the world, and a good number of them lies in India alone. The study is focused on building a platform where all these manuscripts can be found at once. In other words, here we are trying to develop and design a web portal with a runtime database so that all the manuscripts can be accessed more easily by a single search. In other words, this is an attempt to create a blueprint of "the GOOGLE for manuscripts".

5. FACILITIES OF WEB

In the early phase, the web portal was used to describe the Internet search. They signify a gate, a door or an entrance. In the modern context of the World Wide Web, a portal would be the next logical in the evolution of digital culture. Web pages are no more self-advertising or self-referential elements but, in fact, a platform that allows personalisation, workflow, integration of information and application. A web portal basically collects data from different sources and puts it up in one platform. The main aim is to make it easily available for the specific users or anyone who requires that specific information. By creating a web portal for manuscripts, we can create a single point of access to documents from different sources. This would be categorized and specialised as per the developer and as per the need of the user. To put it in a better way, it is the idea of a personalised filter into the web.

A portal is the first page that the user gets to see the moment the user connects to the web. The look and feel of the portal is designed in such a way that, not only does it give them the required information but also the latest news, a well trained concierge who knows where to find what, the market information about surfers stocks, free provision of communication or discussion forums and all as the surplus. So from the traditional search engines, now it is the digital era of gateways. It is the one stop to get on board for the daily activities of the surfers where in they start their flight into the web and find their way to their destination without much difficulty.

6. POORVANIVASANUSMRITHI WEB PORTAL

The Poorvanivasanusmrithi Web Portal will contain the following two interfaces:

- The librarian interface
- The user interface

6.1. Administration

Administration interface is the librarian interface which will deal with the submission, approval transaction, and the account details. The administration will be comprised of all the libraries and the web portal in charge will set the permissions. The members in the administration are categorised into two:

The submitter : who only has the credentials to submit the documents. This constitutes of the staff of the member libraries or archives.

The approvers : who can submit, edit and review a document. The approvers are generally the director / head of the archive.

The credentials of these both accounts and types of administrators will be set by the portal in charge.

Administration Home Page : The Librarian Interface is the administrator home page. This will be common for the approver as well as the submitter. The first search tab at the top left is for searching the documents available. The second search tab is to search the member libraries either by the name of the library or by the location.

The collection search tab is to search the materials by the given fields. It includes the title, author, year and keywords. The notifications tab scrolls the new events and news.

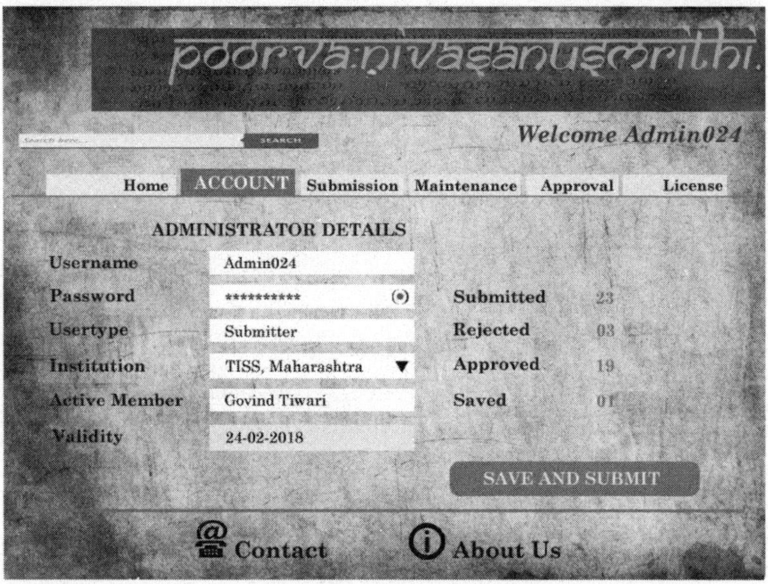

Fig. 1. The Accounts Page

This is the page that deals with the accounts. Here the accounts are totally different from the normal ones. They are of the number of documents submitted, approved etc. The Administrator details generally consist of the username, password, user type, the institution, member and the validity. The user type decides whether it is the submitter or the approver. The right side has the account of the total number of documents submitted by the submitter and the ones that are approved, the number of documents rejected by the approver and the pending ones that are saved for future editing. By clicking the numbers in violet (faded), it will take you to the list that gives further details of the documents.

6.2. Adding Manuscripts

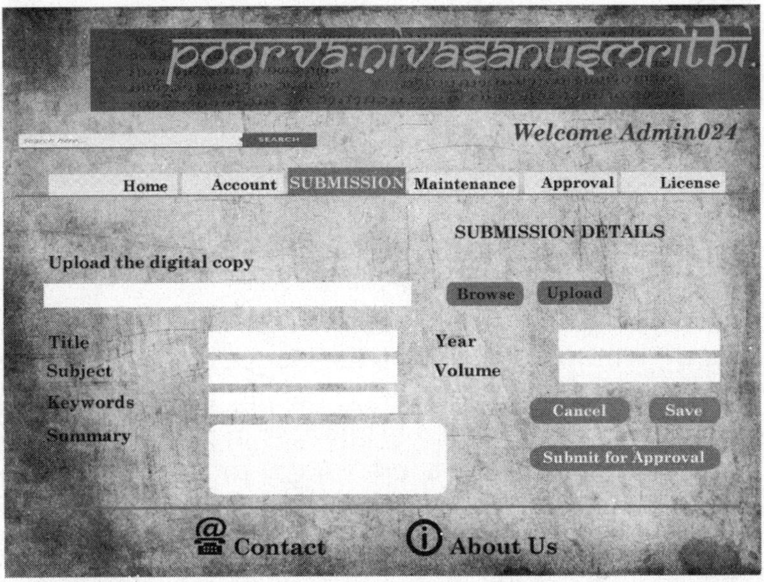

Fig. 2. The Submission Page

The submission page is meant for the submission, as the name says it. Here the submitter can upload the documents and enter the metadata. Here the submitter is given the option to save the document and can edit the metadata later or he/she can submit it for the approval by the approver. The metadata tags are as given: the title, author, keyword, subject, year, volume and summary.

6.3. Maintenance

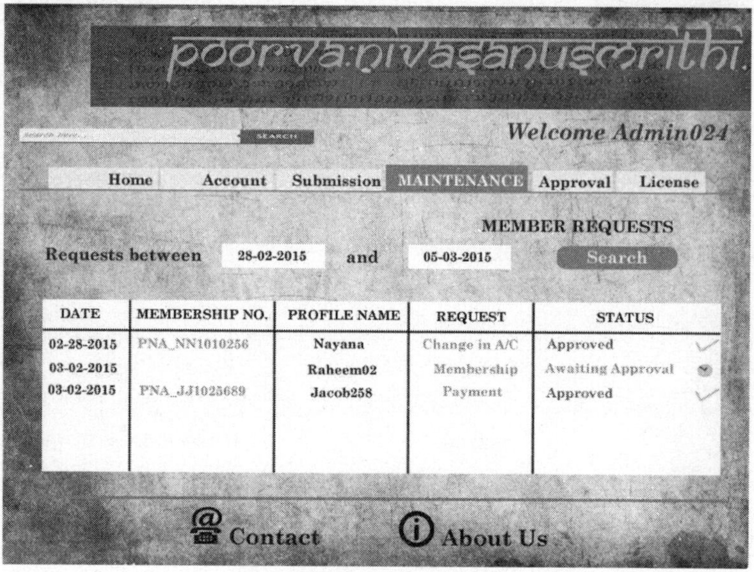

Fig. 3. Maintenance Page

This page keeps a tab on the members and creation of new members. Clicking on the 'Request' will take them to the page which has got all the details. The above image gives the number of requests from 28th of Feb 2015 to 5th of March 2015. So here the administrator can limit his search using dates. The first member needs a change in the account type, while the second needs an approval for membership and the third wants to get a document.

6.4. The Approval Page

The approval page is only for the approver. Anybody without the approver username and password will not be able to access this account. Every time the approver logins in a one time password (OTP) will be sent to their account or mail and that should be entered in the space given for Security Code, without which the access will be denied. Once that is done, it authenticates the user. The approver as mentioned earlier will usually be the head of the

Fig. 4. The Approval Page

member library. Once it authenticates, the page will look somewhat like the image below:

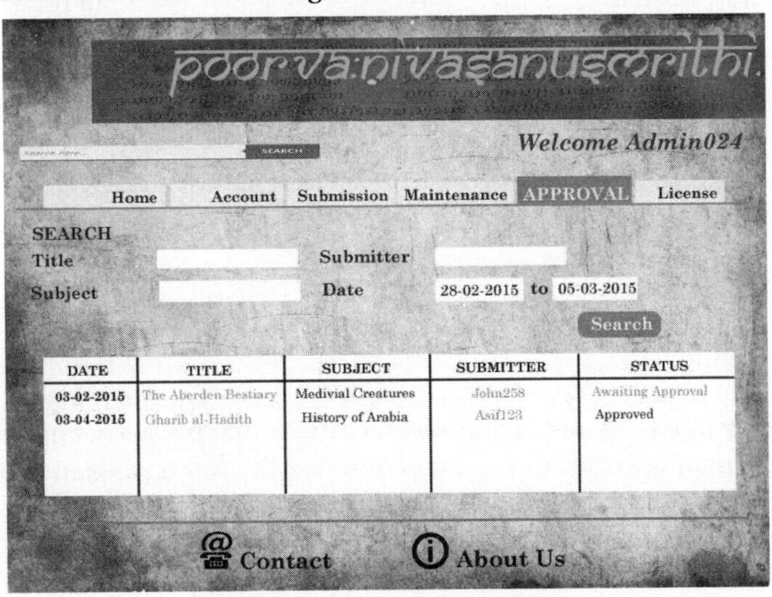

Fig. 5. Page Listing Approved Item

Here the approver does his job of reviewing the manuscripts and editing it and later approving or rejecting the same. The approver can limit his/her search by putting the date. The approver can also search by title, subject, and name of the submitter. Again by clicking on the grey coloured or the dull links can take them to the concerned pages as those words act as links. There the approver can accept or reject documents. He can even keep the work for later or may be let some other approver do it.

6.5. The License

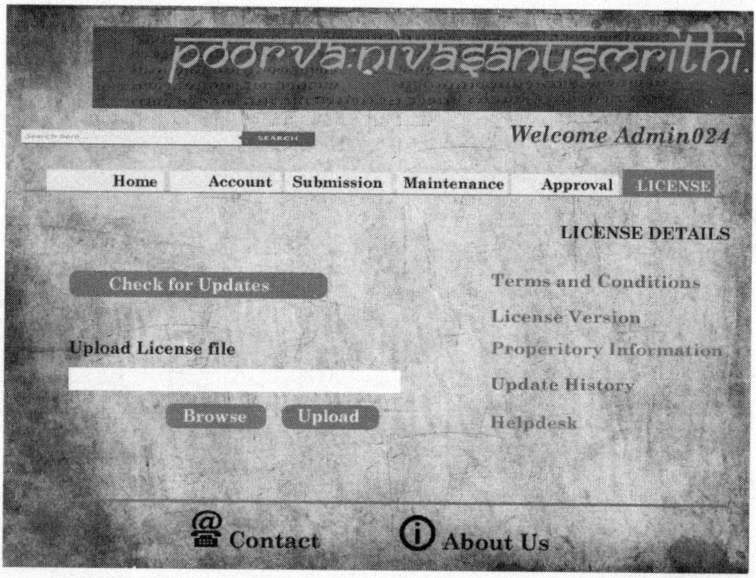

Fig. 6. The License Page

As mentioned before, there are a lot of security issues as well as that of copyrights and intellectual property rights. Hence to avoid these, the license for the library is a must. Hence this page is very important and is for authenticating the validity of the library. Here we can also refer to the terms and conditions, the recent update and all other details of the portal. This concludes the illustrations of the librarian interface. Now moving on to the user interface, the explanation continues.

6.6. The User Interface

The user interface will be for the users who will be allowed to view the document. They are also allowed to download the article provided they pay for the same to the respective account. The transactions will be dealt by a third party and the payment will go to the respective library after the processing. To get a better idea of the portal, it will be discussed with the illustrations in the upcoming pages.

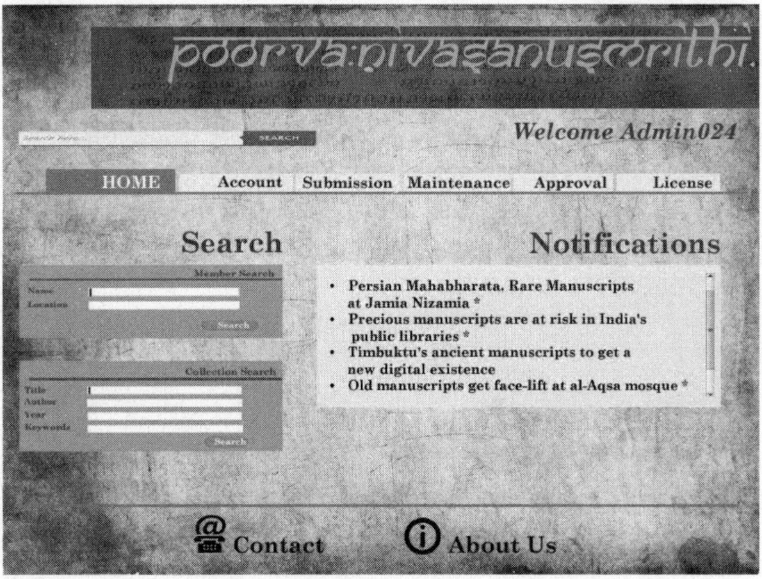

Fig. 7. The Login or Sign up Page

User Registration: The above image is the first page that the user will get while accessing the portal. Here a new user needs to sign in while the already registered user can login with his username and password and can go to the home page.

6.7. The User Interface

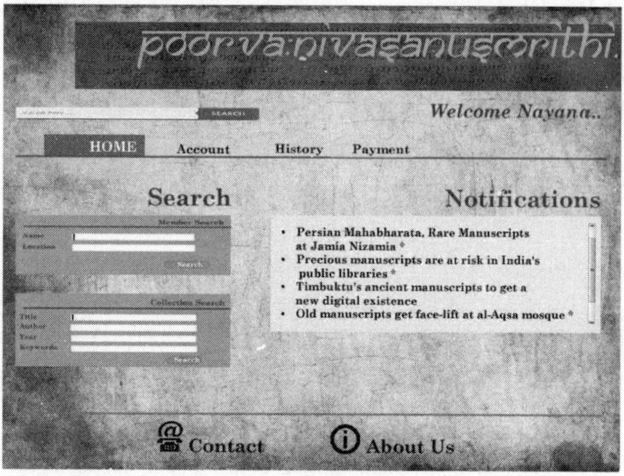

Fig. 8. The User Interface - The home page

The user home page is pretty much similar to the librarian interface. This interface also lets the user search the library. By searching the library by name, the user will be directed to the page that has the details of the library. And again, the user can search the manuscripts by the search tags mentioned.

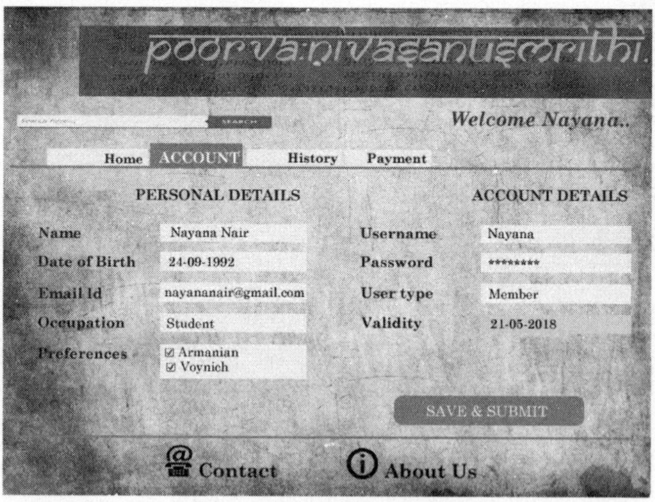

Fig. 9. User Accounts Page

This page, as we can see, deals with the account details of the user. The personal details are filled by the user, while the account details will be generated by the portal in charge. By setting the preferences, any new updates or documents that come under the set preferences will be brought into notice of the users by sending an alert mail to their accounts. The validity is decided by the user type.

6.8. The History

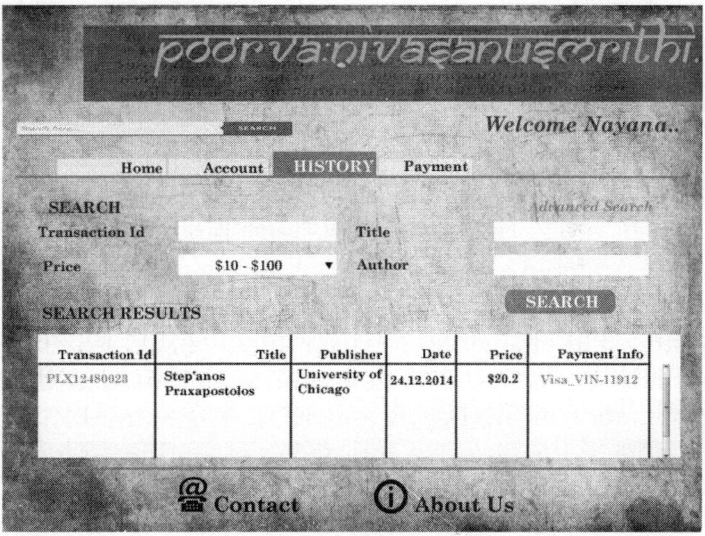

Fig. 10. The History Page

This page gives the history of transactions that are made by the user. By clicking on the discoloured links, the user will be taken to the pages that have more details of the transaction. The search tags help the user make the search easier.

7. SEARCH MECHANISM

By clicking the search tab at the top left navigates the user to the following page:

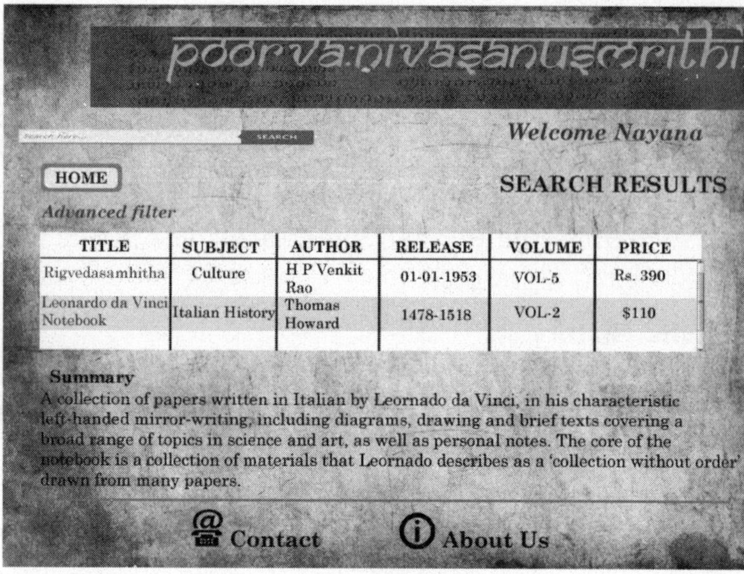

Fig. 11. Advanced Search Page

The above is an example of how the search page looks like, and the results are displayed. Clicking on the option 'advanced filter' enables the user for advanced search with the help of filters, Boolean operators along with the combination of AND, OR and NOT. The same facility is available in the librarian interface.aka.administrator also.

8. PAYING FOR ACCESS

As mentioned before, managing manuscripts is a very expensive business and requires lot of funding. So every manuscript that the users wish~~es~~ to read will be charged and they are given the permission to keep a soft copy. The payment happens in this page; the user ~~is~~ can select his mode of payment and can get the document. The transactions are done by a third party, usually someone assigned by the portal developers and in-charges and after processing, the money is transferred to the library that holds the respective collection.

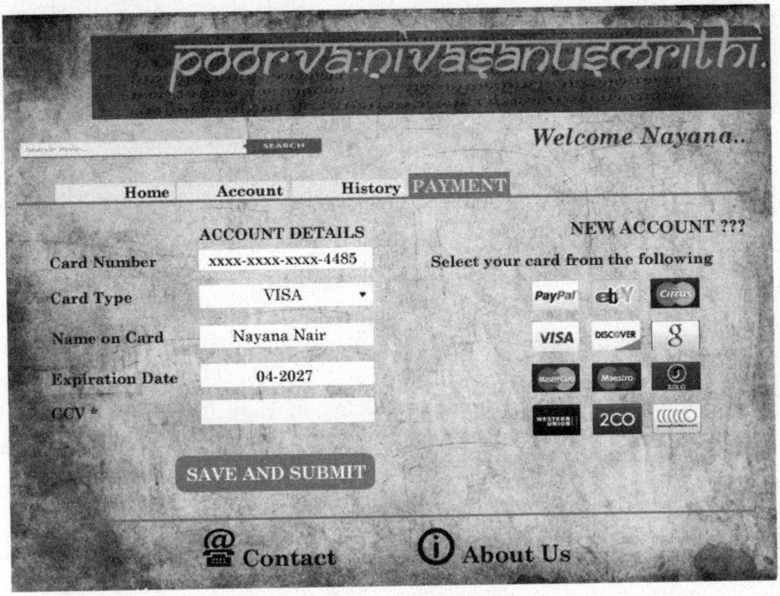

Fig. 12. The Payment Page

9. CONCLUSION

From the study and the prototype web portal Poorvanivasanusmrithi, it can be concluded that creating a web portal will help a lot in better storage and dissemination of information contained in the manuscripts. There will be a few problems like the possibilities for anyone copying the rare documents which may contain very valuable knowledge. But resources are for use. So misuse is something that can be taken care of later rather than not bringing the recorded knowledge into use. In this age where we tend to forget our past and our tradition, such attempts can become strings that connect us to the knowledge heritage of the past. The manuscripts are storehouses of knowledge generated by our forefathers' efforts through centuries. It is also tested knowledge. Ancient sciences are sustainable sciences. By discovering their knowledge, by publicising their existence and by bringing them to use in the present, we will be fostering new information and ideas that can help to conserve life in this planet.

REFERENCES

[1] Anand Narayan. Words From Another Era. Thiruvananthapuram, The Hindu, December 18, 2013

[2] Michael Forstrom. Managing Electronic Records in Manuscript Collections: A Case Study from the Beinecke Rare Book and Manuscript Library. The American Archivist: Fall/Winter, Vol. 72, No. 2, pp. 460-477. 2009.

[3] Raman Nair, R. Digital archiving of manuscripts and other heritage items for conservation and information retrieval. All India oriental Conference (42nd Session), 4 th to 6th November 2004, Sampurnanand Sanskrit University, Varanasi, 2004.

[4] Ranjan, Mazumdar Nirmal. Management of manuscript collection in Assam in digital era a practical approach using ICT tools. (PhD Theses) Gauhati, Gauhati University, 2015.

[5] Richard H. Lytle, Richard H. Management of archives and manuscript collections for librarians. New York, Society of American Archivists, 1980

[6] Sulochana Devi, L. Information System for Research in Sanskrit and Indology. In the Proceedings of the National conference on Vedic Sciences. Madras, JGRCVS, 1997.

12

Designing Library Automation Package : In-house

Akshay K
Geo Kevin Rubison
Josbin Simon

ABSTRACT

Library automation is automating the house keeping operations of a library like entering the records of new book, retrieving the details of book available in the library, recording the book transactions in the library, preparing book selection lists, automatically generating supply orders from the selection lists, management of data related to periodicals received etc. This paper proposes a framework for development of a library automation package in-house. Library automation packages can maintain centralized repository of information about the collections as well as transactions related to the central library and all departmental libraries of a college or university. The Library automation package can keep track of records related to current books, members, book issue / returns etc and numerous other aspects. The proposed automation package can allow a library to efficiently manage all house keeping operations in an easy and convenient mode.

Keywords : Library, Library Automation, Transactions, Management, Circulation, Information Retrieval, Software Development

1. INTRODUCTION

Currently ~~the~~ most college libraries are using manual system for tracking the day-to-day activity. This project focuses on the automation of the library, which monitors and controls the transactions in a library. The proposed package can be used to issue books to the library members and maintain their records and can also check how many books are issued and stock available in the library.

It can provide the information on any book to the students & faculty members of the department. It can also keep track of books issued, returned & newly added to the library.

The college admin. can anytime view total book status. This can overcome the entire library problems, which we are facing currently. The software is easy to use for both beginners and advanced users. It provides facilities to students or faculty to search for the required books and it allows the administrator or librarian to issue & return books to students and can create & delete membership of students.

An important aspect of library management is planning and maintaining library facilities. Planning the construction of new concepts or remodeling those that exist is integral as user needs are often changing. This paper is based on an attempt by students in the Dept. of Computer Science & Engineering, TocH Institute of Science & Technology, Arakkunnam, Kerala, to develop a Library Automation package for use in the college. The package was initially tested in the Dept. of Computer Science in the small collection of books the department was having and after finding it successful tested at the central library collection. It was tested for single library as well as pooling catalogue and member information of the different departments and central collection. There is provision to transfer student member information from the administrative system immediately after the admissions. Staff details also can be transferred from staff database of automated administration files.

2. EXISTING SYSTEM

The existing system is totally based on manual operations. Currently two registers are maintained. One for keeping information related to books and the other for maintaining book issue details. Thus all day-to-day transactions are recorded in those registers. Also a copy of book information is stored in MS Excel files. This creates data redundancy, insecurity, inconsistency, insertion, deletion anomalies etc., as there is no central database to handle data. Another important problem with the existing system is difficulty in tracking the correct location of a particular book in the library. Most of the books are not arranged in an orderly way. For searching a book we need to search the entire library, which is time consuming. Due to the lack of appropriate software fast report generation regarding the available book list, borrowed book list etc is also not possible. Also the current system does not maintain information about issue/return of books properly. Increased user expectations for faster and easier access to relevant information goes hand in hand with institutional demands for increased operational efficiency.

3. PROBLEM STATEMENT

The manually managed existing system has several drawbacks like low accuracy, difficulty in data access and manipulation and lack of user interaction. Chance of errors is more in the existing system. Our project is to manage the library database and to reduce the drawback of the existing system. It also increases the user interaction with the system to deliver a better output.

4. OBJECTIVES OF THE SYSTEM

The primary objective of the system is the library management and authenticating system. The most time consuming task in the existing system is the management of the huge database of the books present in a library, which is simplified here. The user can also check the availability of books at any time.

The librarian can login to the system and can add the users to this system. Librarian is given the priority and has the privilege of adding books in the library. The users can login through web and get details of the books required.

5. SYSTEM DESIGN

In system design phase we had undergone through various steps which are described as under :

1. Identify the origin of the information at different levels.
2. Identify the expectation of user from computerized system.
3. Analyze the drawback of existing system (manual) system.

5.1. Admin Module

The following aspects are taken care of while developing the administrative module of the library automation packages.

- The admin. is provided with username and password.
- The books in the library are added by the admin.
- The admin. adds the users to the library.
- Manages the database of the books.

- Authenticate users and keep track of them.
- Generate book issue details & handles book returns & renewals.

5.2. User Module

The user module is the highly used one. This facilitates easy use of services and facilities of the library. We have kept in mind the following aspects while developing user Module and are kept simple, user-friendly and attractive.

- The user can login with a username and password
- In this module the user can view the books they have taken.
- User can search for books.
- The users can reserve books.
- Submit a request for new books to the admin.

6. IMPLEMENTATION

6.1. Hardware Requirements

In order to implement a new system the choice of a processor with maximum possible speed is made. There should be sufficient memory to store data and software tools for efficient processing.

Table 1.1

System	Intel Pentium dual core or higher
Primary Storage	1 GB or more
Storage	10 GB or more
Architecture	X86 or x64

6.2. Software Requirements

Table 1.2

Front End Tool	PHP5, HTML
Back End Tool	MYSQL
Storage	WINDOWS XP/7/8/8.1
Environment	DREAMWEAVER CC, NETBEANS 7.0.1

6.3. SCREENSHOTS

6.3.1. User Login

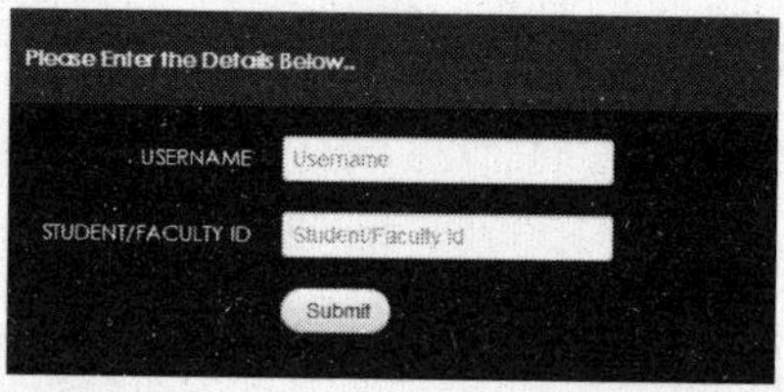

6.3.2. Admin Login

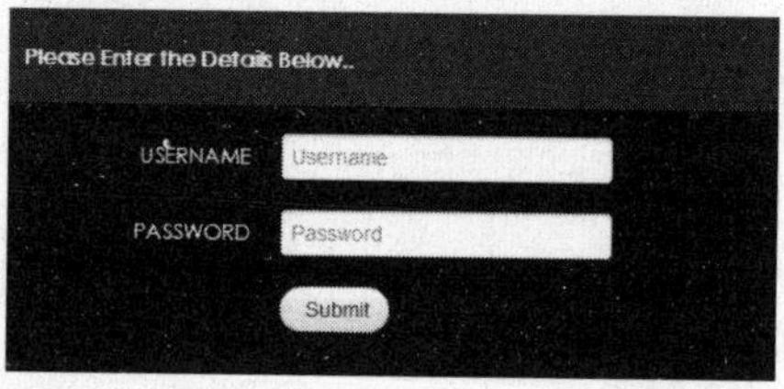

6.3.3. Add Book

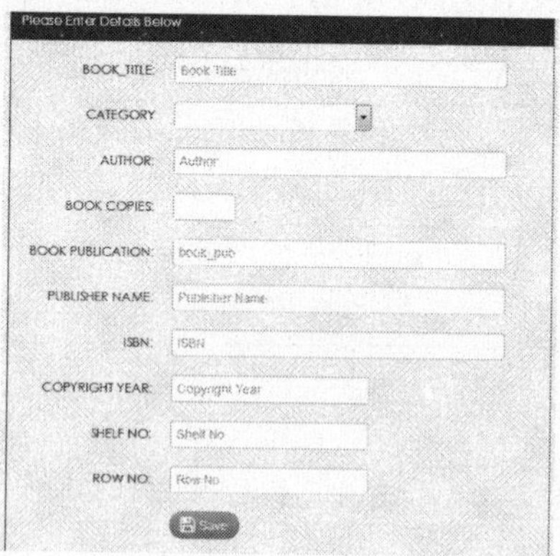

6.3.4. Add Member

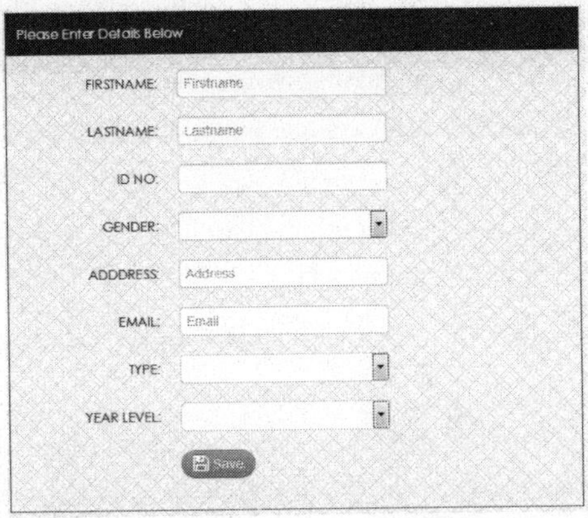

6.3.5. Book Issue

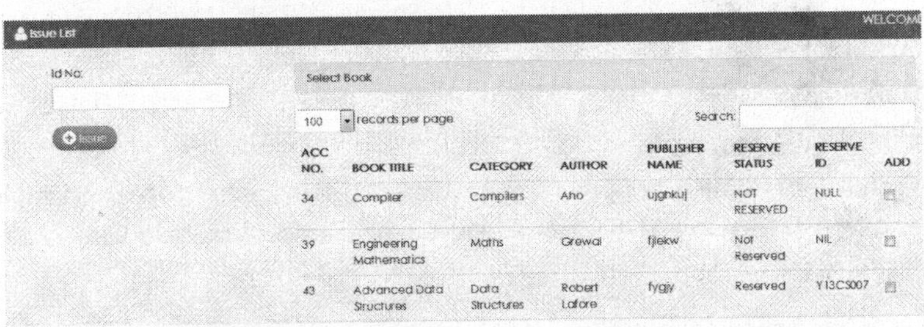

6.3.6. Search Book

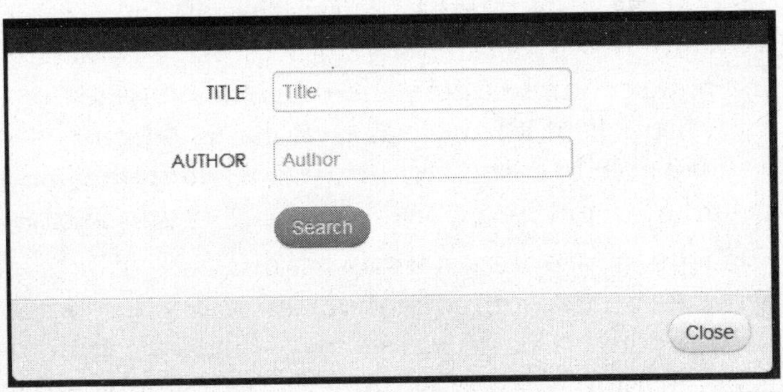

6.3.7. New Book Request

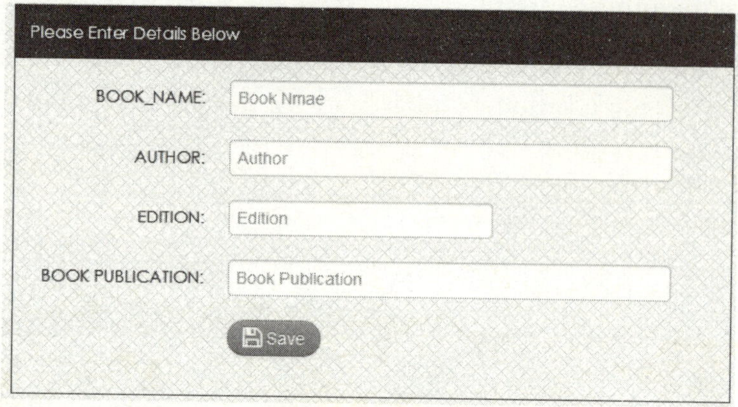

7. CONCLUSION

Software industry is the most dynamic industry at present. The dawn of each day brings new technology that transforms the way we interact with the computers. Computers are crossing every frontier where their presence was unimaginable a few years ago. As the technology is growing day-by-day, hour-by-hour very fast, we have to use those growing technologies to the best.

Using this web application all the details are managed normally and automatically without any risk. Cost of its initialization is very low. Special care has been taken that the system remains user friendly and error free. Our system provides different services like easy access to users, better computations and efficient management. It can keep track of all the transactions in the library. We have been able to complete the project within the allotted time and have put in the best of our ability and hard work

From a proper analysis of positive points and constraints on the component, it can be safely concluded that the product is a highly efficient GUI based component. This application is working properly and meeting all user requirements. This component can be easily plugged in many other systems.

8. FUTURE DEVELOPMENT SUGGESTED

This system has been made or designed keeping the present requirement in mind. It helps the user to get the current status of the book, his/her transaction details, submit request for a new book, reserve a book etc. They can verify the correctness of the system by further clarification.

The renewal of the book can be done through web. The QR code can be used as mean of authentication and the system can be further developed on android platform, which increases the usage and provides better experience to the user.

In case of inserting bulk data at a time instead of adding each entry individually the entire data can be uploaded from an excel sheet using suitable software.

When a new book is added its position such as its shelf no and row no can be automatically updated according to the number of books in the shelf and row.

9. REFERENCES

[1] Computer Application to Library and Information Services. New Delhi: Ess Ess, 1992

[2] Raman Nair, R. CDS/ISIS for DOS. New Delhi, Ess Ess, 1999.

[3] Elmsri and Navethe, "Fundamentals of Database systems", 3rd edition, Addison-Wesley, 2001

[4] RajibMall, "Fundamentals of Software Engineering", 3rd edition, PHI Learning, 2009

[5] Robert Vieira, "Beginning SQL Server Programming", Wiley Publishing, 2008.

13

Digitizing Heritage: An Account of the Digitization Projects of Kerala State Central Library

Sobhana P K

ABSTRACT

The importance and advantage of Digitization as a method of preservation is far reaching and is now considered as one of the major innovative work of any library. State Central Library, Kerala established in 1829, is one of the pioneer institutions in the country and holds very unique rare and valuable document collection of the State. The Library started the digitization project in 2006. This paper discusses two projects: Rare books Digitization and State Gazette Digitization. The paper explains the historical value of this special collection of the State Central Library and the reasons for digitization. It also discusses the methods and the technology used in digitization and also the formation and working of the digital library.

Keywords : Library Digitization: State Central Library ; Trivandrum Public Library; Gazette Digitization; Kerala Gazettes; Rare book Digitization, Nitya Digital Archive;

1. INTRODUCTION

During the past ten years, the State Central Library has been involved with the Digitization projects. Library Digitization is one of the most innovative concepts in the present library situation. But Digitization is an expensive process too. Digitizing means converting print or image or manuscripts or any type of hard copies into electronic information. The major purposes are to preserve the data for a long time and retrieve from it more efficiently and to increase the data access and dissemination facilities. Before digitizing, the data was accessible only to a few who could physically visit the location where it kept. But Digitization make it accessible from more access points in the library itself and by web hosting it can be accessed any corner of the world. Digitization provides electronic access to fragile but heavily used heritage collections without harming the originals. Hence the documents, which are having heritage value, should be preserved through digitization.

For the Libraries planning to develop a digital collection, the IFLA 2002 guidelines are very useful. The libraries should consider certain important things. The answer to the following four questions are important .What is to be digitized? Why digitize? How to digitize? Who are the targeted users of the Digital collection?

2. EARLY HISTORY OF STATE CENTRAL LIBRARY

State Central Library previously known as Trivandrum Public Library was established in 1829 seven years before National Library Calcutta (1836) was established. Though, Maharaja Swati Tirunal encouraged the library, the library functioned at the sheer interest of then British high level officials of the Travancore State. The library was started by the then British Resident Col. Cadogan, who was the grandson of Sir Hans Sloan, the founder of the British Library & Museum. The Trivandrum

Trivandrum Public Library: The first Public Library in India

Public library had tried to function in similar way as the British library of UK. The local people had no access to the library. The membership pattern, and collection development procedures had been followed as in the British Museum and Library. There were three categories of memberships like Members, Readers and Nominees. Readers were the users who could not take books but could read the books. Nominees are the nominated people mostly the family members of the privileged people. Members and Readers were not permitted to take the books, they can read only. (Karl Marx was a Reader of the British Library and was not permitted to take books outside) There were disputes between the Public Library Authorities and the Govt. regarding the compound of the library. Finally the issues were resolved and in 1897, Travancore Government decided to construct a new building on the occasion of celebrating the Diamond Jubilee of Queen Victoria's Commemoration and took over the library from Trivandrum Public Library Association with all its collections and other equipments. In 1902, the library started functioning in the new building and was opened to the public. Later, when Travancore University was established, Trivandrum Public Library functioned as Travancore University Library till 1948.

The old Library Advisory Committee reports show that the collection of books and periodicals and the circulation rules were that of any internationally prevailing library standards. But the big question arises is that whether this rare and huge collection is properly maintained? Travancore State under British had gone and the Kerala State under the Indian Republic was established. And the library had functioned under the Travancore University for a long while. But there had been no policy for Government for preserving the valuable documents its collections contained. Interestingly, it could be seen from the old Gazettes , the auction notices of the public library collection listing the valuable books. Only during the 1980s library authorities decided to maintain a separate collection for these rare and valuable collections. It is known as Closed Reference Collection. As the name suggests, the entry of this section is restricted.

The oldest book in the library was a book published in 1569, the English translation of a Greek book titled Righte Noble and Pleasant History of the Successors of Alexander Surnamed the Great by Diodore the Sicilian (In Greeke) Stocker, Thomas(Tra). Some of their lines written by the wife Plutarch - Original in Greeke and translated to French then to English. There are lots of such valuable books in the Trivandrum Public library Collection. Most titles in the collection are unique and very rare. Most of the books are out of print.

When it comes into the digitization work, State Central Library considered this old rare and valuable book collection as the first priority and started the process in 2006.

3. FIRST PHASE : DIGITIZATION OF OLD AND RARE BOOKS

The common problems encountered by the old print digitization are the following

- The color of the paper mostly changed to yellowish
- Chances of missing pages in the originals
- Some of the print is obscured by aging, folds etc
- Some the pages are torn and brittle
- The holes in the pages causing loss of data
- The joints and binding of the books may be loose or detached

A total collection of 707 ancient and rare documents - 644 English and 63 Malayalam books were digitized. The digitized collection includes 3,28,268 pages and opened for use of the public in 2007. The unique feature of this collection is its Malayalam indexing and retrieval system known as Nitya Digital Archive of M/s Beehive developed exclusively for State Central Library Digital Collection. It is possible to use vernacular language for the retrieval. Full text retrieval is possible using Malayalam Script. This is the first multilingual bibliographic information system compliant to Unicode.

State Central Library outsourced the digitization work to M/s Beehive and the project used the unique digitization software mentioned above.

4. DIGITIZATION METHOD USED FOR RARE BOOKS

As stated above M/s Beehive Concepts was entrusted with this work. In the process the documents are first scanned and converted to Portable Document Format (PDF) using Adobe Acrobat. Images of the pages are later converted to text ('Captured') and book marked/annotated. A database is created for the documents selected for the digital library and indexed using CDS/ISIS. The efficiency of the search depends on Indexing Techniques were applied to build up Inverted File (Dictionary of indexing terms). Nitya provides facilities for searching archived documents using Inverted File and the search results are displayed in full bibliographic details. Keywords for query building can be elected from the Inverted File under different categories like author, title, subject, etc.

The search can be performed using Malayalam script is a great advantage of this system.

5. SECOND PHASE: DIGITIZATION OF GAZETTES

Digitization second phase started in 2010. Gazettes are the most important government records. These historically valuable, authentic official records remain as the most reliable record too. The public get the access of government work through the gazettes. It is the history of public administration.

The word gazette indicates public journal of the government. Gazettes are the unique publication of the Government. Not everyone knew that the publication of Gazettes started in 1665 in U K,with the worst outbreak of plague in England, which killed 15% of the population in London. When rumors were spread through independent pamphlets about this, Govt. was compelled to provide the state of events . It resulted in the birth of the London Gazette.

When State Central Library functioned in the present building from 1902, we could collect all these gazettes of various governments. They are St.George Gazettes, Travancore Gazettes (1903), Travancore-Kochi Gazettes (1942) and the Kerala Gazettes (1956). Historically and socially these documents are very important old collections of the library. A separate section is maintained in the library for these documents and these are heavily used documents. From layman to Chief Secretary need this document for various purposes. Though the information is open to public, the format and intricacies of the content itself make people to move away from the records.

The type of information contained in the Gazette are the deeds and agreements of the government, the utilization and loans of government lands to private , charitable institutions etc, the list of inheritance, take over of private lands ,vegetations ,agriculture etc are published in the Gazette. It records the variations and transformation in the names of places. Socially important place name-to-name changes of the public are announced in it. PSC notifications, promotions, various Government department orders etc are also published in it.

Gazettes are published in four parts. They are

Part I : Departmental Notifications, Government orders, Acts, Ordinance , Bills etc

Part IA : Statutory Notification of Election Commission

Part I B : Official Notifications, orders and results of Kerala Public Service Commission

Part II : Extra Ordinary gazette of declaration of conducting election

Part III : Notification by Heads of Departments (Disputes, Certificates, heir ships etc,)

Part IV : Private and Miscellaneous Notification (Change of Name, Change of Signature etc.)

6. DETAILED APPROACH AND METHODOLOGY

The search and retrieval of the Gazettes address the following access points, which are different to each part:-

- Volume no., Issue no, and date of publishing are common to all parts
- Notification No. Date of Notification and Department are common to majority of items

Digitization and archiving are done through the following for stages:-

1. Scanning the document
2. Indexing each item in the pages
3. Developing the Database
4. Web hosting the database

The planetary scanner using digital camera does scanning.

Though these documents are authoritative and carefully monitored throughout its publication, the internal structure is not standardized, not indexed and it is poorly coordinated. So it is very difficult to retrieve a document from the traditional print version of the Gazettes. Added to it the complications of the vernacular language make ~~the~~ digitization and retrieval more complicated . Hence a special feature Book Marks has been introduced in the digitization.

7. FEATURES OF NITYA DARCH DIGIAL LIBRARY SOFTWARE

As in the Digitization of Rare Books, Nitya Digital Software developed by M/s Beehive is used for the Gazette digitization too. Front end of the archive is capable of retrieving pages related to queries addressing each of the above access points taking single or pair wise. Fields of the database are defined in parallel to each part.

Nitya DArch, which is employed in the Digitization of rare books, is thoroughly redesigned to achieve these goals. It is programmed in Python and web enabled using Django Mysql and is chosen as back end database.

8. DEEP INDEXING

Search and retrieval of the digital archives still follows the ways of traditional catalogues. A few subject headings are given in the materials of an archived document and searches roam around these keywords in title and subject fields. When a document is searched using these limited words, the whole document is retrieved and presented to the user. It is the job of the user to browse from one end to the other to locate a paragraph he needs essentially.

Deep indexing works at two levels. In the first level, documents are extensively book marked for chapters, sections, tables, figures, charts, maps etc., hyper links established through bookmarks enable navigation through the content. In the second level, bookmarks are extracted into the database as a relational sub table. The searching mechanism of 'Nitya- D Arch' treats these book marks as distinct titles, extending the retrieval beyond the main title, going deeply into the content and catching individual pages. Once relevant page is displayed, other bookmarks in the document lead the user to other parts of the document. Bookmarks are Gateways for internal navigation of e-Books. The access points of Parts/ Pages in the document are made possible through this.

Table 1. Gazette Digitization Details

Year	*Gazette*	*Pages*	*Amount (Rs in Lakhs)*
2010-11	1903 - 1935	2,33,968	40
2011-12	1935 - 1954	2,33,968	40
2012-13	1955 - 1973	4,11,064	70
2013-14	1973 - 1985	2,44,337	39.99
2014-15	1985 - 2005	4,88,698	79.99
2015-16	2006 - 2014	299452	50

9. CONCLUSION

Government of Kerala spent Rupees 3.2 Crore for the Digitzation project of the State Central Library and from the feedback we are getting from different sections proves it is the worth the cost. By digitizing State Central Library collection, we could preserve the unique, fragile heritage materials by the digital reproduction and creation of a digital collection of Kerala State Government primary data, which is essential for the Public. While the rare books reference is a boost for the researchers all over the world, the use of the Gazette is more for the lively need of the common people. The user can easily locate the gazette details for the change of name, legal heir ship, PSC Examination and old transaction from the Travancore State onwards etc. As these Digital collections are viewed in our site, it is more visible and the use is also increased. This collection at the same time, gives the users an accurate idea of our Gazette holdings in order to better plan for an onsite visit.

As the State Central Library is the only Public Library under the direct control of the Kerala Government, it is an asset of the State and this model can be followed by all other State Central Libraries of India

REFERENCES

[1] IFLA "Guide lines for digitization projects for collections and holdings in the public domain, particularly those held by libraries and archives March 2002

[2] Proposal submitted to the State Central Library by M/s Beehive Concepts 2010

[3] Raman Nair, R. Developing Digital Libraries: Need For Proper Strategies. Advances in Library and Information Science. V5. Ed by D C Ojha and D V Kothari. Jodhpur, Scientific Publishers, 2005. Ch 21, P 259-271. http://eprints.rclis.org/8039/ Accessed on 01.06.2016

[4] Kerala, State Central Library. http://statelibrary.kerala.gov.in/gazette/index.php Accessed on 01.06.2016

14

Extended Vigenere Cipher Using ASCII Values to Enhance Security in Libraries

Steffy Livera

ABSTRACT

Libraries have made significant investments in computer based resources, training and services. However, such investments need to be protected from misuse or mistake by taking an active role in information security. The Vigenere cipher is a method of encrypting alphabetic text by using a series of different Caesar ciphers based on the letters of a keyword. It is a simple form of polyalphabetic substitution. It is a method consisting of a vigenere table with 26 ciphers. In vigenere table,each of the 26 ciphers are laid out horizontally,with the key letter for each cipher to its left. But with the advent of powerful computers, this method gets weaken against the cryptanalysis. In this paper I introduce an extended version of vigenere cipher using ASCII values with the aim of building a strong barrier for the cryptanalysts. Computers can only understand numbers, so an ASCII code is the numerical representation of a characters such as '@' or '$'. In the proposed technique, I will be using a table of an extended version of vigenere table with 256 ciphers. In the extended version of vigenere table, each of the 256 ciphers are laid out horizontally with the key letter for each cipher to its left. The strength of this cipher is that there are multiple ciphertext letters for each plain text letter, one for each unique letter of the keyword. The proposed cipher is expected to give more security than the existing vigenere cipher.

Keywords : Cryptography, Vigenere cipher, American Standard Code for Information Interchange (ASCII)

1. INTRODUCTION

Today, library environments are increasingly reliant on computer technology. Many libraries of all sizes have discontinued use of card catalogs in favor of electronic versions and many of the electronic versions previously accessible only via terminals within library buildings are now web accessible. The proliferation of the Internet and other computer technologies has been highly beneficial to libraries. Investment in everything from online databases and computing equipment to personnel and training is significant. Libraries need to have policies, protection measures and trained staff in place, in order to safeguard their investments in computer and computer related technologies, personnel and services. Traditionally, the most sensitive data that libraries collect are circulation records. By necessity, these are linked to identifying information for individual patrons who borrow books or other materials.

Online Public Access Catalogs (OPACs) are centralized systems that handle circulation and holdings information, as well as a variety of other data ranging from acquisitions budgets to cataloging modules.

Modern OPACs include functionality to make the holdings information searchable via a Web interface. Here lies the substantial security risk. Reasonable and prudent steps should be taken by libraries to insure that private data are kept private. The greatest risk might come from outside the library via an Internet connection, an unattended modem or from staff who abuse their access rights. To prevent packet sniffing, network switches should be used in place of network hubs. A switch provides a single network channel for each computer, removing the opportunity for sniffing. All areas of information security risk must be assigned to specific personnel. For example, if there is a public use computer workstation, someone needs to be responsible for its security. Similarly, someone needs to be responsible for the security of circulation data.

Cryptography is defined as the art and science of generatingsecret messages. An original plaintext is coded into the cipher text through the process of enciphering or encryption and the plaintext is restored from the cipher text through the process of deciphering or decryption. The many schemes used for encryption constitute the area of study known as cryptography. Cryptanalysis is " Breaking the code" without the knowledge of any encryption techniques. The areas of cryptography and cryptanalysis together are called cryptology. Encryption or enciphering is the process of using the key to produce ciphertext from plaintext. Decryption or deciphering is the process of using the key to produce plaintext from ciphertext. To encrypt a message requires knowing two things, the method of encryption such as simple substitution and the key such as the letter substitutions. If the messages were no longer secure, leave the method unchanged such as simple substitution but change the key by using different letter substitutions. Solving the messages not knowing the key is called cryptanalysis.

Cryptanalysts take up the "implied challenged to the ingenuity" that is tossed down by secret writing. The encryption algorithm point of view, two main techniques are used to implement in the secret key cryptography which is symmetric cipher system. Those are Substitution cipher and Transposition cipher. The Vigenere cipher is a method of encrypting alphabetic text by using a series of different Caesar ciphers based on the letters of a keyword. The Caesar Cipher works with replacing each letter with the letter standing three places further down of the alphabet order. Vigenere cipher is a simple form of polyalphabetic substitution. Polyalphabetic cipher a cipher in which there is more than one ciphertext alphabet and a rule that describes how to use them.

2. BACKGROUND

Substitution technique is one that the letters in the plaintext will be replaced by other letters or by numbers or symbols. A simple substitution cipher involves a single mapping of the plaintext alphabet onto ciphertext characters . The earliest use of substitution cipher is also the simplest one that is proposed by Julius Caesar, called Caesar Cipher.

Simple substitution ciphers, Caesar ciphers are all examples of monoalphabetic ciphers . In monoalphabetic ciphers, only one ciphertext alphabet is used. The Caesar Cipher works with replacing each letter with the letter standing three places further down of the alphabetic order.

Simple substitution ciphers like Caesar cipher use a single mapping from plaintext to ciphertext letters, that is the same plaintext will have the same ciphertext. This characteristic is always not good in cryptography from the security point of view. Polyalphabetic cipher solves this problem by using multiple substitutions. Polyalphabetic cipher a cipher in which there is more than one ciphertext alphabet and a rule that describes how to use them. Using different substitution mappings on various portions of the plaintext results in so called polyalphabetic substitution. Vigenere cipher is a simple form of polyalphabetic substitution cipher. It is a method of encrypting alphabetic text by using a series of different Caesar ciphers based on the letters of a keyword. The Vigenere Cipher works on the set of 26 English alphabets.

3. JUSTIFICATION

Vigenere ciphers use sequences of shift ciphers, whose use is facilitated through a rectangular array of letters referred to as the Vigenere square *with 26 ciphers.* The Vigenere cipher is a method of encrypting alphabetic text by using a series of different Caesar ciphers based on the letters of a keyword. Vigenere cipher is a simple form of polyalphabetic substitution. Polyalphabetic cipher a cipher in which there is more than one ciphertext alphabet and a rule that describes how to use them. In vigenere table, each of the 26 ciphers are laid out horizontally, with the key letter for each cipher to its left.

But with the advent of powerful computers, this method gets weaken against the cryptanalysis. In this paper I introduce an extended version of vigenere cipher using ASCII values with the aim of building a strong barrier for the cryptanalysts. I will be using a table of an extended version of vigenere table with 256 ciphers. In the extended version of vigenere table, each of the 256 ciphers are laid out horizontally with the key letter for each cipher to its left. The strength of this cipher is that there are multiple ciphertext letters for each plain text letter, one for each unique letter of the keyword. The proposed cipher is expected to give more security than the existing vigenere cipher.

4. LITERATURE SURVEY

History

The Vigenere cipher is a method of encryption invented by Giovan Batista Belaso and described in his 1553 book, "La cifra del. Sig. Giovan Batista Belaso". It was misattributed to Blaise de Vigenere in the 19th century, and given his name.

The "de" in his name simply indicates that his family came from the village of Vigenere. He was born in the village of Saint Pourcain, about halfway between Paris and Marseilles, on April 15, 1523. At the age of 17, he was taken from his studies and sent to court and, five years later, to the Diet of Worms as a very junior secretary. This gave him an initiation into diplomacy, and his subsequent travels through Europe broadened his experience. At 24, he entered the service of the Duke of Nevers, to whose house he remained attached the rest of his life, except for periods at court and as a diplomat. In 1549, at the age of 26, he went to Rome on a two year diplomatic mission. It was here that he was first thrown into contact with cryptology, and he seems to have steeped himself in it. He read the books of Trithemius [1462 – 1516], Belaso [known to have published in 1553 a booklet in which he proposed a polyalphabetic cipher], Cardano [1501 – 1576], and Porta [1535 – 1615], and the unpublished manuscript of Alberti [1404 – 1472]. He evidently conversed with the experts of the papal curia in 1566 and he was sent again to Rome as the secretary to King Charles IX. Here he renewed his acquaintance with the cryptographic experts, and this time seems to have been admitted to their chambers. Finally in 1570, at the age of 47, Vigenere quit the court , married the much younger Marie Vare and devoted himself to writing. He turned out some 20 books before he died of throat cancer in 1596.

The book which is constantly cited by workers in its field is his Traicte des Chiffres, which was written in 1581. It was a curious work . Vigenere was scrupulous in assigning credit for material from other authors and quoted them accurately and with comprehension. Each of his used a Trithemius like table which he improved by adding mixed alphabets on the sides. He also improved upon the autokey system of Cardano. Vigenere's system [3] works well and affords fair guarantees of security . In spite of Vigenere's clear exposition of his devices , both were entirely forgotten and only entered the stream of cryptology late in the 19th century after they were re-invented. Writers on cryptology then added insult to injury by degrading Vigenere's system into one more elementary. This system is more susceptible to solution than Vigenere's original. Nevertheless, a legend grew up that this degenerate form of Vigenere's work was the indecipherable cipher par excellence, a legend so hardy that as late as 1917, more than a half century after it had been exploded, the Vigenere was touted as "impossible of translation" in a journal as respected as Scientific American.

For many centuries, cryptography was a kind of secret technology practiced in black chamber by some special party or governments. Secret key cryptography and public key cryptography are two main ideas to do encryption .There are three main purposes in cryptography listed as following in[2] First, creating confidentiality. Second, giving authentication which is used to recognize if the message sender is the legal one or not. And the third is integrity.

Modern cryptography relies on Kerchoff principle says that one should always assume that all details about the cipher are known to the enemy, the exact algorithm and all its inner workings, except one small piece of data called key. From the encryption algorithm point of view, there are two main techniques we used to implement in the secret key cryptography system.

They are Substitution cipher and Transposition cipher. Substitution ciphers replace bits, characters, or blocks of characters with substitution. Transposition ciphers rearrange bits or characters in the data.

Substitution technique is one that the letters in the plaintext will be replaced by other letters or by numbers or symbols. The earliest use of substitution cipher is also the simplest one that is proposed by Julius Caesar, called Caesar Cipher. The Caesar Cipher works with replacing each letter with the letter standing three places further down of the alphabet order. For example,

plaintext : a b c d e f g h w x y z

ciphertext : e f g h i j k l z a b c

So if the plaintext is " meet me after the party " , then the ciphertext would be " phhw ph diwhu wkh sduwb ". If we assign each letter a number from 0 to 25 (from A to Z). Take the Ciphertext as C, Encryption as E, and plaintext as P. Then we can describe the Caesar Cipher as ,

$$C=E(p)=(p+3)mod(26)$$

A shift could be any amount, so the general shift algorithm is,

$$C = E(p) = (p + k) \bmod (26)$$

where k takes on a value in the range from 1 to 25.

And the decryption algorithm is simply,

$$p = D(C) = (C - k) \bmod (26)$$

If it is known that a given ciphertext is a Caesar cipher, then a brute force cryptanalysis will be easily performed. Just try all the 25 for the possible value of k. In this example, there are three reasons for us to use the brute force cryptanalysis. First is that the encryption and the decryption algorithms are known. Second is that there are only 25 keys to try. Third is that the language of the plaintext is known and easily recognizable. Simple substitution ciphers like Caesar cipher use a single mapping from plaintext to ciphertext letters, that is the same plaintext will have the same ciphertext. This characteristic is always not good in cryptography from the security point of view.

Polyalphabetic cipher solves this problem by using multiple substitutions.

Transposition technique is achieved by performing some kind of permutation on the plaintext letters. It is very simple to realize this kind of cipher. If the plaintext is "meet me after the party", it can be rearranged it by this way:

m e m a t r h p r y

e t e f e t e a t

The plaintext and the ciphertext like this:

plaintext: meet me after the party

ciphertext: mematrhpryetefeteat

Another simple transposition cipher is called Columnar transposition. If the plaintext is "data encryption", we will compose the sentence into a 3*5 matrix.

Existing system

The Vigenere cipher is a method of encryption invented by Giovan Batista Belaso and described in his 1553 book, "La cifra del. Sig. Giovan Batista Belaso". It was misattributed to Blaise de Vigenere in the 19th century, and given his name. The cipher is a keyword-based system that uses a series of different Caesar ciphers based on the letters of the keyword. It is a simplified version of the more general polyalphabetic substitution cipher, invented by Alberti ca 1465. This cipher is well known because while it is easy to understand and implement, it often appears to beginners to be unbreakable. Consequently, many programmers have implemented encryption schemes in their applications which are essentially Vigenere ciphers, only to have them broken by the first cryptanalyst who comes along.

The Vigenere cipher is a method of encrypting alphabetic text by using a series of different Caesar ciphers based on the letters of a keyword. It is a simple form of polyalphabetic substitution [2]. It is a method consisting of a vigenere table with 26 ciphers. Vigenere type cipher should theoretically be difficult to break if mixed alphabets are used in the table, if the keyword is random, and if the total length of ciphertext is less than 27.6 times the length of the keyword. These requirements are rarely understood in practice and so Vigenere enciphered message security is usually less than what might have been. Use and cryptanalysis of the Vigenere cipher is therefore frequently introduced at the beginning of courses on cryptography.

In the Vigenere cipher, the first row of the table is filled out with a copy of the plaintext alphabet, and successive rows are simply shifted one place to the left. Such a simple table is called tabula recta, and mathematically corresponds to adding the plaintext and key letters, modulo 26.The keyword is then used to choose which ciphertext alphabet is to use. Each letter of the keyword is used in turn, and then they are repeated again from the beginning. So if the keyword is 'CAT', the first letter of plaintext is enciphered under alphabet 'C', the second under 'A', the third under 'T', the fourth under 'C' again, and so on. In 1863, Friedrich Kasiski published a method, which enabled the calculation of the length of the keyword in a Vigenere ciphered message. Once this was done, ciphertext letters that had been enciphered under the same alphabet could be picked out and attacked separately as a number of semi independent simple substitutions complicated by the fact that within one alphabet letters were separated and did not form complete words, but simplified by the fact that usually a tabula recta had been employed. As such, even today a Vigenere type cipher should theoretically be difficult to break if mixed alphabets are used in the tableau, if the keyword is random, and if the total length of ciphertext is less than 27.6 times the length of the keyword.

These requirements are rarely understood in practice and so Vigenere enciphered message security is usually less than what might have been. Use and cryptanalysis of the Vigenere cipher is therefore frequently introduced at the beginning of courses on cryptography.

How to use the Vigenere square

First choose a secret keyword at random, e.g. DOG. This keyword is made up of plaintext letters at positions 3, 14 & 6 in the alphabet. So we use the Caesar shifts in rows 3, 14 & 6 to encipher our message. These rows are shaded yellow in the square below.

	a	b	c	d	e	f	g	h	i	j	k	l	m	n	o	p	q	r	s	t	u	v	w	x	y	z
1	B	C	D	E	F	G	H	I	J	K	L	M	N	O	P	Q	R	S	T	U	V	W	X	Y	Z	A
2	C	D	E	F	G	H	I	J	K	L	M	N	O	P	Q	R	S	T	U	V	W	X	Y	Z	A	B
3	D	E	F	G	H	I	J	K	L	M	N	O	P	Q	R	S	T	U	V	W	X	Y	Z	A	B	C
4	E	F	G	H	I	J	K	L	M	N	O	P	Q	R	S	T	U	V	W	X	Y	Z	A	B	C	D
5	F	G	H	I	J	K	L	M	N	O	P	Q	R	S	T	U	V	W	X	Y	Z	A	B	C	D	E
6	G	H	I	J	K	L	M	N	O	P	Q	R	S	T	U	V	W	X	Y	Z	A	B	C	D	E	F
7	H	I	J	K	L	M	N	O	P	Q	R	S	T	U	V	W	X	Y	Z	A	B	C	D	E	F	G
8	I	J	K	L	M	N	O	P	Q	R	S	T	U	V	W	X	Y	Z	A	B	C	D	E	F	G	H
9	J	K	L	M	N	O	P	Q	R	S	T	U	V	W	X	Y	Z	A	B	C	D	E	F	G	H	I
10	K	L	M	N	O	P	Q	R	S	T	U	V	W	X	Y	Z	A	B	C	D	E	F	G	H	I	J
11	L	M	N	O	P	Q	R	S	T	U	V	W	X	Y	Z	A	B	C	D	E	F	G	H	I	J	K
12	M	N	O	P	Q	R	S	T	U	V	W	X	Y	Z	A	B	C	D	E	F	G	H	I	J	K	L
13	N	O	P	Q	R	S	T	U	V	W	X	Y	Z	A	B	C	D	E	F	G	H	I	J	K	L	M
14	O	P	Q	R	S	T	U	V	W	X	Y	Z	A	B	C	D	E	F	G	H	I	J	K	L	M	N
15	P	Q	R	S	T	U	V	W	X	Y	Z	A	B	C	D	E	F	G	H	I	J	K	L	M	N	O
16	Q	R	S	T	U	V	W	X	Y	Z	A	B	C	D	E	F	G	H	I	J	K	L	M	N	O	P
17	R	S	T	U	V	W	X	Y	Z	A	B	C	D	E	F	G	H	I	J	K	L	M	N	O	P	Q
18	S	T	U	V	W	X	Y	Z	A	B	C	D	E	F	G	H	I	J	K	L	M	N	O	P	Q	R
19	T	U	V	W	X	Y	Z	A	B	C	D	E	F	G	H	I	J	K	L	M	N	O	P	Q	R	S
20	U	V	W	X	Y	Z	A	B	C	D	E	F	G	H	I	J	K	L	M	N	O	P	Q	R	S	T
21	V	W	X	Y	Z	A	B	C	D	E	F	G	H	I	J	K	L	M	N	O	P	Q	R	S	T	U
22	W	X	Y	Z	A	B	C	D	E	F	G	H	I	J	K	L	M	N	O	P	Q	R	S	T	U	V
23	X	Y	Z	A	B	C	D	E	F	G	H	I	J	K	L	M	N	O	P	Q	R	S	T	U	V	W
24	Y	Z	A	B	C	D	E	F	G	H	I	J	K	L	M	N	O	P	Q	R	S	T	U	V	W	X
25	Z	A	B	C	D	E	F	G	H	I	J	K	L	M	N	O	P	Q	R	S	T	U	V	W	X	Y
26	A	B	C	D	E	F	G	H	I	J	K	L	M	N	O	P	Q	R	S	T	U	V	W	X	Y	Z

Fig. 1. Vigenere Table

To encipher the plaintext "the message". To encode the first letter, 't', find the column labelled 't' and follow it down until it intersects the first Caesar shift row 3, to find the cipher letter 'W'. Following this procedure for each letter in turn enciphers the plaintext "the message" to "WVK PSYVOMH". To decipher the message, the correct Caesar shifts have to be applied to the ciphertext in reverse.

Thus, the person receiving the cipher has to know the secret keyword in order to decipher it. Deciphering is done by reading off the red plaintext letters on the top of the square, one by one, while locating each cipher letter on rows 3, 14 & 6 over and over.

Operation of Vigenere cipher

The Vigenere was described as "impossible of translation" in the respected journal, "Scientific American". "The Alphabet Cipher" provides a good description of how to use a table for encryption and decryption using arbitrary keywords, but here is an alternate description:

- The encipherer chooses a plaintext: VIGENERE
- The encipherer chooses a keyword and repeats it to become the length of the plaintext. (e.g. the keyword, "CIPH") which is CIPHCIPH
- The encipherer finds the letter that corresponds to plaintext and the key. Thus V becomes X.
- This is repeated for each letter in the plaintext and its corresponding letter in the key will be VIGENERE + CIPHCIPH ⇒ XQVLPMGL

To encode a message, one locates the plaintext letter in the top row, and then reads the ciphertext letter from one of the alphabets below, using each one in turn. One can also write out the entire set of these shifted alphabets, picking the right row for any letter of the key, the resulting block of alphabets is known as a tabula recta. This use of multiple alphabets in rotation to encrypt a message is called as a polyalphabetic cipher. The systematic and repeated use of multiple alphabets is not as secure as polyalphabetic ciphers.

Cryptanalysis of Vigenere cipher

Cryptanalysis is the methods to attack cryptographic protection. There are several ways to achieve this goal. A cipher is breakable if it is possible to determine the plaintext or key from the ciphertext, or to determine the key from the plaintext ciphertext pair.The first step in cryptanalysis of vigenere cipher is to find the length of the key. To obtain the key length, Kasiski method is used. After the key length is obtained, the proposed algorithm will be applied on ciphertext to get the correct key and to recover the original plaintext.

KASISKI/KERCKHOFF Method

Vigenere like substitution ciphers were regarded by many as practically unbreakable for 300 years. In 1863, a Prussian Major named Kasiski proposed a method for breaking a Vigenere cipher that consisted of finding the length of the keyword and then dividing the message into that many simple substitution cryptograms. Frequency analysis could then be used to solve the resulting simple substitutions. Kasiski's technique for finding the length of the keyword was based on measuring the distance between repeated bigrams in the ciphertext.

5. RESULT AND ANALYSIS

Modified Vigenere table generation

In the vigenere cipher proposed by Blaise de Vigenere, the vigenere table consists of 26 * 26 matrix. While comparing the generation of vigenere table in the earlier cipher, an average of 15 milli-second was taken to generate a 26 * 26 matrix . But, the Kasiski test can be easily try in this technique. In the extended vigenere table consisting of 256 * 256 matrix, an average of 200 milli-seconds was analysed. Eventhough this much amount of time is taken, it is a good sign indicating the difficulty to a kasiski text to happen.

Encryption Time

The time taken to encrypt the plaintext in both techniques are almost similar. The time taken in the vigenere cipher to encypt the plaintect is less than a second. The time taken to encrypt the plaintext in the extended vigenere cipher takes also a time of less than a second. Thus it concludes that the extended vigenere cipher is more efficient in terms of encryption time.

6. CONCLUSION

For many centuries, cryptography was a kind of secret technology practiced in black chamber by some special parties or governments. Cryptography is defined as the art and science of generating secret messages. The Vigenere cipher is a method of encrypting alphabetic text by using a series of different Caesar ciphers based on the letters of a keyword. It is a simple form of polyalphabetic substitution. Conventional vigenere ciphers use sequences of shift ciphers, whose use is facilitated through a rectangular array of letters referred to as the Vigenere square with 26 ciphers.

In vigenere table,each of the 26 ciphers are laid out horizontally,with the key letter for each cipher to its left. Vigenere cipher, being poly-alphabetic cipher was one of the most popular ciphers in the past because of its simplicity and resistance to the frequency analysis test of letters that can crack simple ciphers like Caesar cipher. But with the advent of powerful computers, this method gets weaken against the cryptanalysis. In this paper I introduce an extended version of vigenere cipher using ASCII values with the aim of building a strong barrier for the cryptanalysts. I will be using a table of an extended version of vigenere table with 256 ciphers. In the extended version of vigenere table, each of the 256 ciphers are laid out horizontally with the key letter for each cipher to its left.

The strength of this cipher is that there are multiple ciphertext letters for each plain text letter, one for each unique letter of the keyword. The proposed cipher is expected to give more security than the existing vigenere cipher. Libraries need to have policies, protection measures and trained staff in place in order to safeguard their investments in computer and computer related technologies, personnel and services. The extended vigenere cipher helps to provide security in all aspects to store the private data in libraries by encryption.

Scope for future study

The Vigenere cipher is a method of encrypting alphabetic text by using a series of different Caesar ciphers based on the letters of a keyword. It is a simple form of polyalphabetic substitution. Conventional vigenere ciphers use sequences of shift ciphers, whose use is facilitated through a rectangular array of letters referred to as the Vigenere square of size 26 and in extended vigenere table, the size is 256. In both systems the vigenere table is static.

This can be modified to a dynamic table which makes this system more secure in future by providing a more complex encryption schemes.Lot of applications , systems and techniques can be make tight secure using the ASCII characters. It can be applied to double encryption, triple encryption, DES, AES and in lot of areas where real time applications need more secure than the existing security. There is a lot of scope in this area.

REFERENCES

[1] K.Senthil, K.Prasanthi, R.Rajaram "A Modern Avatar of Julius Ceasar and Vigenere Cipher " of the 2013 IEEE International Conference on computational Intelligence and Computing Research.

[2] William Stallings: "Cryptography and Network Security: Principles and Practices" 4th Edition, Prentice Hall".

[3] Dara Kirschenbaum: "Advances in Cryptography History of Mathematics"1ST Edition.

[4] Beutelspacher, Albrecht (1994). "Chapter 2". Cryptology. translation from German by J. Chris Fisher,Washington, DC: Mathematical Association of America. pp. 27–41. ISBN 0-88385-504-6.

[5] Luciano, Dennis, Gordon Prichett, "Cryptology: From Caesare Ciphers to Public-Key Cryptosystems", The College Mathematics Journal, vol.18, No.1, Jan.1987, pp.2–17.

[6] Wobst, Reinhard, "Cryptology Unlocked", Wiley, 2001,ISBN 978-0-470-06064-3.

[7] Reinke, Edgar C, "Classical Cryptography". The Classical Journal,vol.58, no.3, Dec.1992, pp.114-118.

[8] Pieprzyk, J., Thomas Hardjono, Jennifer Seberry, "Fundamentals of Computer Security", . Springer. ISBN: 3-540-43101-2, 2003.

[9] Singh,Simon, "The Code Book", ISBN 0-385-49532-3,Anchor, 2000.

[10] Alexander Poltorak, "Mezuzah and Astrology", Retrieved2008-06-13.

[11] Kahn, D, The Codebreakers, ISBN 978-0-684-83130-5,1967.

[12] Wobst, Reinhard, Cryptology Unlocked, Wiley,ISBN978-0-470-06064-3.

[13] Leyden, John, The Register, Retrieved 2008-06-13..

[14] Beutelspacher, Albrecht, Cryptology Mathematical Association of America, ISBN 0-88385-504-6.

[15] Leighton, Albert C, "Secret Communication among the Greeks and Romans". Technology and Culture, vol. 10,no.2, Apr.1969, pp. 139-154.

[16] Gregory B Newby, "Information Security for Libraries"

15

Innovative Library Management Using Holographic Projection Technology

Hariharan S

ABSTRACT

This paper describes an algorithm for innovative library management. Within this paper we suggest a method of speeding up 3D Holograms formation. In this paper, the holographic projection technology is used to implement the mid air glass less projection of the library management system. The innovative library management algorithm uses light blue optics technology to provide touch facility. The user of the library can touch the mid air projected holograms to perform required tasks, such as; book search, book returns. The idea being that we only need to uses the holographic interface for performing the book search, returns, and other library operations, such as; issue of book, and fine management.

1. INTRODUCTION

3D Holographic Projection is one of the latest innovations in projection screen technology; it focuses on displaying images in mid air rather than conventional projection screens. 3D Holographic Projection system designed to project video, products, information, and people in mid-air. It is available in various dimensions in accordance with various applications it might have, for example 3D Holographic Projection models with screen sizes to display a two meter tall person is available, thus ensuring a more lifelike and interactive form of communication. 3D Holographic Projection does not affect the environment as it works using the existing air that is already in the room to create the image. The book maintenance, staff maintenance, student maintenance, journals maintenance, issue & return maintenance, fine maintenance, attendance of staff maintenance, date & time maintenance, and internet access maintenance are the important function that should be performed by a efficient library management tool. The "Innovative Library Management Using Holographic Projection Technology" is an efficient application for maintainig the library efficiently with advanced mid air based user interface.

2. HISTORY

Before computer is implemented, registers are used to maintain the library details, such as; date of issue and returns. After computer is implemented, the computer is used to maintain the library details. A single computer can replace many numbers of registers. In current scenario, the person who needs a book can find the availability detains using the computer software such as LibSoft. In future the person who needs a book can find the availability detains by simply using the mid air projected library management tools.

3. RELATED WORKS

3.1. Pepper'S Ghost

Pepper's ghost is an illusion technique used in theatre, amusement parks, museums, television, and concerts. It is named after John Henry Pepper, a scientist who popularized the effect in a famed demonstration in 1862. It has a long history, dating into the 16th century, and remains widely performed today. Notable examples of the illusion are the Girl-to-Gorilla trick found in old carnival sideshows and the appearance of "ghosts" at the Haunted Mansion at Disneyland. Teleprompters are a modern implementation of Pepper's ghost. Examples of concert illusions based on Pepper's ghost are the appearance of Tupac Shakur onstage with Dr. Dre and Snoop Dogg at the 2012 Coachella Music and Arts Festival and Michael Jackson at the 2014 Billboard Music Awards.

3.2. IBM Research

IBM surveys 3,000 researchers to find out what they think are going to be big in the future. This year, everyone's caught the Face Time bug, and is looking forward to 3D hologram video calls. The video calls will be projected from cell phones using Pico-projector technology, according to the survey. Other "likely" technologies we can look forward to using in just five years' time are batteries powered by air (which will last 10 times' longer); computer programs crunching numbers for real-time traffic and heat-generation for homes, from computers and data centers.

3.3. Aerial Burton

Most of the 3D displays reported until now draw pseudo-3D images on 2D planes by utilizing the human binocular disparity. However, many problems occur, e.g., the limitation of the visual field, and the physiological displeasure due to the misidentification of virtual images.

To overcome the mentioned problems, we tried to research and succeed in developing "True 3D Display" which can produce bright dot in the air so audience can see 3D images in true 3D space. Our display device uses the plasma emission phenomenon near the focal point of focused laser light. By controlling the position of the focal point in the x, y, and z axes, it displays real 3D images constructed by dot arrays in the air.

3.4. Holus

Holus is a tabletop holographic platform accepts any multimedia content from your smart phone, tablet or PC and creates a hologram that is visible from four sides. Normally holograms are notorious for being visible from specific angles but Holus get round this problem by projecting images from four different perspectives in a pyramid-like structure resulting in 360 degree viewing angles. The pyramid structure is made out of tempered glass to make it durable. If you are using Holus solo, it can detect your movement around the room and project the content from your perspective in real time. Skype and Face Time calls become much more immersive with the 3D image projection of the person on the other end. Holus supports third party controllers like Emotive Brain Sensor and Leap Motion that help you interact with the hologram with brain waves and gesture recognition respectively. Holus will be able communicate with your smart phone or PC with the help of Wi-Fi and Bluetooth. Holus has cleverly added USB charging docks and a tablet holder dock that not only house the smart device but also charge it ensuring longer hologram sessions. The product will be sold in two variants. The Holus Home Edition as the name suggests is a smaller variant with wireless connectivity for end users who just have to download the Holus app for their respective platforms to get started. The Holus Pro Edition is aimed at businesses and developers who are interested in developing their 3D hologram experiences using the Holus Software Development Kit that supports platforms like iOS, Android and Windows and gaming engines like Unity and Unreal Engine. The Pro Edition is bigger and has an additional HDMI port.

3.5. Illumiroom

It uses a Kinect for Windows camera and a projector to blur the lines between on-screen content and the environment we live in allowing us to combine our virtual and physical worlds. For example, our system can change the appearance of the room, induce apparent motion, extend the field of view, and enable entirely new game experiences.

3.6. Skype

Skype is working on a technology that will no doubt be impressive when used once and then promptly ignored for the rest of time – 3D video calls. The project was revealed in an interview with the BBC to commemorate Skype's 10th anniversary but it could be another decade before we see that project bear fruit. Microsoft's Corporate VP for Skype Mark Gillett told BBC that Skype's labs has been doing work on both 3D capture and 3D display of video calls, and while it's impressed with the progress made in monitors and TVs that can produce a 3D image, the company still believes there's a lot of work needed to be done before the 3D capture technology is where it needs to be. That's because there's too much tuning required to get the multiple cameras you need for producing 3D images angled as you need them for live video calls. Gillett said in the BBC interview that Skype has the tech working in the lab, but needs the hardware ecosystem to be able to support it before it's introduced. But he also said that 3D video chat would take longer to catch on with consumers than other 3D video tech in all likelihood, which begs the question of whether it ever really will. 3D movies and broadcast television efforts have been seen by many industry watchers as something of a flop, after all. The BBC abandoned plans to use 3DTV tech for its programming, citing weak demand and the need for glasses as part of the problem, neither of which helps encourage the massive cost related to filming and airing 3D content. Sony also seems pretty much to have discontinued (though no official proclamation has been made) its dedicated 3D display for PlayStation gaming, despite 3D gaming being one of the best use-case scenarios for the tech.

3.7. Sixth Sense

Sixth Sense' is a wearable gestural interface that augments the physical world around us with digital information and lets us use natural hand gestures to interact with that information. The Sixth Sense prototype is comprised of a pocket projector, a mirror and a camera. The hardware components are coupled in a pendant like mobile wearable device. Both the projector and the camera are connected to the mobile computing device in the user's pocket. The projector projects visual information enabling surfaces, walls and physical objects around us to be used as interfaces; while the camera recognizes and tracks user's hand gestures and physical objects using computer-vision based techniques. The software program processes the video stream data captured by the camera and tracks the locations of the colored markers (visual tracking fiducials) at the tip of the user's fingers using simple computer-vision techniques. The movements and arrangements of these fiducials are interpreted into gestures that act as interaction instructions for the projected application interfaces. The maximum number of tracked fingers is only constrained by the number of unique fiducials, thus Sixth Sense also supports multi-touch and multi-user interaction. The Sixth Sense prototype implements several applications that demonstrate the usefulness, viability and flexibility of the system. The map application lets the user navigate a map displayed on a nearby surface using hand gestures, similar to gestures supported by Multi-Touch based systems, letting the user zoom in, zoom out or pan using intuitive hand movements. The drawing application lets the user draw on any surface by tracking the fingertip movements of the user's index finger. Sixth Sense also recognizes user's freehand gestures (postures). For example, the Sixth Sense system implements a gestural camera that takes photos of the scene the user is looking at by detecting the 'framing' gesture. The user can stop by any surface or wall and flick through the photos he/she has taken. Sixth Sense also lets the user draw icons or symbols in the air using the movement of the index finger and recognizes those symbols as interaction instructions. For example, drawing a magnifying glass symbol takes the user to the map application or drawing an '@' symbol lets the user check his mail. The Sixth Sense system also augments physical objects the user is interacting with by projecting more information about these objects projected on them. For example, a newspaper can show live video news or dynamic information can be provided on a regular piece of paper. The gesture of drawing a circle on the user's wrist projects an analog watch.

3.8. Holho

The holographic communication can be a suspended tridimensional hologram or a real object holographic projection mapping, always granting your products the attention of the audience.

3.9. Femto Second Laser

A lot of work is currently going into creating Star Wars

3D holograms that can be seen by the naked eye without wearing 3D glasses, and now researchers have found a way to make safe, touchable mid-air displays using femto second lasers. it is possible to create holograms in mid-air using a laser-induced plasma display, which works by ionizing air molecules so that they release extra energy in the form of bluish-white photons that can be seen easily. The plasma photons are known as 3D pixels, and at the moment, the lasers used to make 3D holograms are nanosecond lasers, meaning they fire tens or hundreds of thousands of times per second to heat up specific points of air.

4. HELIO DISPLAY

This technology can be used as a touch interface when it is connected to a PC via USB cable. Strictly speaking, the surface of projection is not air! It is a layer of mist in mid-air that gives rise to a 2D display that seems to be floating. This mist is formed as a layer using a series of metal plates. The source of projection of this technology is water. Here are some of the basics and ideas of the issuing technology..

4.1. Materials and Methods

4.2. 3D Holographic Projection

Holographic projection is the new wave of technology that will change how we view things in the new era. It will have tremendous effects on all fields of life including business, education, science, art and healthcare. The 3D Holographic Projection is used to represent 2D data in 3D and display it in middle of the air. Generally Holograms are 2D canvas which can display 3D objects. You can find them in many places in real life such as your credit card and driving license. There you can see 3D object in 2D sticker and depending on the angle you look at it you can get different views, same as in real 3D object. Those holographic stickers are difficult to reproduce and used to indicate originality of products. Using the same underlying fundamental concept laser devices can create 3D images in thin air. This is a brand new experience to us. Every time we see a reproduced image its 2D and there is a screen. Even if you experience Wi-Max 3D, still there is a screen. But with Laser hologram there is no physical screen. It juts appear 3D objects in air. Normally in a Smartphone we see images in 2D display and touch responsiveness is also limited to 2D surface. Yes, some applications are capable of displaying 3D images, but still they are virtual 3D and displayed on 2D surface. The day engineers equipped a Smartphone with a Holographic display, the images stuck in 2D display will pop out of the phone as real 3D objects. Smartphone home screen will spread out in air and menu item will start floating near them. Once this becomes reality it will be the next big thing in Mobile handset evolution. Display real 3D images in air won't be adequate to deliver a great user experience. There has to be motion sensor which can understand hand gestures and control the UI accordingly. When you combine this kind of motion sensor to a Holographic display, you will be able to actually touch a 3D object which popped out from your phone and turn it around with your fingers. Same concept will work even better with large screens in tablets.

4.3. Light Blue Optics

The light blue optics is to convert the projected screen into a touch screen. The Hand is used for the keyboard typing on the projected screen. The corresponding Value of the character will be passed to the system using simple 2D Camera. The light blue optics enable the user to touch the mid air projected holographic library management tools.

4.4. Gesture Recognition

It is a technology which is aimed at interpreting human gestures with the help of mathematical algorithms. Gesture recognition technique basically focuses on the emotion recognition from the face and hand gesture recognition. Gender recognition technique enables humans to interact with computers in a more direct way without using any external interfacing devices. It can provide a much better alternative to text user interfaces and graphical user interface which requires the need of a keyboard or mouse to interact with the computer. An interface which solely depends on the gestures requires precise hand pose tracking. In the early versions of gesture recognition process special type of hand gloves which provide information about hand position orientation and flux of the fingers. Once hand pose has been captured the gestures can be recognized using different techniques. Neural network approaches or statistical templates are the commonly used techniques used for the recognition purposes. This technique has a high accuracy usually showing accuracy of more than 95%. Time dependent neural network will also be used for real time recognition of the gestures.

5. LIBRARY MANAGEMENT

Library Management System is an application which refers to library systems which are generally small or medium in size. It is used by librarian to manage the library using a computerized system where he/she can record various transactions like issue of books, return of books, addition of new books, addition of new students etc. Books and student maintenance modules are also included in this system which would keep track of the students using the library and also a detailed description about the books a library contains. With this computerized system there will be no loss of book record or member record which generally happens when a non computerized system is used. In addition, report module is also included in Library Management System. If user's position is admin, the user is able to generate different kinds of reports like lists of students registered, list of books, issue and return reports. All these modules are able to help librarian to manage the library with more convenience and in a more efficient way as compared to library systems which are not computerized.

6. Innovative Library Management Using Holographic Projection

Innovative library management using holographic projection is simply a library management system, which uses holographic interface for managing the library. The library management system will be projected into the mid air as holograms, by using gesture, and touch interface the user can easily manage the library in a more efficient way as compared to library systems which are computerized.

6.1. Applications

Proposed applications for the real-world 3D Holographic Projection include:

- Advertising and Promotion, e.g.: trade shows; in-store displays; museum, movie and casino displays; theme parks.
- Collaborative Decision Making, e.g.: board meetings and presentations; air-traffic control;
- Military command and control; architectural and engineering design; teleconferencing.
- Simulation & Training, e.g.: virtual targets; pre-operative planning; virtual surgery.
- Consumer, e.g.: video games; home theatre.

- Heads-up displays in new fields, e.g.: a patient's vital signs could hover above the chest during open heart surgery.
- Build one into a door jamb and have a walk through image or virtual privacy screen.
- An in-store end cap advertising display and demonstration through which the customer can reach and grab shown product.

7. DISADVANTAGES

7.1. Needs controlled lighting for best working conditions

Needs controlled lighting for best working conditions is the main disadvnatage. Darker the ambience the better the clarity of the image projected by 3D holographic projection. External light sources can seriously affect the visibility of the 3D holographic projection. The projection screen being transparent other light sources will pass through making the image characteristics hard to distinguish .So 3D holographic projection units are used only in controlled lighting conditions to ensure greater clarity of viewing.

7.2. Wind and bright lights interfere with image visibility

3D holographic projection projects images in to a layer of air, acting as an invisible screen in the path of the projector. Since the screen is suspended in mid-air wind around the screen may affect the image projected, a certain amount of waviness is imparted in the displayed image and this is another drawback of 3D holographic projection affecting the visibility of the image. This waviness created is small under less extreme conditions as the projection screen for the image to be projected is sandwiched between two layers of clean air that is continuously flowing out of the base unit. These layers of clean air will give more steadinesses to the image.

7.3. Expensive

Like any other mid-air projection technology 3D holographic projection is in its developing phase. Various 3D holographic projection units are made available for common people but it is out of reach of most of the common people as it is expensive. A single 3D holographic projection unit cost ranges from $19000 to $39000.As technology develops further it is likely to get cheaper and same is about to happen to 3D holographic projection. It is because of this high cost 3D holographic projection technology is mainly accepted and implemented in various institutions or multinational companies or museums, casino's etc where interaction and attraction of clients are very important. But, the proposed system is cost effective. It costs around $ 75 (nearly 5000 Indian Rupees).

8. CONCLUSION AND FUTURE WORK

This 3D holographic interface will provide a computerized version of library management system which will benefit the students as well as the staff of the library. It makes entire process holograms where student can search books; staff can generate reports and do book transactions. It also has a facility for student login where student can login and can see status of books issued as well request for books or give some suggestions. It has a facility of teachers' login where teachers can add lecture notes and also give necessary suggestions to library and also add info about workshops or events happening in our college or nearby colleges in the online notice board. There is a future scope of this facility that many have more features such as 3D holographic lectures; video tutorials can be added by teachers as well as holographic assignments submission facility, a feature of group chat where students can discuss various issues of engineering can be added to this project thus making it more interactive, more user friendly and project which fulfills each users' need in the best way possible. 3D Holographic Projection is a good projection unit which does not require any special hardware and support videos and jpg images, flash, quick time etc. We can also play games on 3D Holographic Projection. This unique technology, developed by a former architect, creates one of the most convincing open-air holographic-like images in existence. 3D Holographic Projection can work as a free-space touch screen when connected to a PC by a USB cable. A PC sees the 3D Holographic Projection as a pointing device, like a mouse. With the supplied software installed, one can use a finger, pen, or another object as cursor control and navigate or interact with simple content. As advocated by IO2 technologies, 3D Holographic Projection is just the beginning of the future generation displays to come. 3D Holographic Projection therefore can be considered as the foundation blocks for the future generation display technology. A future generation display might incorporate the best of 3D Holographic Projection with some additional features like open-air display with 3D capability, higher resolution and accurate interactive capabilities.

ACKNOWLEDGMENTS

This is a product of experience and it goes a long way in shaping up a person in respective profession and it is not only who gains that experience but a group of kind heart behind success. If words are considered as a symbol of approval and token of knowledge, then these words play heralding role in expressing our gratitude. First, my sincere thanks to Toc H Management for giving me free education and HOD (IT) DR. Sherly K K for the constant care and support, my special thanks to Asst. Prof. Smitha Mohan,

Asst. Prof. Dipu Jacob. Last but not the least, a very special thanks are due to all the teaching and non teaching members of the Toc H Arakkunnam.

REFERENCES

[1] Wu, W., Blaicher, F., Yang, J., Seder, T., Cui, D. A Prototype of Landmark-based Car Navigation Using a Full-windshield Head-up Display System. In Proc. AMC 2009, ACM Press (2009), 21-28.

[2] Productivity Future Vision. *http://www.youtube.com/watch?feature=player_embedded&v=a6cNdhOKwi0.*

[3] 2012 GM Advanced Tech Window. *https://www.youtube.com/watch?v=9G4cYYlIaCc.*

[4] Olwal, A. Unencumbered 3D Interaction with See-through Displays. In Proc. NordiCHI 2008, ACM Press (2008), 527-530.

[5] Anupam Alur et al, / (IJCSIT) International Journal of Computer Science and Information Technologies, Vol. 5 (5), 2014, 6039-6043

[6] Bergmann Tiest, W. M., & Kappers, A. M. L. Cues for haptic perception of compliance. IEEE Transactions on Haptics, 2, pages 189–199, 2009.

[7] F. I. Parke, "Computer generated animation of faces", Proc of ACM National conference, vol. 1, pages 451-457, 1972.

[8] F. I .Parke, "Parameterized models for facial animation", IEEE computer graphics and applications, vol. 2, no. 9, pages 61-68, 1982.

[9] Freyberger, F. K. B., & Färber, B. Compliance discrimination of deformable objects by squeezing with one and two fingers. In Proceedings of EuroHaptics, pp. 271–276, 2006.

[10] S. Dong, T. Haist, W. Osten, T. Ruppel and O. Sawodny, "Response analysis of holography-based modal wavefront sensor," Appl. Opt. 51, 1318-1327(2012).

[11] S. Dong, T. Haist, W. Osten, T. Ruppel and O. Sawodny, "Response analysis and experimental results of holography-based modal Zernike wavefront sensor," Proc. SPIE 8165, 816506 (2011).

[12] Sindhuja Raghupatruni, Niharika Nasam, Keerthi Lingam, International Journal of Computer Applications, International Journal of Computer Applications, Sixth Sense Enabled Campus -Possibilities and Challenges, Volume 75, No.8, August 2013

[13] Vignesh.M, SaravanaJothi.M, International Journal of Advanced

Research in Computer Science and Software Engineering, Implementation of Holographic View in Mobile Video Calls, Volume 2, Issue 10, October 2012, 2277 128X

[14] Hariharan S, Advanced 3D Holographic and Haptic Interface for 3D Video Calling, Technoareate conference, IRF proceeding, 30th oct 2015, Hyderabad

[15] Hariharan S, video calling using Haptic technology, International research journal of engineering and technology, volume 2, issue 6, September 2015 edition, 2395-0056

[16] Hariharan S, Accident controlling for vehicle using Haptic technology, International research journal of engineering and technology, volume 2, issue 6, September 2015 edition, 2395-0056

[17] Boring, S., Baur, D., Butz, A., Gustafson, S., & Baudisch, P. (2010). Touch projector: mobile interaction through video. *SIGCHI Conference on Human Factors in Computing Systems (CHI'10)*, 2287–2296.

[18] The Cicret Bracelet: It's like a tablet...but on your skin! (n.d.). Retrieved December 05, 2014, from *http://www.cicret.com/wordpress/?page_id=17920*

[19] Touchjet. (n.d.). Retrieved December 05, 2014, from *http://www.atouchjet.com/*

[20] TouchPico: Turn Any Surface Into A Touch Screen | Indiegogo. (n.d.). Retrieved December 05, 2014, from *http://tinyurl.com/k3pcvpm*

[21] Dell. (n.d.). Dell Interactive Projector | S520. Retrieved from *http://tinyurl.com/le64sp4*

[22] Tsai, C. J. (n.d.). 3D & Mobile Interactive Projection Hot Topics of LED in Display.

[23] Touchjet. (n.d.). Retrieved December 05, 2014, from *http://www.atouchjet.com/*

[24] The Cicret Bracelet: It's like a tablet...but on your skin! (n.d.). Retrieved December 05, 2014, from *http://www.cicret.com/wordpress/?page_id=17920*

[25] TouchPico: Turn Any Surface Into A Touch Screen | Indiegogo. (n.d.). Retrieved December 05, 2014, from *http://tinyurl.com/k3pcvpm*

[26] *www.io2technologies.comb*

[27] wwHYPERLINK "http://www.wikipedia.com/"wHYPERLINK

"http://www.wikipedia.com/".HYPERLINK "http://www.wikipedia.com/"wHYPERLINK "http://www.wikipedia. com/"iHYPERLINK "http://www.wikipedia.com/"kHYPERLINK "http://www.wikipedia.com/"iHYPERLINK "http://www.wikipedia.com/"pHYPERLINK "http://www.wikipedia.com/"eHYPERLINK "http://www.wikipedia.com/"dHYPERLINK "http://www.wikipedia.com/"iHYPERLINK "http://www.wikipedia.com/"aHYPERLINK "http://www.wikipedia.com/".HYPERLINK "http://www.wikipedia.com/"cHYPERLINK "http://www.wikipedia.com/"oHYPERLINK "http://www.wikipedia.com/"m

[28] *www.heliodisplay.com*

[29] wwHYPERLINK "http://www.google.com/"wHYPERLINK "http://www.google.com/".HYPERLINK "http://www.google.com/"googlHYPERLINK "http://www.google.com/"eHYPERLINK "http://www.google.com/".HYPERLINK "http://www.google.com/"cHYPERLINK "http://www.google.com/"oHYPERLINK "http://www.google.com/"m

[30] Ahmed Elmorshidy, Ph.D., Holographic Projection Technology: The World is Changing, Journal of telecommunication, Volume 2, Issue 2, and May 2010

16

A Security Mechanism for SaaS Cloud Service Model Using Dynamic Network Strategy Plan

Teenu Jose

ABSTRACT

Cloud computing is a computing paradigm, where a large pool of systems are connected in private or public networks, to provide dynamically scalable infrastructure for application, data and file storage. With the advent of this technology, the cost of computation, application hosting, content storage and delivery is reduced significantly. Now a days the organizations are trying to migrate into a cloud system, so the cloud system should be secure enough to deals with the organizational services. The SaaS model is easily vulnerable to attacks. The main cause for the attack is the static network configurations. These static network configurations may open the attackers to study the weakness of the network and this will help the attacker to launch the attack. The cloud models mainly suffer DoS attack. The main reason behind it is the static network configuration. So the paper suggests a security mechanism to protect SaaS model from DoS attack. For this a dynamic network strategy plan is used. In dynamic strategy plan, the network configurations can be done dynamically. To avoid DoS attack, we are changing the IP address of the network host using NOX controller algorithm. It is very difficult to implement the traditional network; so software defined networking is adopted.

Keywords : software defined networking; Cloud Computing; DoS attack.

1. INTRODUCTION

Cloud computing is an innovative technology. Cloud computing refers to the use of networked infrastructure software and capacity to provide resources to users in an on-demand environment. With cloud computing, information is stored in centralized servers and cached temporarily on clients that can include desktop computers, notebooks, handhelds and other devices. Cloud infrastructure can reside within the company's datacenters or on external cloud computing resources. It encompasses any subscription based or pay per use service that extends existing IT capabilities. By design, cloud computing is scalable, flexible and elastic –offering a way to easily increase capacity or add additional capabilities on demand without investing in new and expensive infrastructure, training new personnel or licensing more software..

The characteristics of cloud are 1) Resource pooling: the resources are pooled by the cloud providers and shared between multiple customers according to their requirements. 2) Broad network access: These resources on the cloud are accessible through standard network protocols over the Internet. 3) Rapid Elasticity: In a matter of minutes resources may be provisioned to scale out and released to scale in. Therefore, elasticity of resources are very rapid. 4) Measured service: The cloud provider measures and generally charges for usage of CPU, memory, disk, network bandwidth, or other resources. 5) On-demand self-service: Resources can be provisioned via automated mechanisms at the time of their demand only. Combining these two concepts give a great advantage to business application as well as IT industry.

Software Defined Networking (SDN) is an emerging network architecture where network control is decoupled from forwarding and is directly programmable. This migration of control, formerly tightly bound in individual network devices, into accessible computing devices enables the underlying infrastructure to be abstracted for applications and network services, which can treat the network as a logical or virtual entity. Network intelligence is (logically) centralized in software-based SDN controllers, which maintain a global view of the network. As a result, the network appears to the applications and policy engines as a single, logical switch. With SDN, enterprises and carriers gain vendor-independent control over the entire network from a single logical point, which greatly simplifies the network design and operation. SDN also greatly simplifies the network devices themselves, since they no longer need to understand and process thousands of protocol standards but merely accept instructions from the SDN controllers.

The SDN architecture mainly contains 3 layers application layer, control layer and data layer. Application layer contains application in the network. The control layer contains the SDN controller software that controls entire network. The data layer contains the network devices. The main difference between the traditional network and the SDN is the separation between the control plane and data plane. In traditional network each network device has separate control plane and data plane. In SDN the control plane is moved into a centralized controller.

SDN has several advantages over traditional networks. First it provides centralized control of multi-vendor environments: SDN control software can control any Open Flow-enabled network device from any vendor, including switches, routers, and virtual switches rather than having to manage groups of devices from individual vendors. Second, it reduces complexity through automation; SDN offers a flexible network automation and management framework, which makes it possible to develop tools that automate many management tasks that are done manually today. Third, it allows higher rate of innovation; SDN adoption accelerates business innovation by allowing IT network operators to literally program and reprogram the network in real time to meet specific business needs and user requirements as they arise.

The paper concentrates on providing a security mechanism to SDN based SaaS cloud model for avoiding DoS attacks. The main security aspects of cloud system are availability. So the attacker wishes to compromise the availability of the cloud system, then the attacker launches DoS attacks. In this paper the attack detection and prevention are performed by the SDN controller.

2. RELATED WORKS

The paper by Qiao and Richard[9] specifies the issues in cloud and the security measures. The first issue is the authentication. Authentication ensures that the legitimate users access the resources. In cloud environment, each user has to prove his identity before ~~it~~ accessing the data. There are several authentication methods for cloud like Single password authentication, Knowledge based authentication and Two factor authentication. Second issue is authorization; it ensures that the user submits its own details for the login purpose. Authorization also checks the access level of the user. There is a policy based authorization in which the user can develop a policy in order to protect his data. For securing the data encryption is performed. There are several encryption methods used like hardware based encryption, software based encryption and full disk encryption.

The paper, data security mechanism for cloud [10] specifies a security mechanism; in this the data is classified into private and public data. The private data is stored in the storage space of the respective user. It is accessible by a particular user. If the user wants to share the data with someone, then it is stored on public compartments so it can be accessed by trusted users of the owner of the data.

The paper by Diogo Menezes [4] specifies the attacks on SaaS cloud model. SaaS is one of the service models of cloud computing. SaaS will provide Application and the required databases to the clients. The SaaS service model is highly vulnerable. The attacks are as follows:

DoS Attack : In this attack all the attack nodes will purposefully send flood messages to make the node unavailable to the client machine in the cloud.

Account Lockout : The attacker tries to lock out the valid user account by failing the authentication process several times. So the valid user is unable to use the cloud system.

Buffer overflows : The attacker overflows the buffer. If the buffer is in the stack, the attacker will overwrite the address of the calling function; this will give the attacker the over all control of the program.

Cross site scripting : It is a technique used to add script to a trusted site that will be executed on other users' browsers.

Access Control : Access control functionality decides which request will be granted. If the access controls mechanism is not enough to restrict unauthorized request, it will compromise the entire network.

Privilege Escalation : A privilege escalation attack is a type of network intrusion that takes advantage of programming errors or design flaws to grant the attacker elevated access to the network and its associated data and applications.

Network Penetration : The attacker will find out the security weakness of the network and then try to get access to the network for future attacks.

Session Hijacking : The attacker will take the control over the user session after the user successfully entered into the session. For this attacker should know the session IDs.

The paper by Hyojoon[1] specifies what is SDN and how SDN manages the network. This paper proposes SDN as a key for network management and network configuration. SDN separates the dataplane and controlplane. The network is controlled by the controller and the dataplane devices just forward the datapackets. SDN supports frequent changes to network conditions and state, providing support for network configuration in a high level language, and providing better visibility and control over tasks for performing network diagnosis and troubleshooting. SDN brings several advantages, first is through a software program change the behavior of network devices. Second, it will give a centralized control so there is a no need to configure individual devices to change the network behavior; instead the controller make the forwarding decision. This paper also proposes a method to implement high level policies in SDN called Procera. Procera is based on functional reactive programming (FRP). Procera allows operators to express high level policies with this language, and translates such polices into a set of forwarding rules, which are used to enforce the policy on the underlying network infrastructure, using Open Flow.

The paper SDN controller mechanism for flexible and customized networking [2] is a reference for SDN controller (SC) functionality. Controller mechanism forms the base for autonomous network operations. It is possible to deploy any application directly on SC, due to security reasons application for network management and provisioning of network devices are allowed to deploy on SC. Routing is done by the SC, for SC it is a simple task because it knows the status and all information about the network. There is an exception case; for external routing it requires routing via border interfaces. In such situations an application is run on a host that takes care of the external routing. B4 SDN is an example for a network that uses such an application. Other functionalities of SC are: Access Control for Flows (AC4F), Multipath Unicast and Anycast Routing for QoS and Load Balancing Control (MPR), Multicast Routing for QoS Control (MCR), Path Selection for End-to-End QoS Flows (PS4Q), Transactions for Flow calendaring (T4C), Energy Savings Control (ESC), & Co-operation with other SDN controllers (C2C).

The paper Towards Secure and Dependable Software-Defined Networks [3] defines 3 threat vectors that are significant to SDN and the security measures. The first threat vector is attack on control plane communication. The weakest link between the controller and the device may introduce DoS attack. Once the attacker gets an access to control plane then it will launch DoS attack. Several papers recommended that the TSL/SSL mechanisms are not the optimal solution. The proposed solutions are diversity, dynamic switch association and trust between controller and devices. Second threat vector is attacks on and vulnerabilities in controller. This is considered as the severe threat. If an attacker is able to attack the controller then he or she can compromise the entire network. The solutions are trust between controllers and apps, security domains and secure components. The last threat vector is lack of mechanisms to ensure the trust between the controller and management application. Possible solutions are secure components, security domains and replication. The SDN introduces two interfaces southbound and northbound. Southbound is an interface between dataplane and controlplane. Northbound is between policy and the control layer. OpenFlow[3] is a well known southbound interface. There are a variety of OpenFlow controllers, for example, NOX, Floodlight, and Maestro. NOX is a framework that allows developers to program their software program with C++ or Python, using a set of application programming interfaces (APIs) to interact with OpenFlow-capable switches, while Floodlight is a Java-based controller. Maestro focuses on achieving better performance and scalability in a centralized controller using multithreading.

FRESCO[5] is a security framework for SDN. It allows composition different modules. It provides an API that allow the security practitioners to program different modules such as monitoring, detection module these modules are then known as modular library. These modular libraries are combined to form a security framework. FRESCO have 16 library modules and each module has 5 interfaces, by assigning value to these interfaces and connecting several modules FRESCO can create different security framework.

There is authentication and access control mechanism for SDN[6]. This mechanism involve authentication using datalink layer protocols. The proposed mechanism applies IEEE 802.1X standard and Extensible Authentication Protocol (EAP). A virtual router sends an authentication request, standardized by IEEE 802.1X, and POX controller redirects it to the Authenticator. Then, the Authenticator responds it and the Supplicant host sends its credentials. The Authenticator checks the credentials of the Supplicant against RADIUS server, running the authentication method defined in EAP. If credentials are correct, the Authenticator sends a success message for Supplicant host and sends an authorization and confirmation message for POX via a SSL secure channel. This message identifies the Supplicant by its MAC address, confirms the success of the authentication, and also informs the identity of the Supplicant. After authentication, our application running over POX allows the supplicant host to access network resources. In case of revocation of the credentials of the supplicant host, the Authenticator communicates POX, which immediately denies the host access to the network.

There is some security mechanism for SDN [7]. First method is Ethane it is similar to basic SDN architecture; there is a centralized controller that implements the security mechanism and the Ethane switches simply forward the datapackets. The drawback of this method is that the application traffic compromises the network security. Another mechanism is FlowTag architecture that uses minimally modified middleboxes. There is an API that is used by the middlebox to communicate with the controller. The FlowTag contains traffic flow information in packet headers that provides flow tracking and controlled routing. The disadvantage is it works on predefined policies and does not support dynamic action.

3. PROPOSED SYSTEM

The proposed system detects DoS attack in SDN based cloud and prevents the attack by changing the IP address of host dynamically. The main reason for the DoS attack is the static IP address of the host. Once the attacker finds the IP address of the target host the attacker can launch the DoS attack. The proposed system also avoids this problem by detecting the ongoing attack and changing the IP address dynamically.

A. Architecture

The proposed system will detect and prevent DoS attack in SDN based cloud system. The main feature of SDN is the separation of control plane and data plane.

The main advantage of SDN is that it provides centralized control and it also allows to change the network configuration whenever the network needs. These benefits force the business organization to adopt SDN.

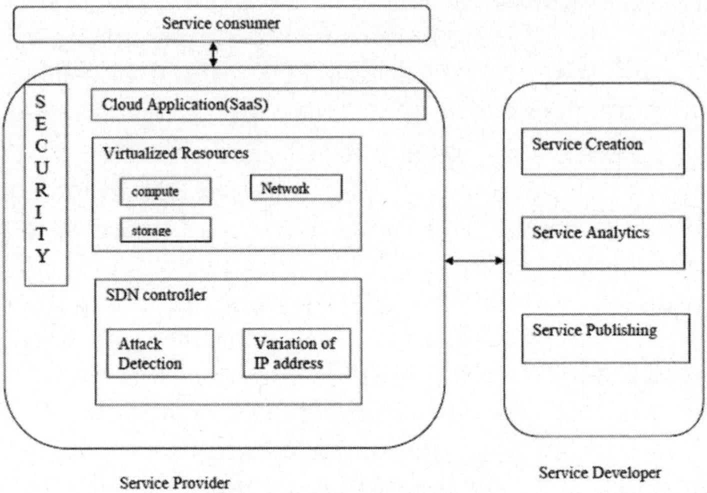

Fig. 3.1. System Architecture

The architecture of the proposed system is shown in figure 3.1. The architecture mainly contains 3 components service consumer, service provider and service developer. Service consumer refers to the client that uses the service provided by the service provider. Service provider is to act as a server; service provider will provide the service requested by the client application. Service provider contains the cloud application, virtualized resources and other cloud computing functionalities. It also contains an extra functional module SDN controller. SDN controller is a software that contains sub module like load balancer, routing, topology manager, accounting, attack detection and variation of IP address. Attack detection sub module is used to detect DoS attack in the cloud system. When an attack is detected, the controller will immediately change the IP address of the host, and then update the flow entries.

B. Module Description

The proposed system mainly contain 2 modules first is attack detection and second is variation of IP address. Attack detection is performed using IDS. For changing the IP address NOX controller algorithm is used. The core function of these modules such as IDS and NOX controller algorithm are appeared as the functions of SDN controller. The modules are resided in the controller. Whenever the controller finds any abnormal traffic in the network, the attack detection module collects attack information (whether the abnormal behavior due to DoS attack) from IDS. If the attack is DoS attack then the network variation module implement the NOX controller algorithm.

1. Attack Detection

For detecting the DoS attack Intrusion Detection System is used. IDS on SDN environment mainly contains 2 components. First is OF collector and second is anomaly detection. The Collector module is responsible for data gathering, a prerequisite in order to perform flow-based anomaly detection. This module collects flow information and periodically exports them to the Anomaly Detection module. In anomaly detection module, Data produced by the previous module are subsequently fed to the Anomaly Detection module at periodic time intervals, thus creating discrete time windows. For every time-window this module inspects all flow entries, exposing any flow-related network anomaly and identifying a potential attacker or the victim of the attack.

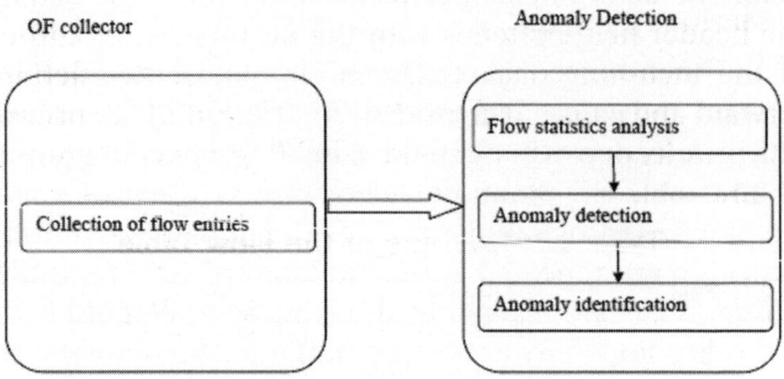

Fig. 3.2. Anomaly Detection

2. Variation of IP Address

To change IP address dynamically NOX controller algorithm is used. In this algorithm all OF packets are checked. If the source IP address of the packet is real IP then the packet is forwarded according to the flow entries. If the IP address is virtual, then the switch forwards the packet to the controller and installs new flow entries to the flow table. This algorithm mainly deals with how the flow table entries will be changed after the variation of IP address occurred. For routing flow table entry is required. The routers make the routing decision depends upon the entry in the flow table. The flow table entries are updated or installed by the controller rather than the routers it self. This feature reduces the overhead of routers to maintain their routing information. In SDN the router just forward the packet does not do anything on the flow table. In traditional network whenever there is a change in the route, each router needs to update their flow table. But in case of SDN the change should be made in the controller only. The controller will provide these updates to the router. The flow table entry mainly contains 3 fields such as header field, Actions and priority. Header field contain the IP address or the port number; whenever a packet is arrived the destination IP address is compared with the header field. The action field specifies what action to be taken if the header field matches with the destination IP address of the incoming packet. There are mainly two actions, forward and cancel. The priority field specifies the priority. The priority depends upon the host IP address. An example of flow table as follows.

Table 4.1. Example of the Flow Table

Header Field	Action	Priorities
If in_port = 1	Output: 2	100
If IP = 10.1.2.1	Rewrite to 129.4.5.1 and output:6	200

The explanation of the table as follows: if a packet comes in port 1 then output packet via port 2. If a packet has IP address 10.1.2.1 then rewrite the address to 129.4.5.1 and output via port 6.

NOX Controller Algorithm

1. Determine unused ranges
2. Determine range to subnet assignments
3. For all packets p from OF-switches do
    a. If p is a DNS response for host h_i then
        i. Set DNS addr to current vIP(h_i), TTLH"0
    b. Else if p is a TCP-SYN or UDP from host h_i to h_j then
        i. If p.src is internal then
            1. Install in flow in src OF switch with action srcIP(p):=vIP(h_i)
            2. Install out flow in src OF switch with action dstIP(p):=rIP(hi)
        ii. End if

iii. If p.dst is rIP then
   1. If h_i access to h_j is authorized install in and out flow in dest OF- switch
iv. End if
v. Else[p.dst is vIP]
   1. Install in flow in dest OF switch with action dstIP(p):=rIP(h_j)
   2. Install out flow in dest OF switch with action srcIP(p):=vIP(h_j)
vi. End if

c. End if
d. For all mutation of each host hi do
   i. Set vIP(hi) to a new vIP
e. End for

4. End for

4. CONCLUSION

Cloud computing implements the concept of anything as a service. Most of the businesses organizations are now migrate into SDN based cloud because of the advantages of both SDN and the cloud. The main disadvantage of SDN and cloud is they are easily vulnerable to attacks. The main attack is the DoS attack because this attack compromises the availability of the cloud system. This paper proposes a security mechanism to detect and recover from DoS attack. The studies show that the main reason for the DoS attack is the static network configuration. To avoid this, the proposed system adopts a security mechanism that dynamically changes the IP address of the host. NOX controller algorithm is used to change the IP address dynamically. The proposed system also avoids the problem of static environment. The proposed system dynamically avoids the DoS attacks.

REFERENCES

[1] Hyojoon Kim and Nick Feamster: "Improving Network Management with Software Defined Networking" IEEE,communication Magazine, February 2013

[2] Jacek Wytr²ebowicz, Thorsten Ries, Khoa Truong Dinh, and S³awomirKukli´nski: "SDN Controller Mechanisms for Flexible and Customized Networking" International Journal of electronics and Telecommunications, Volume 6,September 2014

[3] Seugwon Shin, Phillip Porras, Vinod Yegneswaran, Martin Fong, GuofeiGu, Mabry Tyson: "FRESCO: Modular Composable Security Services for Software-Defined Networks", appeared in the ISOC Network and Distributed System Security Symposium February 2013

[4] Diogo Menezes Ferrazani Mattos, Lyno Henrique Gonc¸alvesFerraz: "AuthFlow: Authentication and Access Control Mechanism for Software Defined Networking" September 2013

[5] Diego Kreutz, Fernando M. V. Ramos, and Paulo Verissimo: "Towards Secure and Dependable Software-Defined Networks" proceedings of the second ACM SIGCOMM workshop on hot topics in SDN, August 2013

[6] Sandra Scott-Hayward, Gemma O'Callaghan and SakirSezer: "SDN Security: A Survey" IEEE publications,November 2013

[7] RowanKloti, VasileiosKotronis and Paul Smith: "Openflow : security analysis" IEEE publications, April 2013

[8] Rodrigo Braga, EdjardMota and Alexandre Passito: "Lightweight DDoS Flooding attack detection using NOX/Openflow", IEEE 35th conference, October 2010

[9] Qiao Yan and F. Richard Yu: "Distributed Denial of Service Attacks in Software-Defined Networking with Cloud Computing", communication magazine vol.53, April 2015

[10] Philip Porras, Seungwon Shin: "A security enforcement kernel for openflow networks"

[11] S. Sezer, S. Scott-Hayward, P. Chouhan, B. Fraser, D. Lake, J. Finnegan, N. Viljoen, M. Miller, and N. Rao,"Are we ready for SDN? Implementation challenges for software-defined networks,"Communications Magazine,IEEE, vol. 51, no. 7, 2013.

[12] .Jajodia et al. Moving Target Defense, Springer, 2011

[13] k.Giotis et al. Combining OpenFlow and sFlow for an effective and scalable anomaly detection and mitigation mechanism on SDN environments, computer networks vol.62, October 2013

[14] JH Jafarian et al. Openflow random host mutation: transparent moving target defense using software defined networking, Proceedings of the first workshop on Hot topics in software defined networks, 2012

17

Automated Library System: Toc H as A Simple Base Model to Start With

Binod Kumar N
Dileep Rajan
Fr.Bibi Alias
Jitha Thankachan

ABSTRACT

Equitable access to education, reach of education to far-flung remote areas and the like have been identified as the core areas marked for the overall development a nation. In this noble and arduous task of nation building, Toc H Institute of Science and Technology, Arakkunnam is contributing its share in the thrust areas of education especially in Technical & Managerial education. The need to excel diverse disciplines taught at an institution cannot be achieved without a technologically advanced library equipped to meet the ever growing information needs of academic community. The automated system and net work of Toc H libraries with e-books, online journals & a Digital Library connecting learning materials developed in-house as well as acquired serving the concerned community in an admirable manner is presented here as a model any library can adopt at the initial stage.

1. INTRODUCTION

Bridging the traditional and the modern has essentially become very complex in the present scenario struggling to meet the demands of the traditional requirements of the library and retrieval and dissemination of knowledge and information in the digital age.

Simply put, information retrieval is finding information. It is done through organizing, processing and providing information in its entirety. But technology driven retrieval allows the users to locate any specific information. With this end in view, information retrieval systems can be designed. Information searching and user behavior are given paramount importance in the Toc H Library as technology is all pervasive in the modern library world.

2. OPAC SYSTEM

OPAC - Online Public Access Catalogue is an important facility provided by the library to the members for easy access to the documents. Through this facility user can search for books by author, title, subject, accession number, publisher, ISBN etc. In the Information retrieval menu, there are 3 columns, viz., FIELD NAME, OPERATOR and LOOK FOR. Users can change the field name according to their need. If the user knows the title of the book, he can consider the field name as Title and enter the first few letters of the title in the column 'Look For'. Or if users know only the author, then can select the field name as Author and give the name of the author in the column' Look For'. Then the user can click on 'Search', and he will get the result. Then can check its shelf number, accession number and its place.

3. SEARCH METHOD

OPAC - Online Public Access Catalogue is to help the users for easy access to the documents. Through this facility user can search for books by author, title, subject, accession number, publisher, ISBN, etc. For example, if user would like to search the book "Engineering Graphics" authored by P I Varghese, the user needs to follow the following procedures:

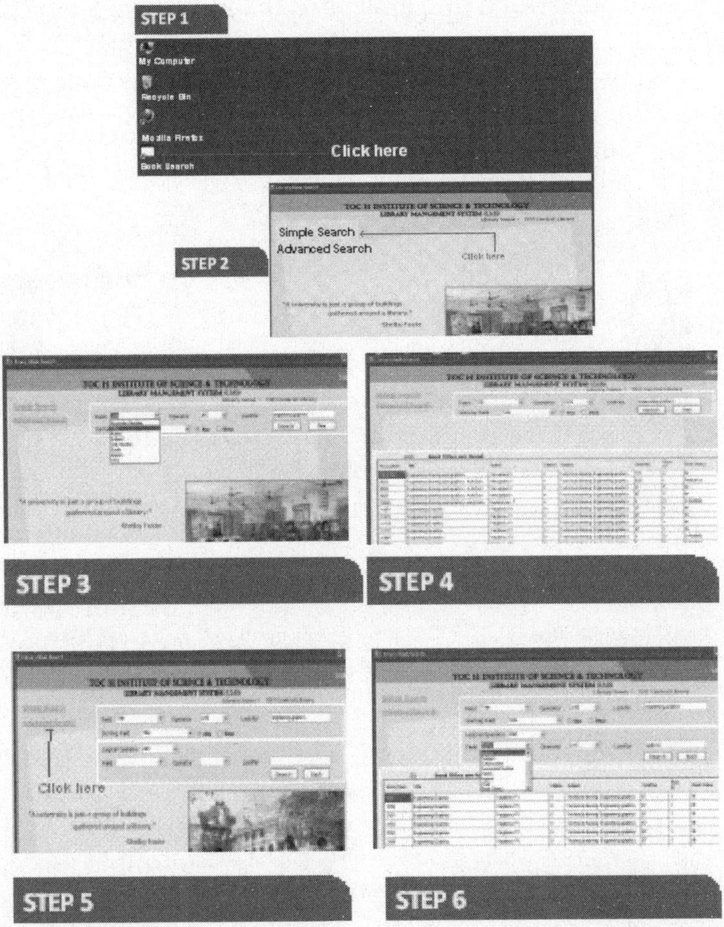

4. WEB OPAC

TIST Central Library provides Web OPAC facility to its users. This is a Web based service through which anybody can access TIST library catalogue and collections like books, journals, multimedia, seminar reports, project reports, research books etc from anywhere in the world. This facility is very much useful to the students and faculty because they can know if the books of their interest are available or not in the library through this Web OPAC. The students need not come always to the library for searching the books; they can access it from anywhere via internet search the site *http://www.tistcochin.edu.in* our college site to get the same. In this, both search and advance search are available. In advance search every type of activity is done.

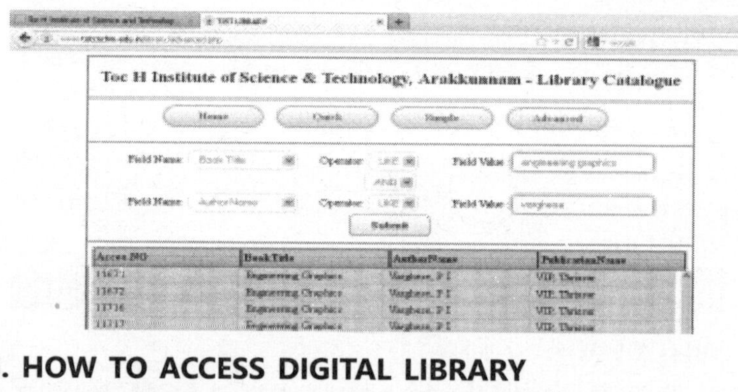

5. HOW TO ACCESS DIGITAL LIBRARY

It is very easy to access TIST digital library. First user has to open the browser and give the term "digital library" in the address bar; then user can get the home page of

Digital Library. From there user can access and use the library collections. TIST Library collections include the following categories:

Videos, Project Reports, Seminar Reports, E Journals, E books and Question Papers

6. E JOURNALS & E BOOKS

In the present scenario of information technology, paperless society is a growing concept. To provide an insight into the onslaught of paperless society, most of the reputed e-journals are available with the TIST Sarabhai Digital Library.

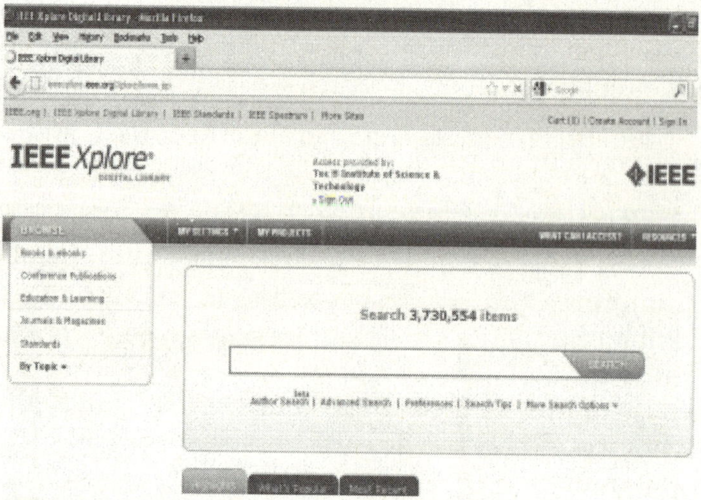

7. USER ORIENTATION

User education is an important service in a library. Instructions are given to the users to help them to make the best use of the library. By educating the user, the quality of library services can be improved. Thus there is an utmost need for user education which provides the knowledge and skills necessary for a user to find out information in his own way. So user educ.0ation is given its due importance in the beginning of every academic session.

TIST Library gives an orientation to every first year student at the beginning of the session in which oral and computer aided methods are used. User orientation is given inside the Digital library, which makes the user practically aware of the nuances of the library. All information about the services and functions offered by the library are provided with graphic aids, and thereby the users can understand how to use the collections in the library, how to search books in the OPAC system, use of Web OPAC, arrangement of books in the shelves etc. Most importantly, they are given instructions on information retrieval system whereby they can retrieve any information from any part of the globe. Through this orientation service, the users get all information about the library rules, fines, book circulation, renewal, return etc. Thus this orientation programme is very helpful to the users to know all about the library and its various services.

8. USER STUDY

TIST Library system conducts user studies regularly and improves the system according to the responses in accordance with the changing needs of users. User study is the study relating to library use in all aspects. The purpose of user study is to improve existing conditions in the library. It helps to identify users and their specific information requirements. The main objectives are

- To determine the type of users
- To identify their information needs
- To establish priorities in relation to these needs
- To establish the level of satisfaction
- To determine user behavior in relation to information
- To evaluate the services provided and the establishment of new services.

The TIST Central Library follows Questionnaire Method for user study. And through this, TIST library prepares a user satisfaction index and takes necessary steps to address the weak points appearing in the questionnaire.

9. AFTERWORD

That education provides the foundation for development of peoples and nations is now a well acknowledged and accepted theory. This is more so for developing countries where education is perceived as a growth driver while combating important issues with an eye on equitable development.

No doubt the thrust areas of equitable access to

education, reach of education to far- flung remote areas etc.... have been identified as the core areas marked for the overall development of one and all. In this noble and arduous task of nation building, Toc H Institute of Science and Technology, Arakkunnam is contributing its share in the thrust areas of education especially in Technical & Managerial education. Realising their relevance in the modern times, this Institute is endeavoring continually to improve and excel at imparting Curricular, Co-Curricular and Extra Curricular education and training to Undergraduate and Post graduate students in Engineering, Technology and Management Studies by synergizing state-of-the-art infrastructure, teaching and learning support systems to achieve and sustain societal acceptance and acknowledgement.

The need to excel in all the diverse disciplines taught here cannot be achieved without a technologically advanced library equipped to meet the ever growing challenges of the highly competitive world accessible to all. The TIST library admirably meets the demands and pressures of every type from any corner. Spread over a total sprawling area of around 10000 square feet, the Central, Digital and the MBA Libraries with additional departmental libraries with a collection of over 34000 scrupulously chosen books along with e-books, online journals& a Digital Library cater to the ever growing needs of the inquisitive minds. The library with its numerous volumes of books, CDs, IEEE, ASTM, IJSOM, ASME, ASCE, McGrawHill, Elsevier, EBSCO Online facility, NPTEL Learning materials complement the learning process in an admirable manner.

Committed to educating the youth to make them better actualized so as to make a difference in the world, the TIST Library is doing yeomen service to every inquisitive scholar to outshine by updating all the facilities here at par with the best in our country. Rabindranath Tagore rightly said, "The lantern which I carry in my hand makes enemy of the darkness of the farther road".

REFERENCES

[1] Glancing through TIST Library; First Edition, January 2012; published by Toc H Institute of Science & Technology, Arakkunnam

[2] Raman Nair R. Developing Digital Libraries; need for Proper Strategies/2005 In: Advances in Library and Information Science. Jodhpur, Scientific Publishers, pp. 259-271

[3] Student prospects 2013-14, Toc H Institute of Science & Technology, Arakkunnam

[4] TIST Library Brochure; 2nd Edition May 2015, published by TIST Library & Information Center, Toc H Institute of Science & Technology, Arakkunnam

18

Survey on DNS Amplification Defence Mechanisms

Jincy Kurian

ABSTRACT

A DNS amplification attack is a kind of distributed denial of service (DDoS) attack that takes advantage of the fact that a small DNS query can generate much larger response. An attacker can direct a large volume of network traffic to a victim's system by sending relatively small DNS queries. The attacker spoofs the IP address of the victim to reflect the network traffic using the DNS server. This makes it difficult to trace the attacker. The security of amplification attacks has grown in recent years.9 defense mechanisms for DNS Amplification Attacks are discussed in this paper. While DNS amplification attacks are well understood, the best defensive strategy is less obvious.

Keywords : DNS Amplification attack, IP Spoofing, DNS Dampening, RRL, BGP route flap dampening

1. INTRODUCTION

Internet has designed without taken into security consideration about any security issues. For providing services to end-hosts, the internet follows a client-server model. This design model was utilized for executing threats such as Denial of Service and Distributed Denial of Service which used to disrupt the functionality of the serving entity. DNS amplification attack [12] is a type of distributed denial of service (DDoS) attack.

In this attack, the attacker sends a DNS query packet to a DNS server. In the process of creating this query packet, the attacker forges source IP address field of DNS query packet so that it contains the IP address of the targeted victim, rather than the actual sender of the packet. On receiving and processing the query packet, the DNS server sends a response back to the indicated source address of the query, which is the address of the victim. When the response packet arrives at the victim, the victim will process the packet, and then discard it. But, at this time, the DNS amplification attack has occurred and the DNS response consumed a portion of the victim's bandwidth and computational resources. And this attack is difficult to detect and mitigate.

In this paper, we focus on various DNS amplification defence mechanisms. Each mechanism has its own advantages and disadvantages. The rest of the paper is organized as follows. Section 2 focuses on DNS Amplification Defence Mechanisms. Finally in section 3, we conclude the paper.

2. DNS AMPLIFICATION DEFENSE MECHANISMS

Although DNS amplification attacks are quite powerful, but there are certain mechanisms that can defend against such attacks. The purpose of the presented solutions is to protect the victim machines from the DNS amplification attack caused by spoofed DNS queries. A proper defence mechanism will need to remove the amplification factor, while continuing to service legitimate requests. The 9 defence methods are as follows.

2.1. DAAD(DNS Amplification Attack Detector)

DAAD mechanism [1] monitors the real time DNS traffic and alert the security supervisors when necessary. This scheme is based on the one-to-one mapping of DNS requests and responses. The mechanism uses a monitor to record DNS requests and responses using the IPTraf tool. IPTraf is a simple tool used to monitor inbound and outbound network traffic passing through interface. The captured network data is stored in a MySQL database. When a DNS message is received the DAAD determines whether the message is a response or a request. For any received {request, response} pair the DAAD tool creates a new entry to the request / response table. When a message is identified as a response the DAAD module checks for the existence of the corresponding request. If the IP address of the response packet does not match with none of the requests logged previously in a given time frame is marked as malicious. Additionally, as soon as the number of malicious messages exhibits a given administrator-specified threshold, an alert is generated and use firewalls to block attackers IP address. All the parameters in the procedure that is, timeframe, threshold are updated depend on the administrative security policies in the specific network domain.

This is a simple scheme that enables administrators to distinguish between normal traffic and attack traffic. The drawback of the proposed mechanism is that it does not scale for large networks because it needs to store all the DNS traffic queries and responses.

2.2. Efficient and Low Cost Hardware Defence against DNS Amplification Attacks

This approach [2] makes use of semantic nature of DNS protocol that is one-to-one mapping of DNS requests and responses. The hardware approach includes two phases: Detection and Filter. The number of DNS requests and responses are counted in each time interval during the detection phase. The approach uses the as the threshold to report the attack if number of responses is th+1 times of the number of requests. Using this scheme, the attack is detected with high accuracy and short response time and with little cost. After detecting DNS amplification attack, the filter scheme starts to work. The main task of the filter scheme is to distinguish the legitimate DNS responses from the attack traffic with an affordable computation and memory cost.

To handle this, we use a two-Bloom filter solution. A bloom filter is a simple data structure which is used to store the DNS queries in each time interval ä. When a DNS request is received, the 4-tuple (destination IP, source IP, destination port, DNS transaction ID) are extracted and insert in to the bloom filter. If an incoming DNS response is received, the scheme extracts its 4-tuple as an item and queries this item from the Bloom filter. If the item is in Bloom filter, then the response is legitimate otherwise not.

This is an efficient and low-cost hardware approach used to defend against the DNS amplification attacks at the leaf router of victim's ISP or organization. This approach works well but the problem with this is that it is hardware-based, which makes it hard to update and extend.

2.3. Best Current Practices 38

BCP38 [4] is a mechanism that prevents spoofing IP addresses by allowing routers to check the validity of an IP address. A customer is assigned an IP address by the internet service provider (ISP). The ISP can then check incoming packets for a valid IP address. If the IP address does not match the range that the customer should have, the traffic can be dropped.

This mechanism prevents spoofing IP addresses

which reside outside the range of the customer or the ISP depending on where BCP38 is implemented. BCP38 would be the ultimate solution because it will prevent IP address spoofing, unfortunately it is unlikely to be implemented throughout the whole internet in the near future.

2.4. Response Rate Limiting

Response Rate Limiting (RRL)[3] is a mechanism for limiting the amount of unique responses returned by a DNS server. This can limit the effectiveness of a DNS amplification attack by dropping responses that exceed the configured rate limit. The rate limiting works as follows. When the server generates a response to a DNS query, the requesters IP addresses are grouped into buckets. By default IPv4 addresses on the same 24 subnet are put into a single bucket. The wild-card, zone name or query name is stored together with the IP address and the boolean error indicator (response code: REFUSED, FORMERR or SERV-FAIL).

The server uses <(IP), (NAME), error-status> to decide how to act upon a request. This information is used as the state. The state is used to count the unique response returned by the DNS server. If the amount of unique responses exceeds the configured limit, the server drops requests for a specific IP or network. The server can also ask the requester to retry using TCP instead. Because TCP is a connection oriented protocol, attacker cannot able perform DNS amplification attack further.

When using RRL the victim might still notice it is under attack, because it receives DNS responses for which no request was sent out for a limited time. The problem with this method is that an attacker might also be able to circumvent this defense mechanism by distributing this attack over a large number of DNS servers, to stay under the RRL limits of the DNS servers.

2.5. Spoof Detection for Preventing DoS Attacks against DNS Servers

An effective defence against spoofing-based DoS attacks on DNS servers requires source address spoof detection [5]. The spoof detection strategies are implemented in a firewall module called DNS guard, which can be deployed without modifying protected DNS servers or DNS requesters. The DNS guard is implemented between the local recursive server and authoritative server. In this strategy, a DNS server sends a distinct cookie to each requesting host, and the requester associates each request it sends to the DNS server with the server's corresponding cookie. . The cookie is computed as follows. For each DNS request whose source IP address is source IP, its cookie is: c = MD5 (source_IP, key).The key is the 76-byte secret key hold by the DNS guard. By checking the cookie that comes with each incoming request, it is possible to determine if a DNS request indeed originates from the source address indicated in the packet.

The spoof detection schemes generate no false positives. And this is the effective mechanism to detect the spoofing DNS requests. However, it can only verify the requests between DNS servers. The requests from general DNS resolver clients, which are the main attack tools in the amplification attacks, cannot be verified.

2.6. DNS Dampening

DNS dampening [6] is based on BGP route flap dampening. The basic idea behind DNS dampening is to collect penalty points per requester based on the query type, the size of the response and other parameters. If the penalty points reach the configured limit, dampening will start. While in dampening state the server drops all queries from the attacker. Penalty points will be decreased exponentially over time. When the penalty point drop below a secondary limit dampening will stop and the server will start to process the request again.

Incoming requests are classified and penalty points are assigned based on the factors such as query type and size of the response. Every query receives penalty points and additional penalty points are added when a query is repeated with the same query ID and based on the size of response. The drawback of this approach is that it provides no mechanism to counter false positives. This could lead to a legitimate client to be blocked from the DNS server.

2.7. Characterizing Optimal DNS Amplification Attacks and Effective Mitigation

The approach [7] creates an off-premises DNS resolver for the victim's organization and creates a tunnel, using virtual private network protocols such as IPSec or SSL, between the off-premise resolver and the organization's on-site DNS resolver. Then configure the on-site resolver to forward all DNS requests through the tunnel to the off-site DNS resolver while configuring the off-site resolver to operate recursively on behalf of the organization. Organizations could then simply request their upstream Internet providers to filter all DNS response traffic to the organization.

This will filter the attack traffic, but will not affect the tunneled traffic between the resolvers, allowing organizations to maintain full DNS resolver functionality. Many cloud providers would allow an organization to cheaply store and run a virtual machine that acts as an off-site DNS resolver. Since the resolver requires minimal computational resources, such hosting would be widely available for less than a dollar per day of use. As long as the organization's upstream provider can filter the attack, organizations could shrug off DNS amplification attacks of arbitrary size with minimal expense. With widespread adoption, the value of amplification attacks would decrease for attackers and their use may decline. That is the victim organization may also monitor the attack, discover the colluding entities, and secure the internal client. The problem with this approach is that it does require the cooperation of a third-party, that third party is the victim organization's ISP.

2.8. Fingerprinting Internet DNS Amplification DDoS Activities

This paper [8] proposes a approach that is used to infer and characterize Internet-scale DNS amplification DDoS attacks by leveraging the darknet space. Darknet traffic is Internet traffic destined to routable but unused Internet addresses (i.e., dark sensors). The approach exploits the idea of analyzing DNS queries that target the darknet space that were originally intended by the attacker to reach Internet open DNS resolvers. The approach consists of 2 components: detection and rate classification. Detection component analyse the DNS queries targeting darknet addresses. By analysing, the detection component calculate packet count, number of scanned hosts, query type, attack duration, packet rate.

The component use threshold value of the parameters as 25. And the component labels a flow of traffic as a DNS amplification DDoS attack if it has sent at least 25 DNS query of type ANY to distinct unused dark IP addresses. The rate classification component classifies the attack rate as low, medium and high based on the packet rate. Using the approach we can find the attack potential of DNS amplification. The drawback with this approach is that it does not provide information about how to mitigate this attack.

2.9. Detecting Reflection Attacks in DNS Flows

This paper [9] proposes a detection algorithm based on Net-Flow data. This algorithm allows for real-time detection of ongoing attacks and identification of the targets. Net-Flow is a network protocol that collects IP traffic information and aggregates this information as Net -Flow records. From the flow record, we get IP address of the host sending the DNS query, IP address of the DNS server, Time of the DNS request, Time of the DNS reply, Size (in number of packets/bytes) of the DNS request, Size (in number of packets/bytes) of the DNS response and Source port of DNS query and destination port of DNS query.

The detection approach is based on thresholds that separate legitimate DNS traffic from reflection attacks and is split up into two parts. The first part focuses on detecting IP addresses generating suspicious DNS requests through the use of a threshold for the amount of requests generated by an IP address and the consistency of the requests size. The second part focuses on detecting IP addresses receiving suspicious DNS responses, also through the use of a threshold for the amount of responses received, but it furthermore looks at the average size of the responses as its second metric.

The problem with this approach is that it does not detect every possible execution of a reflection attack. The reason for this is that the metrics used in the detection approach, the standard deviation of request size and high average response size, become less reliable when based on less data.

3. CONCLUSION

A comprehensive classification of 9 DNS amplification defense mechanisms along with their advantages and disadvantages is presented in this paper.

Even though there are many defensive mechanisms, an effective mechanism is the need of the time. The major disadvantage of some of the mechanisms is that which block legitimate DNS traffic. Another disadvantage is some mechanisms do not scale for large networks. So require a proper defence mechanism to reduce the blocking of legitimate traffic to some extent and which is scalable to large networks. Research work can be focused on attackers' incentives analysis for implementing future defence strategies based on the attacker's motivations.

REFERENCES

[1] G. Kambourakis, T. Moschos, D. Geneiatakis, and S. Gritzalis, "A fair solution to DNS amplification attacks, IEEE, 2007, pp. 38-47.

[2] C. Sun, B. Liu, and L. Shi, "Efficient and low-cost hardware defence against DNS amplification attacks," in Global Telecommunications Conference, 2008.

[3] Thijs Rozekrans, Javy de Koning, "Defending against DNS reflection amplification attacks", University of Amsterdam February 14, 2013.

[4] P. Ferguson, D. Senie, "Network Ingress Filtering: Defeating Denial of Service Attacks which employ IP Source Address Spoofing", 2000. http://tools.ietf.org/html/bcp38.

[5] Fanglu Guo Jiawu Chen Tzi-cker Chiueh, "Spoof Detection for Preventing DoS Attacks against DNS Servers", Proceedings of the 26th IEEE International Conference on Distributed Computing Systems (ICDCS'06), IEEE 2006.

[6] Lutz Donnerhacke, "DNS Dampening", 2012. *http://lutz.donnerhacke.de/eng/Blog/DNS-Dampening*

[7] Douglas C, MacFarland, Craig A. Shue, and Andrew J. Kalafut, "Characterizing Optimal DNS Amplification Attacks and Effective Mitigation", 2014.

[8] Claude Fachkha, Elias Bou-Harb, Mourad Debbabi, "Fingerprinting Internet DNS Amplification DDoS Activities", IEEE 2014.

[9] David Huistra, "Detecting Reflection Attacks in DNS Flows", 2013

[10] Fabrice J. Ryba, Matthew Orlinski, Matthias W¨ahlisch, Christian

Rossowy, Thomas C. Schmidtz, "Amplification and DRDoS Attack Defense A Survey and New Perspectives", 2015.

[11] M. Anagnostopoulos et al,"DNS amplification attack revisited", ELSEVIER Computers and Security, 2013

[12] Randal Vaughn & Gadi Evron, "DNS Amplification Attacks", 2006.

19

Survey on Wireless Intrusion Detection Mechanisms

Moble Jacob
Rasmi P S

ABSTRACT

Wireless communication is technology's one of the promising contributions to mankind. Wireless networks are widely used to transfer sensitive data such as bank details, credit card details, emails etc nowadays. The intrusion detection system for wired network cannot be applied directly for wireless networks. Wireless network does not have specific boundaries since the nodes are moving. Wireless networks are more vulnerable to attacks such as denial of service, spoofing attacks, session hijacking etc. It is easy for the attacker to intrude into the system since no physical connection is needed. This paper deals with the survey of some of the methods used in intrusion detection in wireless network.

Keywords : Wireless Communication, Communication systems, Wide Area Networks, Internet, Intrusion Detection, NOJO, MAC, DCF, MMDS

1. INTRODUCTION

Wireless network has many advantages over wired network such as flexibility, support of mobility of the nodes, easy to deploy, cost effective etc. Since the nodes are moving there is no specific topology in case of wireless networks. Wireless networks are susceptible to malicious attacks ranging from passive attacks to active attacks. Encryption and authentication methods are used to prevent intrusion, but these methods cannot eliminate the problems. Most of the systems focus on the attacks, which threaten confidentiality. In a wireless network the availability as well as integrity is also important.

The intrusion detection systems can be characterized either on the basis of the data being analyzed or on the basis of methods that are used to detect the attack. Based on the data being analyzed, the intrusion detection systems can be classified as the one, which works on the data in the physical layer, the one, which works on the data in the MAC layer, or the system, which works with the data from the physical as well as from the MAC layer. Based on the method used for intrusion detection, the systems can be classified as the one, which uses misuse detection, the one, which uses anomaly detection, or the system, which uses both systems.

The systems, which take physical layer data for reference mainly, focus on jamming attacks. Most of the systems use radio frequency fingerprinting or signal to noise ratio to detect the attacks. The systems, which take MAC, layer data as reference can detect attacks like MAC spoofing, denial of service, session hijacking, etc. There are systems, which use the physical layer data and the MAC layer data. In misuse detection, signatures of attacks were stored. The real time traffic is analyzed and compared with the signatures. If the analyzed traffic matches with the signature, the event is an attack otherwise the event is considered as a normal event.

In anomaly based intrusion detection, a normal model is created. The real time traffic is compared with the normal model. If the analyzed traffic matches with the normal model, the event is considered as a normal event otherwise it is considered as an abnormal event. The detection threshold can be adjusted so as to reduce the false alarms.

2. WIRELESS NETWORK ATTACKS

Attacks can be categorized as either active or passive. Active attacks involve in altering of resources. Passive attacks do not involve in altering resources and are mainly a threat to the confidentiality. Wireless network attacks include probing & network discovery, DoS attacks, impersonation, man in the middle attack etc. Most of the attacks were based on the physical layer as well as the data link layer. The physical layer deals with the radio signals. The data link layer deals with exchange of frames. Frames are of three types, data frames, control frames and management frames.

2.1. Physical Layer Attacks

In the physical layer there can be problems such as hidden terminal problem, capture effect. Hidden terminal problem occurs when a wireless node is visible from an access point, which is not visible from other nodes communicating with that AP. Capture effect is a phenomenon associated with signal reception in which only the stronger of two signals will be demodulated. Both phenomena are caused due to concurrent transmissions and collisions at the receiver side. However, the important differentiation between the two is that the transmitting stations that are causing capture at the receiver are not necessarily hidden from each other.

2.2. Data Link Layer Attacks

In the data link layer, the data frames are encrypted in order protect the data from unauthorized exposure. The management frames are more prone to attacks. There are different DoS attacks such as authentication flood, de authentication attack, association flood etc, which exploit the management frames. In authentication flood attack, authentication requests are sending with spoofed addresses to the access point. At the access point, there is a client association table for each client with a limited size. The requests from the attacker add an entry to the association table. When the table reaches its limit, the legitimate user cannot authenticate and associate with the access point. The attacker spoofs the address of the victim and send de authentication request, which results in the disconnection of the victim from the access point. In case of association flood, the attacker exhausts the association table with huge number of spoofed association requests. Similar to authentication flood, the legitimate user cannot connect with the access point when the association table overflows.

3. WIRELESS INTRUSION DETECTION MECHANISMS

MOJO [1] is a system, which deals with the wireless anomaly detection based on the physical layer data. It proposes a fine-grained algorithm, which is capable of distinguishing the root causes of wireless anomalies. It detects the hidden terminals and differentiates it with the capture effect. In wireless network, there will be interference from other devices such as microwave ovens, cordless phones. It detects noise from other non-WLAN devices, anomalous signal strength variations at access points and the variation of signal strength due to the environmental changes or due to the actions of access point. The signal strength is monitored in each beacon in order to detect abnormal signal strength variations. Faults are observed at different sensors and correlating information is needed from different distributed sniffers.

The system provides detailed information about the faults that occur at the physical layer.

In wireless LAN, MAC address can be easily spoofed. MAC address spoofing can be detected using received signal strength (RSS) [2]. The system proposes an approach based on Gaussian mixture model (GMM) to built RSS profile for detecting MAC address spoofing. Spoofing methods mainly focus on MAC headers since MAC layer encryption is only applied to the payload. Spoofing can be detected by analyzing the sequence number field. It is difficult to match attacker's sequence number to the legitimate device's sequence number. There are some open-source drivers and reverse-engineered firmware, which allows per-frame SN manipulation. Almost all fields in MAC layer can be spoofed. But physical layer information is inherent to radio characteristics. Due to advancements in wireless devices, the RSS based detection technique is not efficient. RSS profiling algorithm is proposed based on Expectation-Maximization learning for GMM. The significant changes in profiled RSS pattern is considered as spoofing attack.

Wireless Network Security can be improved Using Spectral Fingerprints [3]. The system uses radio frequency fingerprints for classification to provide hardware specific identification for detection and mitigation of spoofing. The power-based RSS metric statistics may vary under different conditions such as different physical environments or in case of different hardware. The functionality of radio fingerprinting is divided into four steps. They are Waveform parameter extraction (amplitude and phase), Transient detection (preamble starting location), Feature Extraction (RF fingerprint), Classification of unknown received signals. Among these transient detection is the core functionality. Transient detection reliability is addressed using a Variance Trajectory technique with instantaneous amplitude and phase responses. Then the Power Spectral Density features from signal preamble are extracted to form RF fingerprint. Reference fingerprints are generated from signals from various devices. The unknown signals can generate its fingerprint and classified by correlating it with the reference fingerprints.

Spoofing and Anomalous Traffic can be detected in Wireless Networks via Forge-Resistant Relationships [4]. The system proposes a non-cryptographic mechanism for authentication as well as to detect spoofing. The authentication requires key management or maintenance, which is not possible in case of wireless LAN. Full-scale authentication has the risk of authentication key to be compromised and requires an infrastructure to maintain integrity of authentication methods. The system provides a lightweight security solution for authentication and it detects multiple devices, which use same network identity. The system detects anomaly behavior within the MAC layer. The system verifies the forge-resistant relationships between packets, which are coming from the claimed identity. There are two relationships, which are taken into account in this system. They are relationships that are introduced through auxiliary fields in packets and relationships that result from the use of intrinsic properties associated with the transmission and reception of packets. There are two approaches that use auxiliary fields. They are Anomaly Detection via Sequence Number Monotonicity and One-Way Chain of Temporary Identifiers. The approaches that use intrinsic properties are Traffic Arrival Consistency Checks and Joint Traffic Load and Inter arrival Time Detector. Even though the attacker spoofs any identity it can be easily detected using relationships.

Table 1. Wireless intrusion detection mechanisms and features

Sl. No	*Method*	*Physical/ Data link layer*	*Features*
1	Mutual Observation with Joint Optimization (MOJO)	Physical layer data	Detect capture effect and hidden terminals with the help of signal strength variation. Information from different sniffers were correlated
2	Detection of MAC address spoofing using RSS	Physical layer data	RSS profile for the genuine stations were built based on Gaussian mixture model
3	Detection using frequency fingerprints	Physical layer data	Power Spectral Density features from signal preamble are extracted to form RF fingerprint Reference fingerprints are correlated with the unknown signals finger print
4	Detection using forge-resistant relationships	Data link layer data	Relationships that can be introduced through auxiliary fields of packets and Intrinsic properties associated with the transmission and reception of packets were used
5	Detection using DCF inter-frame space (DIFS)	Data link layer data	Used to detect greedy behavior of a station Checks whether the station transmits before its required DIFS period after last acknowledgement
6	Detection using signal to noise ratio	Physical layer data	Statistical changes in SNR are monitored &

			algorithm executed independently Locally executed results are combined to form a collaborative output in fusion
7	Multilevel Monitoring and Detection System (MMDS)	Data link layer data	Provides hierarchical security agent framework Security node consists of Manager Agent, Monitor Agent, Decision Agent, Action Agent Disadvantage: only allows offline training
8	Detection using spatial correlation with the RSS	Physical layer data	Detect both spoofing attacks & number of attackers Clustering based on RSS-based spatial correlations among normal devices and attackers

DOMINO [5] is a system to detect greedy behavior in IEEE 802.11 hotspots. The wireless Internet service providers provide different security mechanisms. The wireless node needs to be authenticated at the access point. There should be mechanisms to detect the greedy behavior of wireless nodes. A station can attain the bandwidth at the expense of other stations misusing the MAC protocol. The key features of the system are integration with the access point without interfering with the normal functionalities, compatibility with existing networks and applicability to future versions. During monitoring the traffic traces of sending stations are collected at regular intervals of time called monitoring periods. The traced data are analyzed using the DOMINO algorithm. In order to reduce false positives there is a threshold beyond which the suspect is considered as a cheater. In order to reduce the erroneous detection the cheat count will be decremented each time the station does not cheat. There are different tests being done to the traced data. The systems checks whether the station transmits before its required DIFS period after its last acknowledgement. Then it checks for oversized NAV value followed by back off manipulation, actual back off and consecutive back off. Each test keeps its local counter and if it exceeds the threshold the remaining tests are aborted to save resources and the station is considered as cheater.

Effective and robust detection of jamming attacks [6] deals with the wireless anomaly detection based on the physical layer data. Two types of algorithms were proposed. One is a locally executed algorithm and other is a fusion algorithm. In locally executed algorithms, signal to noise ratio is measured. Statistical changes in SNR are monitored and algorithm executed independently. In fusion algorithms the locally executed results are combined to form a collaborative output. Local detection algorithms are categorized into two, simple threshold algorithms and cumulative sum change point detection algorithms. The algorithms consider SNR-based metrics, which include the average SNR, minimum SNR, and max-minus-min SNR, in a short window. The values of these metrics are measured over a small time window and during a large time window another metric is compared. When the considering metric deviates from the normal or expected value, the simple threshold algorithms trigger an alarm. The normal value is the value of the metric estimated in a long time window. A collaborative intrusion detection system (CIDS) system collects and fusses information from the monitors and takes final decision about a possible attack. Depending on the output of the locally executed algorithms, several types of fusion algorithms can be used such as average, product, majority vote etc.

Multilevel Monitoring and Detection System (MMDS) [7] is based on an agent based monitoring in different levels. Different rules were generated using fuzzy decision support system. The system provides a framework based on hierarchical security agent. A security node consists of agents such as Manager Agent, Monitor Agent, Decision Agent, and Action Agent. The Manager Agent coordinates the activities such as sensing, communicating, and generating responses of agents. The security issues of the monitored environment are addressed by performing a unique function at each agent. In case abnormalities or intrusion, Decision Agent can take a robust decision with the help of fuzzy inference engine which provide imprecise and heuristic knowledge since between the normal and abnormal activities are not distinct but rather fuzzy. The action agent reports the state of the monitored environment and generates alerts, heartbeats, etc. The necessary action is taken by Action Agent such as killing a process, block potential intruder from accessing the user, alerting the administrator about the intrusion, etc. The system detects ssh attacks, nmap attacks and MAC spoofing attacks. The system only allows offline training.

Multiple spoofing attackers can be detected and the location can be identified in wireless networks [8] using spatial correlation with the received signal strength. Number of attackers can be determined using cluster based mechanism. Support vector machine is used to improve accuracy of number of attackers. The main contributions are GADE (generalized attack detection model) and IDOL: an integrated detection and localization system. Attack detection is done in the generalized attack detection model by using partitioning around medoids. A mechanism called SILENCE is used to improve the accuracy of determining the number of attackers.

The wireless intrusion mechanisms and its features are summarized in the Table 1.

4. CONCLUSION

Wireless communication networks become an inevitable medium for communication nowadays. Wireless network are more prone to attacks such as spoofing, denial of service etc. These attacks can be detected using different detection systems, which make use of data from physical layer, MAC layer or the data from both layers. This paper dealt with some of the methods, which detect intrusion. The methods take data from the wireless network, then process it and detect the intrusion. The problem in detecting the intrusion is that the accuracy of the system is based on the training of the system in case of anomaly detection systems. In case of signature-based systems, all possible attack signatures should be stored in order to get better performance. Some methods works offline that is the previously collected data is used for detection and the real time traffic cannot be analyzed. In order to improve the performance of the wireless intrusion detection system, it is better to take care of possible frame loss, which may tend to occur during the online evaluation and context dependency during the training phase.

REFERENCES

A. Sheth, C. Doerr, D. Grunwald, R. Han, and D. Sicker, "MOJO: a distributed physical layer anomaly detection system for 802.11 WLANs", in Proceedings of the 4th international conference on Mobile systems, applications and services, June 19-22, 2006, Uppsala, Sweden.

Sheng, Y., Tan, K., Chen, G., Kotz, D. and Campbell, A. "Detecting 802.11 MAC Layer Spoofing Using Received Signal Strength", in Proceeding IEEE 27th Annual Conference on Computer Communications (INFOCOM), April 2008.

W.M.Suski II, M.A.Temple, M.J.Mendenhall, and R.F.Mills, "Using spectral fingerprints to improve wireless network security", in proceedings of the IEEE Global Communications Conference (GLOBECOM), December 2008.

Q. Li, and W. Trappe, "Detecting Spoofing and Anomalous Traffic in Wireless Networks via Forge-Resistant Relationships", Information Forensics and Security, IEEE Transactions on, vol.2, no.4, pp.793-808, Dec. 2007.

M. Raya, J.P. Hubaux, and Imad Aad, "DOMINO: a system to detect greedy behavior in IEEE 802.11 hotspots", in Proceedings of the 2nd international conference on Mobile systems, applications, and services (MobiSys '04), ACM, New York, NY, USA.

A.G.Fragkiadakis, V.A.Siris, and A.P.Traganitis, "Effective and robust detection of jamming attacks". Future Network and Mobile Summit, 2010, vol., no., pp.1-8, 16-18 June 2010.

D. Dasgupta, F. Gonzalez, K. Yallapu and M. Kaniganti, "Multilevel monitoring and detection systems (MMDS)", in Proceedings of the 15th Annual Computer Security Incident Handling Conference, Ottawa, Canada, 2003.

J. Yang, Y. Chen, W. Trappe, J. Cheng, "Detection and Localization of Multiple Spoofing Attackers in Wireless Networks", Parallel and Distributed Systems, IEEE Transactions on , vol.24, no.1, pp.44,58, Jan. 2013.

20

Techniques of Literature Search for Relevance and Efficiency in Research

Humayoon Kabeer P.

ABSTRACT

Literature search is the preliminary stage of research which tries to assess the status of the specific area in which a researcher is going to work. The quality and relevance of a research project is dependent on proper assessment of prior work done. So effective literature searching is critical and will save time and prevent unnecessary repetition of work already done. The paper introduces methods for effective search and retrieval of relevant information.

Keywords : literature search, research, information retrieval

1. INTRODUCTION

A literature search is a systematic and thorough search of all types of published literature in order to identify good quality references relevant to a specific topic. The success of a research project is dependent on a thorough review of the academic literature at the outset. Effective literature searching is a critical skill in its own right and will prove valuable for any future information gathering activity whether in academia or not. Getting the literature search right will save hours of time through the course of one's research project and will also improve the quality of the research carried out.

It is seen that, journals are the main source of information for most in-depth literature searches. However, depending on the topic many other sources will prove equally valuable such as newspaper archives, images, primary data and conference proceedings.

2. OBJECTIVES OF LITERATURE SEARCH

The main objectives of literature search are:

- Review existing critical opinions/theories on the topic
- Identify current research findings on a topic
- Identify potential research methods or models one could use
- Enable to compare with one's own research findings

The literature search can be a time-consuming job – One needs to be well prepared before beginning.

3. THE STAGES OF THE LITERATURE SEARCH

A good literature search involves the following steps which should be worked through systematically:

1. Background reading and preparation
2. Working with your title: identify search terms
3. Identify the resources to search
4. Search using search techniques
5. Collate your results

4. BACKGROUND READING AND PREPARATION

Start by doing some background reading of textbooks, subject encyclopaedia, etc., to get a grasp of the context of the topic and the terminology used in its discussion. What is the starting point that has led you to choose this topic for your extended research project? Is there a seminal book or journal article on the topic you have read? Is the subject currently being discussed in the media? Do you have personal knowledge / experience of the topic?

Start off by identifying a small amount of reading material informed by the above to give you an overview of the topic. If there is a seminal book or journal article related to the topic, this in itself may contain good suggestions for further reading

5. WORKING WITH YOUR TITLE: IDENTIFY SEARCH TERMS

In order to successfully carry out your search it is important to identify at the outset as much of the key terminology associated with the topic as possible. This will include a range of different terms. For example: Important authors, Theories / concepts, Key research reports or legislation, Major genres / movements

The simplest starting point for identifying such terms is to spend some time thinking about the wording you are considering for the draft title of your research. Within any title, it will be possible to identify several key elements. For each of the key elements within your title we can think about:

- alternative terms (synonyms) – words used interchangeably to mean the same thing e.g. a synonym of children is kids
- related terms / concepts e.g. related words such as girls, boys, teenagers

For eg: Crime films Alternative terms: Crime drama, Crime melodrama, Crime movies, Film noir, Detective movies, etc.

Women Alternative terms: Woman, Females, Girls, Ladies

Related terms: Gender Molls Femme fatale

America Alternative terms: United States United States of America US USA

20th Century Alternative terms: Twentieth century

Related terms: Specific time periods e.g. 1940s, 1950s

Remember, no search engine, whether in a database of journals or an Internet search engine, is intuitive. They are merely computer programmes designed to match on the exact words you enter. Unless you think about the range of potential search terms you are certain to miss content that is relevant to your topic.

6. IDENTIFY THE RESOURCES TO SEARCH

Unfortunately, regardless of the subject you are studying, there is no one single source of information that will contain everything you need for your literature search. You will need to give some thought as to which resources are likely to contain the most relevant content to the topic you are researching.

A starting point for your search will be to use the search facility in online databases. This will be useful to identify some initial references. However, just searching online databases will not do an exhaustive and comprehensive search of the literature. You will therefore need to go directly into a small number of individual resources and search them in their own right.

Whilst there are some databases that contain exclusively full text articles, most contain a mixture of full text and abstract only content. Databases however allow you to restrict your search to only retrieve full text results if you choose to.

7. DIFFERENT TYPES OF DATABASES

Multi-disciplinary journal databases Resources such as Academic Search Complete, Academic One File and JSTOR contain journal content across a large range of academic subjects. Often multi-disciplinary databases will contain professional and trade journals as well as academic peer-reviewed journals. You will however usually be able to restrict your search to just find academic peer-reviewed journals.

Subject specific databases contain journal articles and/or other types of content relevant to a specific subject or group of related subjects. Examples include PsycArticles, Education Research Complete, Westlaw and International Index to Performing Arts.

Publishers' databases Databases such as Science Direct, Sage Journals and Emerald contain journal content published by a particular publishing company. Such resources may also have a subject focus or may be multi-disciplinary.

8. SEARCH USING SEARCH TECHNIQUES

Having identified the potential terminology to search with, and which databases to search, the quality of your results will be improved by employing some of the techniques outlined below.

As a general rule avoid using the 'simple' or 'basic' search option (where you only get one box to type your words in). Always use the advanced search (or multi-search box search). This is because it is only in the advanced search that you will be able to use all the techniques that follow.

Use of asterisk (*)

Search engines also won't automatically search for derivatives of the same word.

For example: Searching for the word 'cinema' won't necessarily find 'cinematics'. This may even affect simple variants such as the singular and plural of the same word such as cinema and cinemas.

Often with databases of journal articles if you insert an asterisk * at the end of the 'stem' of the word it will automatically search for all the endings for that word stem.

For example:

Cinem* Will find:

Cinema, Cinemas, Cinematic, Cinematics etc.

If you aren't sure where to insert the asterisk * always include it where the word ending changes.

(b) Linking terms together using Boolean Operators

If you want to enter more than one term into a search engine you should link the terms with either the connecting word 'AND' or the connecting word 'OR'.

Linking two terms with AND will narrow your search to find only results that contain both terms.

Linking two terms with OR will broaden your search to find any results that contain either or both terms.

For example: Television AND Children

The above example will find only the results that contain both the term television and the term children. It won't find any results that just refer to Television on their own or just refer to Children without any mention of television.

Television OR TV

The above example will find any results that just mention television, any results that just mention TV and any results that mention both Television and TV.

8. VARIANT SPELLINGS

Databases will only match on the specific word you enter. In practice this means they aren't capable of coping with variant spellings such as American / English variants e.g. searching for colour won't necessarily find any results containing the American spelling color. Use 'OR' between the two different spellings to find either.

The Boolean operator 'NOT' or 'AND NOT' is used to exclude a term from the search result.

For example: Use of meat NOT chicken by Keralites will retrieve all types of meats except meat of chicken

(c) Finding phrases

If your search terms are expressed as a phrase, i.e. more than one word appearing immediately next to another, insert your search terms in quotation marks "...."

e.g. "University Grants Commission", "United States"

This ensures that our words always appear immediately next to each other in the text of the results:

If you don't insert phrases in quotation marks as in the example above, the database will usually find results that find both words but there may not be any contextual relevance between the words.

(d) Currency

Think about whether currency of the references you find is a factor as to whether they are relevant to your topic. Is up to date material critical or are older references just as valid? This will very much depend on your individual topic and area of study. Nearly all databases of journal articles will allow you to limit your results to only articles published within a certain range of years. This can be a powerful way of limiting the results you find and ensuring that you don't get overwhelmed with too many references. In Google searches we can use three dots (...) to limit the ranges

Eg: 2010...2015

(e) Think about where the database is looking for your search terms

Most databases allow you to choose where in the article / publication your search terms can appear:

Searching for your search term(s) in the title is a good starting point as if your term(s) appears in the title, the publication will have a high degree of relevance to that topic:

If this doesn't find enough relevant material try searching in the abstract / subject / keywords. Abstracts are written in such a way that key terms describing the content of the article are always included. Therefore if your search terms appear in the abstract, the publication will have a high degree of relevancy to them.

Keywords / subject terms are assigned either by the author or the database producer to describe the main topics discussed in the publication. Again, if your search terms appear as keywords or subject terms the publication will have a higher degree of relevancy to your topic.

If you don't choose where the database is searching they will usually search all fields in the publications searched. This will usually mean that the search terms you have searched with will appear anywhere within the full text of the publications found. They may therefore only have cursory relevance to your topic.

10. COLLATING RESULTS

Analyse the material you find and group it in some order of priority. Filter out any peripheral materials and consider storing them separately from your core references.

If any of your core journals references are unavailable

in full text form from the database you have searched, remember that the article/journal may be available from some paid databases by login the publisher's website.

It is essential that at every stage you keep accurate records of all searches and sources, and all references found and used! This will not only help you keep control of your research, but it will be vital when it comes to writing up your final bibliography and citations. And back-up your computer files regularly– every time you update them.

REFERENCES

http://libguides.library.curtin.edu.au/c.php?g=202408HYPERLINK "http://libguides.library.curtin.edu.au/c.php?g=202408&p=1332706"&HYPERLINK "http://libguides.library.curtin.edu.au/c.php?g=202408&p=1332706"p=1332706

http://guides.library.yale.edu/c.php?g=295913HYPERLINK "http://guides.library.yale.edu/c.php?g=295913&p= 1975849"&HYPERLINK "http://guides.library.yale.edu/c.php?g= 295913&p=1975849"p=1975849

https://library.leeds.ac.uk/researcher-literature-search

Shields, Patricia (2000). Step by Step: Building a Research Project. Stillwater, Oklahoma: New Forums Press

21

Report on the Deliberations and Outcome of the Conference

K J John
Sreekumar.N

Greetings from Toc H Institute of Science & Technology! It is with pleasure we present a brief summary of the proceedings of the National Conference on 'Innovative Library Services in Digital Age' LISDA-2016 held on 1st & 2nd of July,2016.

We thankfully acknowledge the support and encouragement from various sources in hosting a conference of this kind for the first time in this region that provided a platform for airing and sharing ideas and experiences on a variety of innovative library services, problems and practices.

The 2 Day Conference that started on the 1st July 2016 at 10 am was inaugurated by Shri. T C Mathew, Vice president of BCCI, and presided over by Prof. (Dr) P J Joseph, President, Toc H Public School Society. Dr. A Ganesan, Director, Knowledge Resource Centre, PRIST University, Thanjavoor delivered the keynote address. On both the days, we were fortunate enough to have many distinguished academicians and administrators from reputed institutions all over India as leading presenters and delegates.

Prof.(Dr) P J Joseph, President, Toc H Public School Society, Cochin, Ms. P K Sobhana, State Librarian, Kerala, Dr. M.G Sreekumar, IIM Calicut, Fr. John Neelankavil, Dharmaram University, Bengaluru, Ms.Laila T Abraham, MG Univeristy Kottayam, Mr. Gireesh Kumar TK, Central University, Kasaragod, Dr. Jayapradeep, VPE, Mavelikkara, Dr. Sainul Abideen P, IISER, Trivandrum, Mr. Humayoon Kabeer, Govt. College, Calicut and Dr. A. Ganesan, Director, Knowledge Resource Centre, PRIST University,Thanajvoor presented ~~lead~~ papers and shared their valuable thoughts and experiences with the participants of LISDA- 2016.

The leading presentations were *Digitizing Heritage : An Account of the Digitization Projects of Kerala State Central Library, Building Digital Libraries using Greenstone, Agricultural Information Systems and its Impact Among the Farmer Community: A Study With Special Reference to Kerala, Library Automation in Contemporary Open Source Environment, Library Space: The Means to Bridge the Gap Between the Recorded Knowledge and the Living Knowledge, Consortium for e-Journals: An imperative for self financing engineering colleges, Techniques of Literature Search for Relevance and Efficiency in Research.*

The presentation on 'Achieving the Objectives of the Public Library Movement Using Information and Communication Technologies (ICT)' by Prof.(Dr.) P.J. Joseph gave a bird's eye view of Kerala's library movement stressing the unique character which is a movement starting at the grass roots level, later getting accepted and supported by Government. The author stated that with the availability of numerous technologies for digitizing content and disseminating it through network, any village library could offer services that earlier only large libraries like State Central Library or University library were able to offer. The presentation gave suggestions for proper use of ICT to extend public library services of required quality and variety to all the people transcending economic and geographical boundaries.

'Digitizing Heritage: An Account of the Digitization Projects of Kerala State Central Library' by Ms. Sobhana P K, introduced the relevance of digitizing library collection in this era. The importance and advantage of Digitization as a method of preservation is far reaching and is now considered as one of the major innovative work of any library. The State Central Library started the digitization project in 2006. In the presentation, she discussed two projects: Rare books Digitization and State Gazette Digitization. She explained the historical value of this special collection of the State Central Library and the reasons for digitization. Also discussed were the methods and the technology used in digitization and the formation and working of the digital library.

'Building Digital Libraries using Greenstone' by M.G. Sreekumar says that the Digital Libraries (DL) are structured storage environments of digital data with a consistent format for index and content abstraction. DLs do enable the seamless integration of the scholarly electronic information, help in creating and maintaining local digital content, and strengthen the mechanisms and the capacity of the library's information systems and services. The penetration of electronic content into our libraries and information centers prompts us to leverage on the latest digital technologies towards building practical digital libraries and in setting up dynamic electronic information systems. In the presentation Mr. Sreekumar portrayed the unlimited potential of digital libraries in real world perspective by trying out open source solutions like

'Greenstone'. Greenstone is an internationally renowned software system for developing digital libraries, promoted by the New Zealand Digital Library project research group at the University of Waikato. It is developed and distributed in cooperation with UNESCO and the Human Info NGO. One of the key features of Greenstone is that it is quite easy to install, configure, customize and administer, even by the novice. It also facilitates seamless aggregation and integration of the digital content possessed by the library. More details of the software and example digital libraries built using the software are available at *http://www.greenstone.org/*.

'Library Automation in Contemporary Open Source Environment' by T.K.Gireesh Kumar reviewed the developmental activities associated with the library automation focusing its growth and justification on adopting open source integrated library system in Indian libraries. It also suggested some measures to enhance the sustainability of open source integrated library system in Indian libraries. The study was based on the perspectives of library professionals from different institutions in India performing library house-keeping operations using any open sources library packages. Online survey method was adopted to examine the perceptions of library professionals. Findings of the study revealed that managerial issues such as knowledge in open source technology, Information and Communication Technology infrastructure, in-house technical expertise, organizational policies and support, experience and training in open source software, trained manpower etc. invariably influence the rate of adoption of open source integrated library system in Indian libraries.

'Agricultural Information Systems and its Impact Among the Farmer Community: A Study With Special Reference to Kerala' by Smt. Laila T Abraham says that the

Agricultural information accumulated in different parts of the nation need to be coordinated and transmitted effectively so that it is utilized by farmer community for enhancing crop production. The services provided by some of the Agricultural Information Systems (AISs) of Central and State Governments were discussed during the presentation. It is found that these AISs play an important role in the development of rural community. The activities of these systems and their impact among farmers in rural development have been examined and suggestions put forward to increase the utility of these Information systems.

'Library Space : The Means to Bridge the Gap between the Recorded Knowledge and the Living Knowledge' by Fr. John N. V. proposed to bridge the recorded knowledge and the living knowledge to protect and promote quality knowledge by good research. The key solution to the widening gap between the recorded knowledge and living knowledge problem is promoting library space – research ecology. The library and information science which spreads knowledge around the world to create a knowledgeable and networked society, LIS should take the initiative to cure the problems of the horizon of knowledge. The researchers are speculating many reasons for this phenomenon like: information explosion, information overload, and limited capacity of human brain. They are wondering about few consequences of the same such as: data mines, skill gap, knowledge monopoly, stagnancy of knowledge, knowledge filtering and unmanageable amount of information waste. *As the* university libraries are symbolically considered as the heart that pumps knowledge to every part of its constituent bodies, the universities have to take special initiative to the bridging of recorded knowledge and the living knowledge to protect and promote quality knowledge by good research.

'Consortium for e-Journals: An imperative for self financing engineering colleges' by Dr M Jayapradeep discussed the need of library e-journal consortium for resource sharing among Self Financing Engineering Institutions in the geographical groups of Kerala State. The consortium aims to diminish library budget vs variety of information services, increasing subscription rates, etc. AICTE-INDEST consortium categorizes private engineering colleges as 'Self supported institutions' and deprives them 'lower subscription rates and better terms of agreement with publishers'. As the price of e-resources being prohibitive, it has become inevitable among the Engineering Institutions to practice resource sharing and cooperation through library consortia in the networked information environment. The issues such as bias, need for and benefits of consortium, operability, pre-requisites and services are discussed and a consortium model is suggested. The author concludes that the experiences, trust and understanding built by the consortium shall benefit the self financing colleges on a long term basis and also equip the libraries and library professionals to the new realms and responsibilities in the technology driven information environment.

'Techniques of Literature Search for Relevance and Efficiency in Research' by Humayoon Kabeer P. introduced methods for effective search and retrieval of relevant information. Particularly for those who do Literature search the preliminary stage of research in which a researcher is going to work, as the quality and relevance of a research project is dependent on proper assessment of prior work done. So the suggested effective literature searching will save time and prevent unnecessary repletion of work already done.

OUTCOME OF THE CONFERENCE

The conference infused interest among the academic and professional community of TIST for implementation of Open Source Library Software, within the TIST campus for having online access to library, which would expand the library space; and the authorities are seriously considering this matter.

The main recommendation of the Conference was to evolve strategies for a Library Consortium for resource sharing among self-financing colleges.

All the presentations threw light on optimizing, synergizing and harnessing the-state-of-the-art technology at our end in meeting the challenges of library applications and innovations.

A common concern expressed by all was the ever escalating and exorbitant cost of e-journals for scholastic pursuits, major and minor projects as well as research. A consensus emerged at the plenary session was the formation of a consortium for e-journals so as to reduce their cost, if done collectively by a group of self-financing colleges. As opined by most of the participating experts and staff from other self financing colleges, TIST has decided to lead the initiatives for forming a consortium which can boost the quality of higher technical education and research promoted by the self financing sector.Two papers presented at the conference on e-journal consortium and resource sharing among engineering colleges also elaborated the topic and invited much discussion and it was felt that further deliberations were required to evolve a strategy and concerted action. Hence a suggestion was mooted for convening a meeting on the issue shortly. We look forward to your response and co-opeartion in the matter.